THE BUDDHIST PHILOSOPHY OF THOUGHT

THE BUDDHIST PHILOSOPHY OF THOUGHT

Essays in Interpretation

ALEXANDER PIATIGORSKY

CURZON PRESS
BARNES & NOBLE BOOKS

First published 1984
Curzon Press Ltd: London and Dublin
and
Barnes & Noble Books: Totowa, NJ, USA

ISBN
UK 0 7007 0159 1
US 0 389 20266 5

Library of Congress Cataloging in Publication Data

Piatigorsky, Alexander.
The Buddhist philosophy of thought.

Bibliography: p.
Includes index.
1, Philosophy, Buddhist. 2. Dharma (Buddhism)
I. Title.
BQ282.P5 1982 181'.043 82-3987
ISBN 0-389-20266-5 AACR2

Printed in Hungary

To my dear parents, Sarra and Moissey

CONTENTS

ACKNOWLEDGMENTS

First of all I would like to express my deepest gratitude to those few friends who from the very beginning helped me very much, not only in the development of my interest in abstract thinking but also in the development of my own abstract thinking. These friends are, in a somewhat quasi-chronological order: Alexander M. P. Lung, Yuri V. K. N. Oroz, Vladimir Toporov, Uku Maasing, Merab Mamardashvili, the late David Zilberman and David S. Ruegg. Without these persons I would never have been able to start this book, not to mention finishing it.

I am also enormously thankful to those in this country who helped me to come, settle and continue here, particularly to Wendy O'Flaherty, Ann Shukman, Martin Dewhirst, I. Golomstock, Kenneth Ballhatchet and Albert Hourani.

FOREWORD

The centrality to Buddhist thought of the theory of *dharmas* or phenomenological units and the primary role assigned in this philosophy to consciousness have long been recognized. In the canonical *Dhammapada* (verse 1) and *Dharmapada* (verse 1/xiii.3) and in the *Udānavarga* (xxxi.23) in fact it is stated that *dharmas/dhammas* are dependent on mind, mind is their chief and they are mind-made

manopubbaṅgamā dhammā manoseṭṭhā manomayā

(or, according, to a widely attested variant, they are fleet as mind, *manojavā*). The Buddhist scholasticism of the *Abhidhamma/Abhidharma*, which is largely devoted to the investigation of the factors termed 'dharmas', has therefore attracted the attention of many scholars for more than a century; but their studies have not seldom encountered serious difficulties owing to a lack of philosophical penetration and method. Recently, despite the problems thus encountered, a revival of interest has been taking place in the literature of the *Abhidharma.* With only a few notable exceptions, however, scholars in the West have tended lately to neglect the Pali Abhidhamma of the *Theravāda*, a school which has not only preserved ancient canonical texts of this division of Buddhist scripture but has also produced on its own account some very significant works on the subject.

The author of this book approaches his study of the *Dhammasaṅgaṇi*, the first book of the canonical Pali Abhidhamma, and of a number of related Pali, Sanskrit and Tibetan texts both as a phenomenologist philosopher and semiotician and as an historian of Indian and Buddhist thought. Alexander Piatigorsky indeed already brought this exceptional combination of qualifications to bear on this subject in an article entitled 'An introduction to Abhidhammic psychology' published in Tartu University's *Trudy po znakovym sistemam*, vol. 6, in 1973. This essay has since been followed by several studies, also in English, on semiotics, general as well as Buddhist, while an earlier version of some parts of the present book have appeared in Italian in the review *Conoscenza religiosa*, 4 (1978), 1–2 (1979), and 1 (1980).

In this volume Dr. Piatigorsky employs methods derived from phenomenological analysis and semiotics to gain an understanding of the dharma-theory and the concept of mind free from what might be called the psychologism that has in the past sometimes superimposed an alien and unsuitable construction on Buddhist thought.

In the Theoretical Introduction the author introduces his readers to the idea of 'dharmas' as 'states of consciousness' which are selfless (*anattā*) in the sense that they are devoid of a thinking subject as their (quasi-objective) counterpart or as their (subjective) constructor or fabricator. A *dharma* is to be apprehended phenomenologically. The dharma-theory is not reducible to ontological or epistemological idealism; and our attention is directed to the risks inherent in any psychological reduction. The term 'meta-psychology' is, then, introduced by the author, who also considers problems concerning the meta-theory and meta-language needed for the comparative philosophical study of the dharma-theory. Special attention is given here to the notion of the 'rise of thought' (*cittuppāda*) in the *Dhammasaṅgaṇi.*

The author singles out for special attention three standpoints in Buddhist thought, the 'sattvic' line concerned with the *satta/sattva* 'sentient being', the 'mentalist' line, and the 'dharmic' line.

The notion of sentient being is examined in Essay 2 on the basis of the Pali *Sutta-Nipāta*, and the resources of semiotics and hermeneutics are applied to the problems of subjectivity and consciousness. The author also considers here the 'de-absolutization of man' and the 'de-anthropologization of consciousness'. Here a key concept is 're-ontologization', a metaterm he uses 'to denote the direction or the chief tendency regulating the change in the Buddhist understanding of thought' and an inherent condition for philosophizing (2.0). With respect to Brahmanical ontology, it is observed that Buddhism never regarded it as something to be denied or refuted but rather simply dismissed it as theoretically incomprehensible and empirically undiscoverable.

Essay 3 is devoted to the 'mentalist line' in Buddhist philosophy and to the question of a meta-philosophical concept—as opposed to an object-concept—in terms of which thought (*citta*) and mind (*manas*) may be interpreted. The author here writes: 'I simply do not know of a concept by means of which it [i. e., thinking] could be interpreted... Thinking which is ascribed to a sentient being is broader as a concept than *any* meta-concept which can be thought of or invented' (3.0).

Essay 4 provides a preamble to the topic of the 'rise of thought'. And the significance of the individual (*puggala*), to whom thought is attributed, is here investigated according to the Abhidhammic scheme of occurrences (*samaya*). Rather than being a subject in the usual sense, the *puggala* is 'objective' since it is thought (rather than an individual subject) that thinks: the thinker is in a sense not only desubjectivized but also 'depsychologized'.

Essay 5 takes up in detail the above-mentioned 'rising of thought' according to the *Dhammasaṅgaṇi*, with special reference to its scheme of 234 samayas. Eight segments are identified and tabulated with regard to the 83 'states of consciousness' (*dhamma*); and the 26 sets of dhammas are enumerated in detail. This elaborate 'positional semantics' (5.1; 5.7.4) of dhammas—which may be homonymous, synonymous and isotopic—is characteristic of the Abhidhamma of the Pali school especially. And the emphasis being on what he terms 'achronic configuration', the author introduces here the concept of topological space.

After having thus investigated the concepts of 'state of consciousness' and 'consciousness' itself with special reference to the Pali sources, the author turns in Essay 6 to a general discussion of the dharma-theory and of some of its Western interpretations from the time of Eugène Burnouf to the present.

In this rich and dense study the reader will find both interesting comparisons and thought-provoking contrasts with modern Western thought. He will also find here a pioneering application of some ideas of contemporary phenomenological philosophy and semiotics to the study of classical Indian thought. Phenomenology and semiotics as well as Indology should gain much from this confrontation and cross-fertilization of ideas and methods which will help to guard against the stultifying inroads of compartmentalization and cultural parochialism.

D. SEYFORT RUEGG

PRELIMINARY TECHNICAL REMARKS

1. In order not to increase the number of marks and notations *ad infinitum*, the Pali and Sanskrit words are not marked, so that a reader would learn from the context which term is a Sanskrit and which a Pali one. So, instead of 'trance (Pali *jhāna*, Skr. *dhyāna*)', we have 'trance (*jhāna*, *dhyāna*)'.

2. The use of a term, either in Pali or in Sanskrit, would depend on the character of a respective text or, even, a context in which this term figures. So, I use the Pali term *jhāna* when speaking about four or five trances in the text of *Dhammasaṅgaṇi*, or in the context of the *Abhidhamma* on the whole. But I use the Sanskrit term *dhyāna* when speaking about trances as mentioned in *Abhidharmakośa*, or referring to the context of the *Abhidharma* on the whole.

3. In a more general case, when I deal with a word taken as a *Buddhist* term, a Sanskrit equivalent is used in preference to a Pali one. So, speaking of 'trance' in general, I use *dhyāna*, not *jhāna*, and *dharma* not *dhamma*.

4. When English derivatives are used, preference is given to Sanskrit terms too. So, I use dhyanic (in the sense 'trancic' 'belonging to trance'), not jhanic. At the same time, when necessary, the derivatives from Pali can also be used, particularly when in a certain juxtaposition to a respective Sanskrit term. So, the term abhidhammic ('belonging to the Abhidhamma') is used side by side with abhidharmic ('belonging to the Abhidharma').

5. In order to minimize the number (yet all the same, immense) of italicized words, italics have been retained only where special (technical) terms are used in the singular form. Frequently recurring names of texts and persons are transliterated without italics and diacritical marks, likewise those in plural form, as derivatives, or in combination with other words.

6. Sanskrit and Pali words figure with their grammatical endings (and *saṃdhi*) only when taken in and together with, their context. So, we have *cittaṃ kusalaṃ* ('wholesome thought'), but *citta* ('thought'), etc.

7. All these rules do not apply to quotations in notes and references, where the terms are given *as they arise* in the original text (including all derivations from adopted systems of transliteration). So, instead of *manas* ('mind') we have *mano* when referring to the article of Rune Johansson, etc.

LIST OF ABBREVIATIONS

General, Special and Technical Terms

(A)	wholesome (*kusala*) states of consciousness (*dhammas*).
(B)	unwholesome (*akusala*) states of consciousness (*dhammas*).
C.	composition of the content of thought.
(C)	indeterminate (*abyākata*) states of consciousness (*dhammas*).
D.	set of *dharmas*.
△	*dharma.*
MS	mental state.
MV	mental variable.
n.	number of reference.
No.	number of case (or occurrence); any other number.
O.	object of thought
S.	sphere (or plane) of thought
T.	nomenclature of thought.
TV.	trancic variable

Titles of Sources

Abhs.	Anuruddha's *Abhidharmārtha Saṅgraha.*
As.	*Aṭṭhasālinī.*
Dhp.	*Dhammapada.*
Dhp. C.	*Dhammapada (Commentary).*
Dhp. CT.	*Buddhist Legends.*
Dhs.	*Dhammasaṅgaṇi.*
Dhs. tr.	*Dhammasaṅgaṇi* (translation).
Dhs. fr.	*Dhammasaṅgaṇi* (the French translation).
SN	*Sutta-Nipāta.*
SNC	*Sutta-Nipāta (Commentary).*
SNT	*Sutta-Nipāta (translation).*
Thera and Therī	*Thera-and-Therī-Gāthā* (the Pali text).
Thera tr.	*Thera-Gāthā* (translation).
Therī tr.	*Therī-Gāthā* (translation).

1. A THEORETICAL INTRODUCTION

Some speculative considerations upon speculation Buddhist and non-Buddhist

1.0. The task upon which I embarked in writing the essays collected in this book was not that of an indologist. For, however exiguous my competence in the realm of Indian philology (is it not one of Nietzsche's 'cheerful sciences'?!) might be, it would not have turned to my advantage here. This is a work of philosophical understanding, not of philology.

Furthermore, I have not tried to pursue an objective as an *historian* of philosophy, though some elements of an historical approach are applied now and then. Very often I do not dare to place in a chronological or, indeed, even in a temporal order the ideas or meanings given, as it were, simultaneously, that is, in the context of *one* text or group of texts.

And least of all am I inclined to connect the ideas or meanings in question *causally* with a social, political, or economic background, or indeed, to put them into the context of such a background, for our knowledge of this historical dimension leaves much more to be desired than our knowledge of meanings and ideas themselves. So, any historical sequences become relevant here only in so far as they reflect the changes in philosophical apperception (see the beginning of Essay 3).

I try here only to understand the Buddhist theory of thought and consciousness as an actual and presently relevant example of philosophical thinking on thinking.

1.1. In these essays I have tried, using some *facts* taken from certain Buddhist texts, to construe some aspects of a Buddhist *theory* of thought-and-consciousness. But first it is necessary to stipulate how these terms—'fact' and 'theory'—will be used here. We must bear in mind the at least twofold meaning of 'fact'. On the one hand, we call 'a fact' such a thing, as the principle of 'selflessness' (*anattā*): hence, we can state that 'there is "no-self" in the Buddhist theory of consciousness'. And this statement would be factual to the point where the meaning of a 'fact' coincides, practically, with that of 'a text'. Likewise, we may call a fact the statement that 'the notion of "thought" is almost the synonym of "consciousness" in the Buddhist theory of consciousness', for in more than one Abhidhammic text they either substitute or are explained in terms of one another. On the other hand, when we state that 'Nirvana is a state of consciousness' (and terminologically it is so, in so far as Nirvana is one of the listed dharmas, i. e., 'states of consciousness'), this statement, however factual it might sound is, in fact, an *interpretation* of a fact rather than a fact itself. The fact itself here is that Nirvana is an *asaṃskṛta dharma*, that *each dharma* is, in one way or the other, *related* to consciousness, and that of all dharmas the *asaṃskṛta* dharmas are related to consciousness in the most complicated and the least comprehensible manner. And, of course, given that the rendering of *dharma* as 'a state of consciousness' is an interpretation more than a translation, and that, though an *asaṃskṛta dharma*, Nirvana is not consciousness (or thought), we must admit that in such a statement as 'Nirvana is a state of consciousness', what we deal with is not a 'textual', but rather an 'interpretational' kind of factuality. It is very difficult, indeed, to remain always aware of these two sorts or levels of facts, yet without such discernment a methodological bias is inevitable (see Essay 6.3.2–3).

1.2.1. The application of the term 'theory' here is even more complicated and methodologically disputable. Setting aside all putative meanings of this term as well as all its modern, purely scientific and positivist implications I espouse a merely phenomenological approach to 'a theory'. Therefore, when I contend that the Buddhist Masters of old had (or may have had) a *theory* of consciousness, I mean first of all their *awareness of the phenomenal character of their own mental activity directed to consciousness as the object of this activity.*[1] This contention I regard as the core and starting point of a phenomenological approach which could be characterized in the following way : despite my cognizing the mental activity as *mental*, i. e., connected with the 'naturally given' psychological mechanisms and modalities, and despite my perceiving the awareness as, though indirectly (i. e., through mental activity), related to these same mechanisms and modalities, I think of them both as already 'processed' through consciousness and, thereafter, got rid of all psychological characteristics and changed into phenomena of consciousness.

The very form and character of the Abhidhammic texts clearly suggests that their exponents were fully aware that what they were dealing with was not a fact of consciousness itself, but the fact of their *awareness* of consciousness or, more rigorously, the fact of *one's being conscious of consciousness.* It was this latter fact that, as Abhidhammic theoretical thinking progressed, became the focus and cornerstone of the Buddhist *theory* of consciousness, thought and mentality, no matter what coeval or later differences and controversies between schools, groups and persons occurred. The triple, non-binary character of the composition of this 'fact' (i. e., 'awareness', 'mental activity', 'consciousness') was so obvious that no epistemological conclusions could be drawn from it until the middle of the first millennium A.D. And indeed, as a theory of knowledge or apperception (*saṃjñā*), Buddhist epistemology had to wait for an opportunity to find its foundations, not in a theory of consciousness or in a theory of dharmas, but in a theory of means or instruments of logically organized intellectual experience.

The awareness of the exponents of Abhidhamma of their own consciousness was analysed and classified by them in the sense and in terms of 'consciousness as object'. That in turn implies that not only were they 'theorizing' in the sense in which I understand the term and meaning of 'theory', but also that they *knew* that they were theorizing, and knew why and how. So, I further contend that their theory of consciousness was not only 'objectively' theoretical, but also 'subjectively' conceived of as a theory. And that is why these two aspects of the term 'theory' ought to be understood as strictly separated from, if not often quite unconnected with, one another.[2] This strange dual character of Buddhist theory of consciousness may from its very birth have prevented it from becoming a *psychological* theory as it has so often and so mistakenly been called. For, any 'normal'(!) psychological science would unavoidably proclaim itself as either purely objectivist, or mostly intuitivist, throwing aside any possibility of a 'methodological combination' of these as two separate aspects of one and the same theoretical understanding.

1.2.2. The discoveries made by the early Buddhist Teachers (fifth–third centuries B.C.) in the realm of thought are extraordinary. When I say 'realm of thought', I do not mean that they found out or founded some new methodology of investigation and applied it to their own or to others' thinking understood as *the object* of such an investigation. Quite the contrary, for, in my opinion, it was *the thing itself* that predetermined their theoretical understanding and induced the type and character of their methodology. *What* was thought of or meditated upon was far more important than *how* something was thought of or meditated upon. The object of thinking prevailed over modes of thinking. So I would assert that thinking about 'Self' (*atta, ātman*) must be 'methodologically' different from thinking about 'Absence of Self' (*anattā*), or from thinking about thought (*citta*), and so on.

This dependence of 'how' on 'what' in Buddhist philosophizing leads to the second idea—that the various and different events taking place within one and the same 'field of thinking' might not have necessarily figured there as deduced from, reduced to, or *causally* linked with, one another. They might have been present to the thought of the investigator as isolated *occurrences* or *series* of occurrences, each of which may be treated as if it were a *separate postulate* (see Essays 4 and 5). It does not necessarily follow from this that there can be no causal linkages there, but that a causal connection is no more than *one* of several possible postulates.

[1.2.3. The last question, it seems to me, is connected in Buddhism (as in some other Indian philosophies) with the unspoken idea of a *quasi-logical* subject containing in itself its own *mode* or *manner* of *predication.* For example, if looked at from an Aristotelian point of view, the 'principle' or 'mark' (*lakṣana*) of *anattā* might be formulated in predication: 'The phenomenal world is devoid of "self" (*atta*)'. However, in Buddhist philosophizing, the phenomenal world may not have figured at all in the context of interpretation of this lakshana, in which case we would reformulate this assertion as 'there is *anattā* there...' And it is *anattā* itself wherein the mode of our thinking is implicitly given as 'subject-postulate' with which one would operate in a quite different way than with, say, *atta.* It would therefore, be very hazardous to apply to *anattā* an *atmanic* mode of thinking, stating, for instance, that 'thou art not that' as a negative paraphrase of 'thou art that' (*tat tvaṃ asi*), however formally correct it might appear.]

1.2.4. Now, however, we have to return to what has been said at the beginning of this essay (1.2.1), and ask ourselves: What *content* can be indicated by such a statement as 'they (the Masters of Abhidhamma) were aware of *phenomenal* character of their own mental activity directed to thought, mind and consciousness?'. And why have I used here the term 'phenomenal' as if my only purpose and aspiration were to confuse initial issues and make the whole problem even more complex than it actually is?

The answer to the first question is a simple and unambiguous one: The contents of Abhidhamma show that *thinking about thinking* was singled out, separated from 'thinking' taken as an *object* of thinking, provided that 'thinking which thinks about thinking' was at least formally opposed to 'thinking which is thought of by it' as *subject to object.* All this, in turn, may imply that there might be *two* psychologies there: one dealing with thought as subject, and another dealing with, in some cases, this very thought, as object.

The answer to the second question is far more difficult. The only thing I would say is that *the mental activity thought of as directed to thought cannot* be reduced to the thought in question or, least of all, to 'thought as object' in general. On the contrary (and this is indicated by some contexts in both the Abhidhamma and Suttas), it is this 'specific' mental activity directed to thought as its object, to which we may reduce 'thought taken as object' on the one hand, and '(their) awareness' on the other. That is, the second and the third would be seen (or 'thought of') as *modalities* of the first. For it is the first, i. e., this mental activity, not 'awareness' or 'thought as object', which has been called 'selfless' (*anattā*). And it is this mental activity whose *states* have been ascribed as states of consciousness (dharmas) to the other two, as well as to itself. For this is its *own* phenomenal character.

1.2.5. All this leaves us with very little, if any, of what *we* are accustomed to regard as psychology proper which (in the context of European scientific tradition) remains strictly reductionist and monistic in its initial postulates. Over the last hundred years the psychological aspects of Buddhist thought have been over-emphasized. I understand psychology to mean the complex of *natural* and organismatic functions and modalities. In my opinion this is not applicable to the Buddhist thought as considered in this book. For, from Descartes to Wundt and from Kant to Wittgenstein, we have been consistently and persistently excluding our own 'thinking about thinking' from the scope, method, object and theory of psychology. That is why I decided, however arbitrary it might appear to be, to introduce the term 'meta-psychology', to denote both the character of the Abhidhammic approach to thought-mind-consciousness and the character and direction of the method applied by ourselves in our endeavour to understand their approach. A further elaboration is necessary here.

There is no doubt whatsoever that the proposition 'Mind-made (*manomaya*) are the dharmas' of the Dhammapada (I, 1) *can be made* present as a psychological theory for the simplest reason, namely, that dharmas here are interpreted in the sense of *mind* (*manas*). But the very next six lines, where mind is going to figure as 'obscured' or 'purified', as bringing about 'suffering' or 'pleasure', would give us an entirely new dimension of this same object, i.e., mind, connecting it with quite another complex of notions (such as 'karma', 'rebirth', etc.), and requiring a totally different approach by an external observer (see Essay 3, 3.2–3.3). This is what the late Mrs. Rhys Davids was referring to as 'psychological ethics' or 'ethical psychology', the late Edward Conze as 'philosophia perennis', and the late Rune Johansson, as 'simply psychology', but what, in my opinion, is a *meta-psychology:* that is, a sphere of *interpretation* where the psychological notions, concepts and terms assume a far broader series of 'meanings', ranging from ontology to anthropology, and from ethnology to sociology. And one of the main functions of the Abhidhamma of the Pali Canon was to *fix* these meanings (with their respective terms) so as to have made them more absorbable for dhyanic (trancic) recollection and transmissable from generation to generation in the course of oral tradition. The very pragmatism of the Abhidhammic texts changes their seemingly psychological content into a meta-psychology, of which fact the Old Buddhist Masters were undoubtedly aware, whereas the majority of the Masters and Apprentices of modern psychology cannot conceive of, speaking strictly terminologically, the *meta-theoretical* nature of their own theories.

Even if we take such a prominent exponent of a humanist and anti-positivist tendency in contemporary psychology as Abraham Maslow, we see that he does not know where he stands with respect to psychology as a science, and when he transgresses its limits and becomes a meta-psychologist. When he writes: 'We have, each of us, an essential biologically-based inner nature, which is to some degree "natural", intrinsic, given, and, in a certain limited sense, unchangeable, or, at least, unchanging'—he is not aware that this very 'nature' is what cannot be found *within* the realm of psychology proper. [It is the nature about which the Buddha would have spoken as 'non-existing, non-intrinsic, non-given, and, in a general sense, changeable and always changing'].[3] A meta-psychological character of his psychology becomes self-evident a little further: 'The question of desirable grief and pain or the necessity of it must also be faced'.[4] Here he puts the suffering (*dukkha*) in a, Buddhistically speaking, *soteriological* context, given, of course, that in Buddhism, 'suffering' has not only the *negative* meaning, as that which we have to discard or to stop originating, but also exists *as such* that is, as a totally neutral feature (*lakkhana*) of the phenomenal world as it is, i. e., as the symptom recognizable and acknowledgeable in a merely diagnostic way.[5] But Maslow (through his anti-positivism) does not understand his own position, marked in his statement by the word 'desirability', as 'psychological' or, shall we say, as a state of consciousness (*dharma*) interpreted in a manner which exceeds the objective limits of his discipline.[6]

1.2.6. And now we have to deal with one more question: what is the type and character of *knowledge* about consciousness, thought and mind contained in these texts? That is, the knowledge taken in its initial, often unspoken, postulates, and considered irrespective of whether it is factual or theoretical, empirical or speculative. In answering this question, I will confine myself to only four points, for a more detailed account will be given in the first, second, and particularly sixth, essays of this book.

1.2.6.1. (1) In our Buddhist 'texts' the 'psyche' (*cetas*) was regarded as not only an object, but also as a *thing* objectively observed and observable.

(2) The 'mind' (*manas*) was regarded as only partly a *substantial entity*, that is, solely to the extent to which it was interpreted in the sense of the *psychic* (see Essay 5, Table VI, △△2, 4). Whereas, when presented as *a state of consciousness*, a *dharma*, the mind remained a *non-thing* par excellence [i.e., when it figures as the dharma of 'thought' (*citta*) or of 'faculty of mind' (*manindriya*), see 5.1, 5.7., and △△5, 16 in Table VI).]

(3) The question of *reality* or *unreality* was never associated with that of *entity* (in the above sense), 'object-ness' and 'subject-ness'-with respect to psyche, mind, thought, consciousness or any other 'psychological' notions.

(4) But this question would inevitably arise when, instead of mind or thought *in general*, or *this* mind or thought taken as an example, we start dealing with *situations* where mind or thought figure as 'mine', 'his', or that of an external observer.

1.2.6.2. These features contrast remarkably with the main features of modern theoretical psychology or of what can be called the *Philosophy of Psychology*.

One cannot assert that philosophy of psychology exists as an independent, self-sufficient science like for example, physics, biology, or, indeed, psychology. Moreover, its scientific status can be in no way equated to that of such stressedly inter-disciplinary disciplines as 'philosophy of physics', 'philosophy of biology', or 'philosophy of science'. This is because in philosophy of psychology, the unity of 'the subject of science' and 'object of investigation' is implied there. That is, the very way or method of thinking of a philosopher over matters psychological, and these very matters themselves taken as concrete object of his thinking, inevitably coincide with or overlap one another. This is regarded as absolutely pernicious to each and every *system* of knowledge and it is Wittgenstein alone who, in his recently published *Remarks*, attempted to overcome it. This attempt, it seems, though being unique in its kind, expresses the very core of European scientific approach to the *thinking of the thinker*. The main features of this approach can be given in the following way.

(1) The main subject of this science is the nature of psychological concepts,[7] not the nature of psychological phenomena, or not 'the nature of nature'. This does not prevent these concepts from having their own 'nature', i.e., from being natural in a certain way (which is more than 'a way of speaking').[8] But these two natures cannot be identified as *one*, be it one state of consciousness (as in Buddhism), or one principle (as *ālayavijñāna* in *Yogācāra* doctrine) or, even, one thinking (as *cogitatio* in Descartes).

(2) *The experience* seems to be implied as a merely formal term—not a contentful concept—covering both 'what is seen' and 'an interpretation of what is seen'. And in order to connect these two in terms of psychological content, one would have to turn to *introspection.*[9] The latter may show one if this or that interpretation of what is seen is... right or wrong.[10] But, of course, the thinker knows the *difference* between what is seen and its interpretation.

(3) This difference implies an absolute *distinction* between the observer of psychological phenomena and phenomena themselves. Or, more exactly, it implies the observer's absolute *knowledge* of this and any other relevant distinction.[11]

He is the user of words denoting these phenomena, and his is their interpretation. He cannot be objectified as these phenomena or as any other *thing*. [For his is the privileged position of an observer who cannot be observed.]

(4) The words and sentences are the *description* of mental states, they are not mental states themselves.[12] That is, they cannot belong to a psychology, for they are irreducible to anything mental or conscious. So, it can be said again that they possess their *own* nature essentially different from that of mental states or 'psychological phenomena' in general. From which invariably follows the absolute reality of the subject (in the sense of 'person') of mental states, for his is their description, and it is he who is experiencing them. [His is, thereby, the language.] He is, therefore, far more real, 'objectively' speaking, than any object of his conscious experience given in his description.

[1.2.6.3. Our own idea of 'objectivity' seems to be twofold. On the one hand, objectivity signifies 'an object outside one's cognition to which the latter is directed'. On the other, it means 'an object other than oneself', i.e., 'other than the individual to whom this cognition is ascribed'. These two connotations of 'objectivity' now coincide with, now overlap, now figure as totally separated from one another. Even one's attempts to cognize 'the mystical' might be cognized in an objective way, if viewed, for example, as fated or otherwise determined by an apperception rooted, as it is, in and conditioned by the culture and time and, of course, by the language used. (This second connotation was by no means alien to the *Prajñāpāramitā*, where we can easily find the contexts where the periods (*kalpas*) of Involution of *Dharma* are mentioned as affecting the propagation and understanding of the *Dharma*). Moreover, it is in the sense of this connotation of objectivity that the clear distinction was drawn between the *cases* when one knew, said or otherwise acted by the Buddha's Might (*anubhāva*), as Shariputra in the beginning of *Hṛdaya-Sūtra*, and Subhuti in the beginning of *Aṣṭasāhasrikā*, and the cases when it was one's *own* power, as it was suggested about Subhuti by Shariputra in the beginning of *Aṣṭasāhasrikā*. The latter are clearly opposed to the former as subjective to objective.

The very Buddhist notion of apperception (*saṃjñā*) seems, however, to be connected with the idea of objectivity in the sense of the first connotation of the term only.]

1.3.0. It is now that we have to pass from what has been, though very vaguely, characterized as 'psychology' (and 'meta-psychology'), to this same material (texts, facts, etc.), but this time viewed in a broader perspective of *philosophy*. Given, of course, that the latter is to be considered from a point of view entirely neutral or even alien to Buddhist philosophy itself, as well as to Western, Eastern, or any other particular philosophy. It is this point of view, that I vaguely define as 'meta-philosophical', and the question of which is going to be treated in Essay 3.

1.3.1. Any attempt at a unified theoretical outlook of Buddhist philosophy, or Buddhism as a whole would, I believe, inevitably fail. For any *general* theory of it would have to neglect not so much some of the 'glorious contradictions' within the Buddhist Philosophy, as some far less glorious and much more essential differences between Abhidhamma and the Suttas. These are, first of all and mostly, differences in *approaches* to the same things. In saying this I do not mean that the Suttas embody one exclusive method, and the Abhidhamma another. What, in fact, we have is a *set of postulates*, some of which belong exclusively either to the Suttas or to Abhidhamma, and some to both while still others are seen by us as implied in the texts or as inferable therefrom as means of *our own* understanding of Buddhist Philosophy. As such, they cannot be identified with any specifically Buddhist term or concept. [It is for these last that I would prefer the term 'Buddhistic' instead of 'Buddhist'.]

1.3.2. And then, bearing in mind this triple *methodological* (i.e. belonging to *my* approach) division of postulates, I would formulate the main philosophical difference between Abhidhamma and the Suttas in the following way: *The philosophy to be seen in the Suttas* (by saying this I do not mean that their content is by any means confined only to philosophy), *reveals its predominant attitude where all things existent are seen as being objects of awareness* (*or consciousness*) *experienced* (*or experienceable*) *by various types of sentient beings, while the Philosophy of Abhidhamma* (the reservation made about the Suttas preserves its strength here) *deals with the various concepts and categories of consciousness as with the primary objects of investigation.* That is, one may say that if in the Suttas one is urged, taught or otherwise instructed how to form the conscious experience of one's life, in Abhidhamma it is the conscious experience itself which is exposed, categorized and classified to be thought of, meditated on, memorized and recollected *as such.* That is, without any returning to the phenomena of *life*, taken outside or without consciousness.

One may even argue that long prior to the time when the *oral* compilation of the main collections of Suttas was completed, there must have been some circulation of the categories, concepts and technical terms which only much later, i.e., *after* this compilation, were systematized and grouped. This is the circumstance which, one might suppose, could be partly, at least, responsible for a still enigmatic fact that there are very many places in the Suttas, where the Abhidhammic terms figure now in a strictly technical Abhidhammic sense, now in a much more general, common way.

1.3.3. The 'postulate of suffering', for instance, is formulated in two quite different ways in the *Sutta of the* (*first*) *Turning of the Wheel of Dhamma.* In the context of the 'Four Noble Truths' suffering is explained as existing, coming into existence, or going out of existence because of various factors which are shown as co-existing, as working synchronically ('horizontal' explanation). In the context of *paṭiccasamuppāda* ('interdependent co-origination') suffering is explained as the final result of the factors originating from one another and working diachronically ('vertical' explanation). However, in various parts of the corpus of Abhidhammic texts and commentaries, suffering figures in a rather non-postulative manner, that is, as no more than one of the very important, but still external, conditions of the rise of thought.

Furthermore, the 'postulate of impermanence' (*anicca*) of every thing in the Suttas, loses its absolute character in Abhidhamma where impermanence is postulated in connection with dhammas ('impermanence of all dhammas'), sharing with them their relational and, essentially, relativistic character.

1.3.4. At the same time, such a postulate as the 'rise of thought'—the fundamental *precondition* of any phenomenal existence whatsoever—is totally absent in the Suttas and could be only secondarily or indirectly deduced therefrom through late commentaries. And now I must refer to one circumstance which seems to be of some importance in respect of the chosen subject of this book: The interval between the completion of oral collections (*nikāya*) of Suttas and the completion of oral texts of Abhidhamma was incomparably longer than the interval which divides the first respective commentaries on them. The very idea of 'Buddhism', 'Buddhist philosophy', or 'Buddhism *as* philosophy', could have come into being and become an *historical* fact only through this late commentation. These commentators (very often one and the same person was commenting on both Abhidhamma and the Suttas) objectively performed the titanic work of systematizing the philosophical content of the text of the Pali Canon in relation to the growing *Mahāyāna* and, perhaps, in some connection with the latter.

1.3.4.1. Perhaps, because of the confrontation or co-existence with the Mahayana, lasting for at least the first four centuries A.D., a certain milieu was spontaneously created where several concepts were circulating on the various levels of the Buddhist philosophizing, i.e., irrespective of a given school of Buddhist thought. Or, more exactly speaking, what we deal with is a set of problems dichotomously formulated between the first and the fourth centuries, in the light of which some other postulates, formulated before and after this period, could be interpreted and explained *Buddhistically* by an external observer of Buddhism. Here I refer to the dichotomy and such oppositions as, '*saṃsāra/nirvāṇa*', '*dharma/svabhāva*', '*lakṣaṇa/alakṣaṇa*', '*saṃskṛta/asaṃskṛta*', 'relative reality of thought or consciousness (*cittamātra, vijñānamātra*)/absolute unreality of its objects', etc. However, if taken out of their Mahayanist-Shravakayanist context and returned to the contexts of the Suttas and Abhidhamma, they would immediately lose all their *dualistic* character. By 'dualistic', I also refer to where the duality of opposite concepts is to be abolished by a postulate of their one-ness. For example, such a postulate as 'Nirvana and Samsara are non-dual' does not mean the duality of postulation, but only indicates a level where this duality is not regarded as relevant.[13]

[1.3.4.2. In European philosophy dualism is seen or figures as a reinterpretation of, a derivation from, or a reaction against, a certain *monistic* principle. The principle which would be unavoidably discovered by means of a simple phenomenological procedure and even without referring to the *history* of philosophy—the principle of a *monistic unity of or within the human microcosm.* Whereas, for example, in the *Mādhyamika* philosophy, non-dualism itself is present as a negation of dualistic distinctions conceived as cosmologically primordial and epistemologically primary. That is why there has never been a monism proper in Buddhist philosophy, but a *non-dualism* which has constantly denied ontological status to any reflexive analysis of human soul, or human psyche, or human nature, or nature in general. And that is why any Indian *advaita* or *advaya* would have been absolutely impossible without such an analysis, so that the very fact that human (as well as any other) mentality was *philosophically divorced* from 'self' (or even 'non-self' where 'self' was denied) could be seen (particularly in the dualistic *Sāṃkhya*) as the basis and foundation for all subsequent non-dualistic re-thinking, be it in the *Mādhyamika*, *Yogācāra*, or *Advaita-Vedānta*.]

1.4. If we look at the Buddhist theory of consciousness from the point of view of an entirely abstract phenomenological approach, we will see that it is the phenomenon of difference, not of unity, which has always played the chief role, and to which very often were reduced even the most 'monistic' ideas of Buddhist thought. Buddhism is *non-monism* par excellence. And this is, probably, due to the fact that it became a theory at a very early stage of its *historical* development. Or, even, that there was practically, no time when it was no theory.[14]

'The theoretical structure of man's world'—says Cassirer—'begins at the point where consciousness first makes a clear distinction between illusion and truth, between what is merely perceived or represented, and what truly "is", between the subjective and the objective'.[15] Here is stated with an utmost neo-Kantian rigidity that there is consciousness the primary *theoretical* task of which is to create *distinctions* between opposite categories of *European* thinking, given, of course, that the subjective is illusion and corresponds epistemologically to what is 'merely perceived or represented'. I would not even refer here to a quite banal fact, that there are quite a few theories in man's world where illusion is theoretically identified with the objective and 'is', while truth is much nearer to the subjective and 'is perceived'. Yet really essential here is that it was Buddhism where consciousness began to produce the clear distinctions between *one thought and another*. I may even aver that it was the thought which started making objective distinctions within itself and theorizing upon them as upon different *states of consciousness*.

1.5.1. However, in order to reconstruct the work which was done by the first Abhidhammic masters, we ought to leave, for the time being, states of consciousness and turn to the *separate thoughts* which seem to have been the first object to which these masters addressed themselves. The idea underlying their 'meditational operations' with thought is that one thought neither appears from nor is a reaction to what is not thought. One thought is *arisen* (*uppanna, utpanna*) in what is present in meditation as a merely *formal* framework of an individual continuum of thought. In stating this I mean that both the fact that one thought arises in connection with another thought, and the fact of attributing this connection to an individual, are formal if related to or compared with, the fact of arising itself (see Essays 4 and 5). This, in turn, means that each and every arising of thought, taken separately, does not imply any causality or intentionality. For it arises *as such*, that is, although the postulate of its *absolute distinction* may be further concretized in terms of causality or individuality (as well as non-causality or non-individuality), such a concretization is not possible, as far as we deal with *this* arising of thought alone.

1.5.2. If we turn now to the *meaning* of the distinction postulated, we will clearly see that it is given to us not as a distinction in *content* of thought (or, in Cassirer's terms, between such *predicative* notions as 'illusion' and 'truth'), but as a distinction between 'there is a thought here and now' and 'there is no thought here and now'. Or, in other words, a distinction between a thought and the 'time-space interval' separating this thought from another one, or from the absence of thought.[16] 'No-thought' is present in this distinction as an *independent fact* (in the sense of its not being dependent on thought!), not as a mere negation of thought or the absence thereof. This 'fact of no thought' was seen by the Buddhist explorers of consciousness, as not any less *conscious* than that of thought itself (see 6.13).

1.5.3. 'Rise of thought' (*cittuppāda*) is a phenomenon that gives to thought a certain dimension which 'no-thought' is lacking, and it is this dimension which leads to the second theoretical distinction made by early Buddhist theorists of thought. This 'rise' was conceived by them not in terms of causality, direction or purpose, but rather in terms of 'what occurred simultaneously with the occurrence of this arising of thought'. They concentrated their attention first of all on conditions of this 'arising'. Conditions, not causes. Or rather, conditions which might or might not have been thought of as causes, and this within various states of discursive thinking.[17] Masters of the Abhidhamma made a powerful attempt to conceive of separate thoughts as arising coincidentally with other factors which, if observed from the point of view of a thought arising, would be seen as co-factors. [Though, if observed as such, these factors themselves might be seen as 'arising thoughts'.] The very notion of 'co-production' (*samuppāda*) means not as much causality as the coincidence of various factors which, by reason of this coincidence become co-factors. Then the second postulate is formulated as saying that 'If looked at in connection with their "arising", the separate thoughts may be conceived either as "coinciding" or as "not coinciding" with other factors' (see Essay 5, particularly 5.4).

1.5.4. One extremely important idea is implied in the second postulate. This idea is that *a separate thought has no mechanism of its own formation.* If I say 'The Prince Siddhartha became the ascetic Gautama because of his subsequent visions of old age, illness and death', or 'The Prince Nanda became an arhat because the Buddha had converted him in Kapilavastu'—these statements would be true only as conventional descriptions of events in the context of which there is no distinction whatever between a thought and deed or anything else. But these same events would lose all their appearance of 'causality' as soon as we see them in the light of the second postulate. In this case, 'becoming an arhat' or 'becoming an Awakened One' would correspond to a thought which is 'unconditioned' (*asaṃskṛta*) and thereby may only *formally* coincide with any event, whether a thought or not. Here we have a point of intersection of various different series of thoughts, for some of which this coinciding is relevant, while for some others it is not.

1.6. Apart from differences in their approach to thought and consciousness in terms of content, the Suttas and the Abhidhamma differ very much in their *fixation* of terms, concepts and ideas. [This difference is shown in Essay 5 which I have tried to make, as it were, Abhidhammist in its tone and subject.] This, however, needs a little explanation. I do not consider the Abhidhamma either as a special part of the early Buddhist teaching i.e., as the philosophy par excellence, taken as *distinct* from the entirety of the *Dhamma*, or as the most technical part of Buddhist philosophy (or, according to Mrs. Rhys Davids, 'ethical psychology of Buddhism'), taken in its distinction from the general philosophical outlook of the Suttas. I am more inclined to hold to the idea that the Abhidhamma has never been intended to be learnt or, indeed, thought as a *separate* theme. Its very *textual* form or, shall we say, the type and character of its fixation in *oral* tradition, might at least indirectly suggest that it was meant to be remembered, memorized, and recollected, first of all as a *form, mould, or framework having no specific content of its own,* that is, as the receptacle of any thinkable content of thought, including thought itself, when the last is thought of by another thought or by itself (this problem is treated in 5.1, 5.3 and 5.4).[18]

Moreover, one may conceive of the Abhidhamma, in the context of what could be called 'religious teaching of Buddhism', as one of the independent and relatively self-sufficient aspects of that teaching. It would, therefore, be inconsistent to say that in order to know Buddhism one would have to learn the Abhidhamma too. Let it be stated rather that one can understand Buddhism *through* the Abhidhamma as one specific, concrete, and particular *case* and *possibility* of its understanding. This would lead once again, to the question of 'rise of thought', but this time, however, understood in a larger Buddhological sense and context.

1.7. The picture of the Teaching as given to us in the Suttas (variegated as it may look), contains one very strange thing, and it is in this that Buddhism differs from Christianity most and first of all. *In Christianity the idea of Religion* itself (Church as Wisdom Embodied, Church as His Body or His Bride, etc.) *was endowed with cosmic dimensions, while in Buddhism the Buddha was conceived as the Observer of the Cosmos of Dharma.*[19] The duality of 'Transcendent-Immanent' is not applicable to Buddhism at all, for such a duality cannot exist without a concept of God as the Absolute Personality. For, when applied to the Buddhas, the very concept of 'person', 'individual', or 'personality' remains very problematic, and can be treated only in the context of a given concrete text, episode or situation (see Essays 3 and 4).

My conjecture is that it is this *idea of Observer* which has made of Buddhism *an open system* to which all criteria applied to close systems are inapplicable.[20]

Speaking figuratively, we may imagine an open system as a sphere with innumerable 'holes' through which one can make observations of its inside. Or, we may imagine that each of these 'holes' is the Observer Himself, for a 'hole' can be thought of as a position of observation only as far as there is an Observer at it.

Or, we can also imagine that a position of observation and an Observer are the same. Then let us imagine that each and every point *within* this sphere *can happen to be a point of observation*, becoming thereby a place wherefrom the whole system might be seen from the outside, so that the very opposition, 'outside-inside' would be made irrelevant or meaningless. And let us, finally, imagine that each and every sentient being (*sattva*) is such a *potential* 'hole' or 'point of observation', and that all incalculable Buddhas are the *actual* 'holes', 'points of observation', which belong to this system, and do not belong to it, at one and the same time. And then, i.e., if looked at from this angle of an open system, Buddhism would be seen as the place where all categories are changing their meaning not because of the 'dialectics' of Buddhist methodology, but because of observations and observers interchanging their places and shifting from one point to another.

1.8. One may only conjecture as to whether or not the problem of subject in Buddhism could be considered outside an ordinary and habitual opposition 'object/subject'. One can, however, state with all certainty that a proposition like 'a *pudgala* ('person') is the subject of thinking' would indicate that the character and the context ('situation') of such a proposition is absolutely *objective*. And if we turn from 'thinking' to 'text' or, more exactly, 'a text of the Buddha', we see that His 'I' (not Self or *atta*) cannot be stated as the subject of this text. Because, as in Husserl, 'I' is neither suspended nor dismissed but remains here as a formal and totally objective condition of this *text*'s being. Even to Husserl it is not a man (or his mentality) who is subject to laws of consciousness, but consciousness itself. For when we say 'our cognition of consciousness' or 'our awareness of action', we treat ourselves as *agents*, i.e., as subjects of a phenomenal activity (as it was stated in 1.2.1 about the ancient Abhidhammists). Whereas when we think of consciousness itself—there can be no agent there, and there can be no 'subject of'... in the sense other than 'agent'. This applies not only to consciousness itself but also to all its derivations and interpretations.

When classical hermeneutics (Heidegger, Gadamer) dismisses the author of a text, it is not aware of what it dismisses, for to it author=agent=subject='I', whereas to a 'free phenomenologist' a text can be reduced ('reducted') to the thinking which, if observed externally, would be seen as a unique fact of consciousness only *nominally* (i.e., in the sense of *nāma-rūpa*) attributable to a 'person', and in no way to an 'I'. The last will remain as no more than a term of conventional description of mental states which correspond or, rather, may have corresponded to this fact of consciousness. Therefore, we can say, anticipating the content of Essay 4 (4.1) that though the dharmas are object of thought, this does not entail the thought being their subject. And all this in turn shows that the terms 'object' and 'subject' are used here not as opposed to one another, but as belonging to a metatheory which is not based on this or any other binary opposition.[21]

NOTES TO ESSAY 1

1 So, for example, speaking of yogacarins, H. Guenther writes: 'For them "mind" was not so much a "particular mind-entity", but a symbol for the particular [*mental-* A.P.] experience...' H. Guenther (1973, p. 93). This is not too bad to start with, but not enough to understand what their (yogacarins') *theory* of mind is about. For, if the *phenomenon* of this 'experience' (symbolized by 'mind') could, in its turn, be *reduced* to mind or one of the synonyms of the last, then there could have been *no theory* of mind in the *yogācāra* doctrine.

2 There is another distinction with respect to theory of consciousness, which now coincides, now overlaps with the previous one, although in some particular cases it seems to belong to a quite different level of our (modern) understanding of what a theory is, the level that could, in a totally conventional way, of course, be called 'semiotical'. Each theory, if regarded from the standpoint of this distinction, would be seen as a theory, only provided that it possesses its *meta-language*, that is, a special language by means of which and in terms of which a theory describes and interprets its own 'facts'. Being clearly aware of an utter vagueness of this 'definition', I would also like to state in a quite unambiguous way that, speaking generally, the criteria of a meta-language of a theory are merely subjective and totally arbitrary with respect to a concrete language used as a meta-language, as well as with respect to the concrete relations between the content of a theory and its meta-language. So, from the point of view of *an external observer* in such propositions as '*dharma* is a state of consciousness' and '1 is a number' we will have one and the same meta-language—English. But if looked at from the *inner* point of view of these two respective 'theories' (i.e., the Buddhist theory of consciousness and the theory of numbers), both 'dharma' and '1' would be seen as two terms of their respective metalanguages which might be thought of as absolutely *neutral* with relation to any *concrete* natural language, in this particular case—Sanskrit and English. And this is totally irrespective of the *fact* that, metalinguistically, 'dharma' remains a Sanskrit word, while '1' does not belong *specifically* to English. However, given all this, I cannot help being entirely aware of the undismissable fact that the very proposition '*dharma* is a state of consciousness'—is rather senseless in the sense of the Buddhist theory of consciousness. Senseless, because in the context of this theory 'dharma' *is* a state of consciousness, a state of consciousness *is* a 'dharma', *dharma* is consciousness (or mind, or thought, for that thing), so that what we deal with in this proposition is a series of fruitless synonyms, if we look at this proposition as belonging to a theory. What it quite certainly belongs to, is our own *meta-theory*, that is, so to speak, our own theoretical understanding and description (or, more exactly, the description of our understanding) of the Buddhist theory.

3 A. Maslow (1968, p. 3). The term 'metapsychology' was used by S. Freud in *The Psychopathology of Everyday Life* (1901), though 'metapsychological' appeared one year earlier, in *The Interpretation of Dreams.*

4 Ibid., p. 8.

5 This unawareness of his culminates in the following passage: 'The ability of *healthier* [A.P.] people to dip into unconscious and preconscious, to use and value their primary processes instead of fearing them, to accept their impulses instead of always controlling them, to be able to regress voluntarily without fear, turns out to be one of the main conditions of creativity' (ibid. p. 209). Particularly amusing is that the term 'healthier' immediately evokes the 'non-sick' of the Dhammapada, though with one difference, that we have 'creativity' instead of 'stopping the production of suffering' (*dukkhasamudayanirodha*) here.

6 Liam Hudson, in this connection, seems to be cleverer and, happily, less 'humanistic' than many others of his generation, though sharing with them some of their *cultural limitations*, but he is, at least, able to be aware that what he deals with, is not, and cannot be, a 'pure' or 'purely objective' psychology. When he says that, 'If the principle of relativism is to apply at all, it must encompass not only the people psychologists study, but the psychologists who do the studying'—he is aware of the *time*, as an undismissable factor of 'meta-psychology', but not of the *type of psychologist* which is culturally conditioned and whose mental activity

is *culturally subjective*. Which means that it works in terms of a certain cultural meta-language and symbolism, see L. Hudson (1972, pp. 158–9). In fact, what has been recently described by Liam Hudson as the double *ethos* of modern psychologists—their division into 'soft' and 'hard' (read—'subjective' / 'objective' or 'personal' / 'impersonal' or humane-ness' / 'thing-hood') seems to be no more than a very temporal *cultural* attitude in his own (and his contemporaries') *self-awareness*. This, as such, has nothing to do with phenomenology which, in principle at least, does not deal with either the personal or impersonal, but only with ways in which *facts of consciousness* are (or may have been) given to their observer. The dichotomy of 'arts/sciences' is as far from being 'a theory' as Marcuse's 'Eros' or Laing's 'divided self' for at least one reason: all these *ideas* cannot be related to any 'given' fact of consciousness otherwise than through or by means of certain, purely cultural, symbolism (though, how tempting it is to call it 'metaphorism' instead!) which in the first case is represented by 'unicorn', in the second by 'Eros', in the third by 'over-grown garden'. Moreover, the very idea of 'fact' with respect to consciousness is, theoretically, related not to consciousness itself, but to its *cultural reflexion*. This, in turn, is tantamount to a situation where, in order to understand 'something' about consciousness, and prior to such an understanding, one would have necessarily to read some texts of *one's own culture*, which would provide one with a symbolic framework—or else, one's theme would never have been formulated.

7 L. Wittgenstein (1980, p. vii). The term 'concept' here is almost synonymous with 'word'. So, he calls 'to feel' a *psychological verb* (p. 11e).

8 'But I am saying: if the facts of nature were different we should have different concepts. That is an hypothesis. I have no use for it', ibid., p. 12e. But he cannot be left with this ambiguity and, as it were, asks himself: 'Isn't it [the nature of concepts—A.P.] the nature of phenomena in disguise?'

9 Ibid., p.8e.

10 We may, by paraphrasing W. James, say in complete agreement with *yogācāra* doctrine, that one and the same 'thing' can be the *interpretation* of the 'seen' in one state of consciousness, and 'the seen' in another.

11 'The content of experience, of experiencing: I *know* what it's like to see red, green, blue..., I *know* what it's like to feel sorrow, fear, joy...' ibid., p. 19e. Knowledge (that is, *his* knowledge) is the only content of experience.

12 Ibid., pp. 86–90. It is when Wittgenstein makes a clear distinction between 'himself thinking' and 'thinking' (which he never ceased to make), that all affinities with Buddhism become absolutely senseless. C. Gudmunsen writes: 'It is just here... where the comparison [of Buddhism—A.P.] with Wittgenstein is particularly fruitful. The organism and its environment are indeed mutually dependent; but that does not mean that I disappear in my surroundings' (C. Gudmunsen, 1977, p. 78). Such a 'naturalistic' interpretation is so typical of a modern Wittgensteinean adept who simply cannot see that, speaking Abhidharmically, there is neither 'organism' nor 'surroundings' in terms of *states of consciousness* (dharmas), and that the only relevant (though not real) distinction is between 'the subject' and 'the object' *in* these dharmas. That is, the subject and the object understood only in respect of *thought* and in no other way. This means (among other things) that both 'organism' and 'surroundings' would be understood in the sense of 'the psychic conceived as the object' [and put under the rubric of the first two dharmas (see Essay 5, Table VI, △△1, 2)—'form' and 'sensation'] and, thereby, *opposed* to 'thought conceived in the sense of the subject' (*citta*, the fifth *dharma*). How naive are the attempts to 'reconvert' the Abhidhamma, with help of Wittgenstein and Russell, into a home-made mystical naturalism!

13 Moreover, what I really mean is that, *behind numerical complexes* covering practically all numbers from 1 to 12, (and many more besides) *met in the Suttas and Abhidhamma lies the triple* (if not trinitarian), *not dual, character of postulation.*

14 I am aware of all arbitrariness of this assertion but, none the less, the more I think about it, the more I am inclined to think that some, even purely religious systems of thoughts, doctrines and teachings might have arisen as *more theoretical* than what they became at later stages of their historical development.

15 E. Cassirer (1955, p. 73).

16 There is no dichotomy 'thought/no thought' or 'one thought/another thought'. The very

structure of theoretical understanding of thought in the Buddhist philosophy is *threefold*—'thought, no thought, another thought'.

17 I.e., the states of consciousness, more or less corresponding to *our* meaning of 'discursive thinking', i.e., *vitakka*, *vicāra* (see Table VI, Essay 5, △△6, 7) and, in different contexts, *saṃjñā* ('apperception' or 'notion').

18 The late Edward Conze, though a brilliant Buddhologist, seems to have failed to understand the most essential feature of the Abhidhamma—its total formality and impersonality. Probably his personal gnosticism (he called it 'philosophia perennis') proved to be incongruous with the neutrality of the Abhidhammic organization of thought, equally indifferent to the differences in *human* mentalities and temperaments and to the differences in the ages or phases in the history of mankind. See E. Conze (1979, II, particularly, p. 38.)

19 Here we have been confronted with the question of 'Absolute Objectivity' in a religion. Marco Pallis (1964) very ingeniously suggests that in Buddhism it is 'the uncreated' or 'incomposite' (*asaṅkhata, asaṃskṛta*) that figures as the *symbol* of this objectivity.

20 To a certain extent 'observer' here is opposed to 'creator' in Christianity and Judaism.

21 From this it inevitably follows that no single opposition, however general or abstract, could be used not only in describing Buddhism but even in describing one's understanding thereof. And nowhere is this 'binary inability' to understand oneself in relation to Buddhism shown clearer than in Lévi-Strauss. He wrote (1976, p. 540): 'This religion of non-knowledge is not based on our inability to understand. It bears witness to that ability and raises us to a pitch at which we can discover the truth in the form of a mutual exclusiveness of being and knowledge. ...It reduces the metaphysical problem to one of human behaviour—a distinction it shares only with Marxism'. Here he failed to understand that the very human behaviour is reduced in Buddhism to *consciousness which is no knowledge*, that knowledge figures as no more than *a way* of understanding the consciousness, and that being does not count as a transcendental category at all. In this connection, L. Kolakowski (1982, p. 42) is *subjectively* much nearer to what can be called 'an authentic European understanding of Buddhism' when he writes: '...a Buddhist contemplative is capable of saying "I do not exist" and of literally meaning it; an utterance which Christians... would normally understand only in a metaphorical way...' In stating this, he, unlike Lévi-Strauss, seems to be able to grasp that there are two (at least) ways of the understanding of 'non-existence', which cannot be worded in the context and in terms of *one* religious postulate.

2. THE CONCEPT OF SENTIENT BEING IN THE SUTTA-NIPĀTA

A Comparative Study

2.0.1. At the very core of the problem—'What is comparative philosophy?'—lies another and far more essential question: *Must thinking be marked, or can it be marked, by anything which is not thinking itself?* If the answer is negative, then we must pack our bags and move elsewhere. But if the reply is in doubt, it gives us an opportunity to look for marks of thinking, at any rate in our own thinking before going further afield to ancient India or even modern England. What I mean by this is that each time I compare Berkeley with Asaṅga, or Buddhism with Kantianism, I have first of all to construct a sort of *meta-system* which, not being either of them, can cover both of them as two different and concrete cases of the same meta-theoretical approach—taking for granted of course, that this approach is broader and, alas, less clear than that of the systems compared. Only with such a meta-theory is it possible to ascertain the criteria which are necessary for philosophical comparison, however unclear and uncertain they may appear. For instance, if I am going to compare the concept of 'form' in Plato with that in early Buddhist philosophy, I must bear in mind that this seemingly nonsensical task is realizable only on condition that my own *meta-concept* of form is neither connected with 'being' (as in Plato) nor non-connected with 'being' (as in Buddhism). That is, it must necessarily be something within my meta-approach, which is *neutral* or 'not thought of' in respect of this connection. Similarly, if I wish to compare the concepts of 'I' in Buddhism and in modern psychoanalysis, I can do so only provided that there is at my disposal a *third concept* of 'I', which includes these two as its varieties.

The problem of 'markedness' or 'non-markedness' of thinking will then undoubtedly be included in this meta-theory of mine as one of its elements, in respect of which the Buddhist concepts of 'thought' (*citta*) and 'mark', or 'sign' (*lakṣaṇa, nimitta*) will be compared with similar, or analogous, or even altogether different concepts of other philosophies. I can also compare these Buddhist concepts with those of my meta-theory, using the latter as already 'not mine', that is, as already estranged from my own approach and, therewith, turned into an *objectified text* external to my immediate philosophizing.

2.0.2. In so far as one's approach remains meta-theoretical in the comparison of various philosophies, it can conventionally be characterized not only as *subjective*, but also as *conscious.* To say 'conscious' here means that I am able (at least, in principle) to reflect upon my *operating with terms and notions as mine* as well as upon my reflection itself. Yet once looked at and speculated upon as *not mine* (that is, as already objectified), this meta-approach reveals its non-specific aspects, which I am aware of as not only not mine, but as positively attributed or attributable to a time, place or manner of philosophizing which I share with other persons, and which I am not able to define as mine or theirs. Because, it is thoughts, not persons that we are in fact dealing with in this case. The problem, formulated as 'must thinking be marked?', then appears as connected with, say, modern semiotical trends in which each and every *thinkable* thing is a sign. Or, with renewed hermeneutical attempts to explore each and everything as having a textual meaning of *its own.* Or with late logico-pragmatical attempts to revise Peircean semiotics in terms of the fundamental duality of all texts (as 'texts of interpretation' and 'texts for interpretation') etc. This leads us to a concept of *apperceptive structures*, which includes in itself all elements inherent in my philosophizing together with the intentions and impulses towards the realization of these elements in other *texts.*

2.0.3. With subjective meta-theory and objective apperception we can at least compare one thing with another in the philosophy—provided, of course, that the very notion of philosophy is no more than a meta-notion here. That is, it is used only when we deal with various *terms and texts* which are *a priori* defined formally as 'philosophical', but are not yet defined as philosophical in their contents. *Terms and texts here are two very different objects of investigation, because they require two completely different methodologies* (the term 'object' here signifies a 'thing' and not an idea).

In the case of *terms* it is necessary to produce a text where a term is interpreted (provided that it is a term within the concrete text) through one's meta-terms and within one's apperceptive structure in the context of which this term is thought to have been used. This term is then to be reconstructed, as it were, from outside, as a primarily given content.

In the case of *texts*, it is necessary to produce a text of interpretation where the field of reconstruction of contents is limited by a given text itself, and the apperceptive structure appears only as the final result of such an interpretation, the meanings of terms (concepts) serving as mere elements of the apperceptive structure. [I also admit here a possibility that a single term can be interpreted as a text or vice versa, but this is another matter.]

2.1.0. For this essay I propose to deal with some Buddhist philosophical concepts *as terms*, using the respective meta-terms for their interpretation. I am going to start with considerations on the group of notions connected with 'being' and its derivatives and then pass to the concept of 'sentient being'. I shall conclude in the next two essays with an investigation of 'thought' as the core of 'the sentient' and the problem of markedness of thought in connection with 'a person' or 'an individual'.

2.1.0.1. 'Re-ontologization' is used here as a mere *meta-term* to denote the direction or the chief tendency regulating the change (only partly historical change) in the Buddhist understanding of thought, mind and consciousnes.

When I say 're-ontologization', I do not mean thereby that there existed, at some time or somewhere, a certain religio-philosophical background which included some ontological categories or postulates, denied, negated or abandoned by Buddhism, and then later acquired, adopted or rediscovered by it in one way or another. The approach I follow is quite different. I observe certain ideas in late Buddhist sources as ontological, then I go back to the early Pali texts, the ideas of which can hardly be interpreted as ontological, and only after that, return again to the late ones in an attempt to discover those trends in early texts, which could be interpreted as leading from an absolute non-ontology to a relative ontology. In my opinion, there are in each philosophy certain *inner conditions* which cannot be reduced either to the socio-cultural factors preceding it, or to the impact of other philosophies and religions. It is these *inherent* conditions of philosophizing to which I attribute all the main changes and modifications we find in late Buddhism compared with earlier Buddhism. In saying this, I do not assert that all extra-Buddhistic circumstances were of no importance for the development of Buddhist religious philosophy. Nevertheless, whenever one looks at Buddhism, one finds already formed its own *apperceptive structure* much superior in strength and persistence to all external factors and influences.

2.1.0.2. For instance, I may say that the apperceptive structure of Brahmanical philosophy was formed around the 'ontological axis' of Being understood not only as Being of Atman–Brahman in the sense of 'thou art that' (*tat tvaṃ asi*, where *tad* is 'Brahman'), but also in the sense of reality of the *relatedness of everything* to Atman-Brahman. This, in turn, means that any relational category —Knowledge, for example—may turn out to be real in so far as it *is* related to what is considered to be the reality par excellence. Even an outright denial of such reality, which is made in many interpretations of Buddhist philosophy, does not change this apperceptive structure. As for Buddhism, it never related itself to Brahmanic ontology as to something to be denied or refuted, but rather dismissed it as theoretically incomprehensible and empirically undiscoverable. This Buddhist attitude was due, as it seems to me, mainly to the fact that the very question of the non-empirical reality of anything never stood at the centre of Buddhist philosophical apperception and remained, as it were, latent, awaiting its hour to emerge within the context of relativistic conceptions of the late philosophical schools.[1] At the same time, it must be borne in mind that the term 'relativistic' (that is, viewed from the angle of *śūnyatā*) was never used by Buddhist scholars in a purely anti-ontological sense. I may add that the usually imagined picture of permanent confrontations of Buddhist philosophy with the ontological concepts of the *Vedānta* can be partly admitted only provided that we look at these confrontations and differences retrospectively. Because, if looked at from the time when one or another Buddhist school actually worked, this 'anti-ontological' situation would be seen in a quite different and much less unambiguous light.[2]

When I call this work a comparative study, it does not necessarily mean that ontology in Buddhism is always compared with ontology in other philosophies. My own philosophical standpoint, however eclectic it may be, remains not only the main criterion and basis for comparison, but also the main object thereof. When comparing, for instance, the Mother *Prajñāpāramitā* with Sophia of Christian gnostics, I am fully aware that it is my philosophical apperception through which both of them are reflected prior to their being compared, and that I have always to bear in mind all the metaphysical consequences of my inability to identify my mode of reflection with that of the philosophies compared. But, at the same time, I strongly admit the idea of *objectivity* of apperception. Moreover, I believe even in a certain objectivity of apperception understood in a quasi-historical sense, in which, for instance, E. Husserl divided the whole 'time of philosophy' into two periods: pre-theoretical and theoretical.[3] And, indeed, the main problem we are facing here is not whether these Buddhist ideas are or are not philosophical, but whether they could be regarded as a *theory* (see 1.2.1.) meta-philosophically, i.e. irrespective of all comparative criteria.

2.1.0.3. The very concept of ontologization differs markedly in Christian theology and Buddist metaphysics. In the former it means the absolute of the personality, as in the case of the Divine Absolute of the Holy Trinity conceived in itself as the objective reality, or achievable subjectively through a process of mystical inspiration or revelation. While in the latter there is a sort of '*de-absolutization of man*', leading finally to the total '*de-anthropologization of consciousness*' achieved or achievable through the process of yogic intuition. It is evident, of course, that neither 'ontology', nor even less 're-ontologization', can be found in the terminology of Buddhist texts. However, we find 'Being' everywhere within the process of our own understanding. There it figures, now as a simple word in practical everyday use ('I *am* looking at the sun', where there is no implication that my 'looking' can exist only on the strength of my 'being'), now as an instrument used in one's empirical self-awareness ('I am *looking* at the sun', where there may be an implication of connectedness of my looking and being),[4] now as a term of philosophical or theological meta-language ('I am looking at the sun', where there is an implication that this or any other described or describable fact can be described or describable only on the strength of some *being* to which 'I', 'looking' or 'am' can be ascribed as its manifestations). Of these three uses only the first can be referred to as *linguistically* (not metalinguistically, that is) present in the texts of Buddhist Suttas. As to the second one, there is a very strong implication in Buddhism that 'to be' or 'being' exist only in the sense of *strict factuality*, that is completely unrelated to any metaphysical reality. Thus, such a purely Buddhistic formula as 'as it is' (*yathābhūtam*), if applied to 'I am looking at the sun', would refer neither to the reality of the 'sun', nor to that of 'I', but reflect the factuality of the situation as a whole.[5] At the same time, we must note that this Buddhist formula, given at least its negative connection with the ontological postulates, might be considered as a term of meta-language of metaphysics.[6] As to the third use, it cannot be discovered in the texts of the Suttas at all, which, nevertheless, should not prevent us from attempting to find some meta-term which would serve as a Buddhistic equivalent to that of 'Being'. It may be that this idea of 'Being' finds its metaphysical counterpart in the Buddhist concept of 'composition', 'complexity', 'synergy' of everything which *is*—a view supported by the fact that in Buddhism *to be* is equivalent to *to be composed of...*, *to consist of...*, or *to be concomitant with...*, However that may be, it is important to stress that, speaking epistemologically, this idea in Buddhism is absolutely devoid of reflective characteristics and presents, as such, a clear instance of *objectification* of each and every subjectivity.[7]

2.1.0.4. Thus, the main *metaphysical* problem of Buddhist philosophy is the problem of *complexity* of... everything. More exactly, every *thinkable* phenomenon is complex, composite, in the sense that it can exist as a phenomenon only in so far as it is complex. Complexity is an indispensable and powerful predicate in a statement where a subject, of whatever kind, is of secondary importance, and where 'is' is no more than a function of complexity of what is conventionally considered as 'being'.[8]

This 'problem of complexity' is presented in the Buddhist philosophical approach from three main standpoints which, though overlapping each other, are distinctly discernible.

2.1.0.4.1. The first view, which I conventionally call the *mentalist* line, can be observed in the philosophical attempts towards understanding of the *mental as complex*, the *mentality as consisting of various mental structures*, and the *mental structures themselves as very complex phenomena* of empirical mental life. However, and this is speaking methodologically, a very important thing to note, the analysis of mentality never began in Buddhist philosophy with the notion or concept of mentality understood as a *definite object of thinking*, called 'mentality', or 'mind' (*manas*). On the contrary, we can clearly trace throughout the texts of the Suttas as well as those of the Abhidhamma that this analytical process started with a very vague idea of 'something which is mentality' as the first step in understanding. Then it goes on with investigation of the various *empirically* observed and observable things, facts and events ascribed to this mental 'something' as its constituents and components. And only after that does mentality cease to be 'something', and become a certain *complex object*, comprising all these things, facts and events, and giving them their own respective transcendental meanings, that is, the meanings of various *mental states*. Yet, once thought of or meditated upon as a complex transcendental object, mentality changes into a 'mental state of all states', that is, it changes from 'something' into, practically, anything. [When I say 'all mental states', I mean also those which were not empirically observed or otherwise detected and described, but were rather thought of in terms of infinitude.] And finally, mentality assumes *its own* transcendental meaning, that is quite independent of that of 'mentality as consisting of ... ', changing thereby, from a 'mental state' into a 'state of consciousness'. It is 'state of consciousness' alone that allows one to leave empirical ground and start thinking phenomenologically. That is, to start analysing thinking itself in terms of consciousness and to start analysing all possible mental structure in terms of *unstructured* consciousness. This state of consciousness is no longer thought of as complex, but as an elementary *dhamma*, an indivisible atomic unit of conscious existence. But however simple and unstructured such a state of consciousness may be, it cannot be prevented from becoming again and again reinterpreted or reinterpretable in terms of mental complexes and structures, when it is needed. These four steps in the analysis of mentality are not to be apprehended as necessarily subsequent — there is no methodological sequence of any kind here. We are dealing rather with simultaneous or achronic acts of apprehension of mentality, so that each given fact finds its place either among mental structures, or within complex mentality as such, or as a state of consciousness (which, of course, is also 'mental', but in a quite different sense and on a quite different level of philosophical approach).

2.1.0.4.2. The second, or dharmic line, that of states of consciousness, is characterized by the permanent efforts in early Buddhist metaphysics to portray everything which is thought to exist in terms of final units which constitute individual streams of consciousness (otherwise called individual continuums of thought). Within the context of this approach each state of consciousness, that is, each *dharma* is, as such, elementary and non-composite, and each individual continuum of thought is composed of states of consciousness of various kinds. Similarly, each thing thought of or thinkable exists only in sequences of various dharmas, and if understood in this sense, might be presented *mentally* as a composition of dharmas closely connected with each other in a sort of time-space sequential configuration. If looked at from this angle, all things which either think or which are thought of, are also dharmic although they are *composite*, as distinct from dharmas proper in the sense mentioned above (see below, 6.1–3).

2.1.0.4.3. The third line conventionally called 'sattvic' (*sattva*—'a sentient being') seems to be particularly difficult for our understanding (though I doubt if its understanding was any easier in Buddha's time), because the idea of the universe never found its positive articulate expression even in terms of 'something', not to speak of some *thing*. In this context the analytical approach was completely forsaken by Buddhist teachers, if of course it ever existed. I think, it is here more than anywhere else, that we can observe a simultaneous multi-aspectedness, so typical of the Buddhist philosophical attitude towards *the things external* (but not externalized). If we follow this line, there is no such 'thing' as 'the whole universe', in distinction from the mentalist line where there *is* something which is mental. But at the same time, there are various sentient beings experiencing various tendencies in accordance with which they find themselves in various planes, spheres and modes (*dhātu*, *avacara*, *gati*) of existence, now placed more or less hierarchically, now overlapping one another. But it is not the whole universe which is hierarchically constructed and classificationally presented here. It is these sentient beings, through and by which only such a construction and presentation is made possible. It is these sentient beings which are primarily, separately and singly given in their beginninglessness—not the universe. For the universe, as such, arises, as it were, as a by-product of their aggregated sentience, having thereby no being of its own. The main problem is that this sentience is not a transcendental category in Buddhist metaphysics, and that is why it often assumes a more naturalistic (naturalistic not in the sense of 'Naturding', but strictly methodologically) than phenomenal interpretation.

2.1.1.0. A sentient being can be cognized neither as something (as in the case of mentality before it has been dealt with analytically) nor as a structure, nor as a transcendental state (as in the case of a *dharma*). A sentient being stays *as it is*, remaining throughout hundreds of texts as an extremely odd notion which presents, as I imagine it, a sort of 'conceptual hole' in Buddhist metaphysical terminology. It preserved its purely pragmatic and soteriological meaning until it found its purely relativistic, and therewith, relatively negative explanation in the texts of *Prajñāpāramitā*, and thereafter assumed its final, relatively positive explanation in the texts of the late Tantric Schools (of so-called New Tantra) in Tibet.

It is in the oldest of the Suttas of the Pali Canon that a sentient being appears as primarily given and uninterpretable, yet it figures there as a *concrete* (and what is a really concrete thing, needs no interpretation) *subject* of various tendencies of a specifically *religious* character. I stress 'religious' here as distinct from philosophical as well as yogic meanings, bearing in mind the Buddhist theory of Liberation (or in Māll's terminology—'lysiology')[9] and the conception of the Path. The whole world then is to be viewed as no more than a mere function of all separate existences of sentient beings, given that all the Buddhas remain *outside* the universe of sentient beings, because Buddhas' sentience cannot be cognized objectively either as objective or as subjective. Strictly speaking, it is to this point that the very beginning of Buddhology, that is, the science about Buddhas, must be traced, the science where Buddhas are thought of in terms of a zero-class of non-sentient non-beings.[10] Yet, in the Pali Suttas sentient beings still figure as definite entities endowing the universe with a relative definiteness, though not making it an entity thereby.

2.1.1.1. The first part of this work is devoted to the interpretation of several passages and concepts of the *Sutta-Nipāta* in the sense of the third line in Buddhist philosophizing. I do not maintain that in such an old Sutta as this the description of sentient beings with their classifications and symbols can be subsumed under the rubric of a theory *per se* (i.e., subjectively conscious of itself as a theory). I am suggesting only that in these descriptions we can discern glimpses of some subsequent theoretical concepts of a quasi-ontological character.

The *Mettā-sutta* of *SN* might well be used as a *basic* text for our understanding —however hypothetical—of the character and the role of the concept of 'sentient being'. In this text we do not find the real concept developed, only a term used in a certain *context*, the interpretation of which is suggestive for the working out of the concept itself.

2.1.1.2. The beginning of *Metta-sutta* contains a short description of a 'person' who has realized (*abhisamecca*) the Calm State (*santapada*), and a few ethical precepts necessary in his behaviour towards *other* persons (which implies indirectly that his *inner mental* qualities have already been perfected with respect to the Calm State). Then this description abruptly comes to a stop and we see, as it were, a direct address to ... and it is here that difficulties start—

May all sentient beings be happy!

This line serving as the refrain to verses 145 and 147 of *SN* still leaves us in uncertainty as to the person to whom it is addressed. That is, whether it is addressed to a person who has already realized the Calm State for himself and is now to be turned towards other beings, or whether it is addressed to all other beings, spiritually assisting them in their natural desire to be happy.

2.1.1.3. I am inclined to think that we are facing here a merely *pragmatic religious situation* in which the whole universe is, as it were, divided into two parts. One part comprises all sentient beings in their separateness from the Calm State, and another comprises those in the Calm State, existing as if the inner mental changes had already been completed whereby they became separated from the world (*loka*) of sentient beings. This 'appeal' to happiness carries the meaning of an intermediary and purely religious action by means of which those in the Calm State are connected with those outside. That is, in this formula (which, by the way, later became the textual basis for one of the most important and widely-spread Mahayanist prayers) we are dealing with the sacred instrument of Compassion (*mettā*), with which the bridge between inner self-perfection and outer natural *status quo* was constructed.

2.1.1.4. Secondly, this religious situation can be interpreted as an *objective* one, that is, as a situation which becomes possible only when there is somebody who can *observe* it from outside, from the point of view of the *third person*. This, in turn, implies that such an Observation (*anupassanā*, *SN*, 477, 723–759; also 'observing'—*pekkhamāna*, *SN*, 39) is performed only by the person who cannot be identified in a *positive way* with either side in this situation, that is, either with those who have realized the Calm State (Arhats), or with all other sentient beings. I stress this objectivity in order to emphasize that 'objective' here is a meta-term, an interpretational instrument quite distinct from the concept of 'objectification' (which is related to a specifically and technically yogic process of changing what is 'the subjective' into 'the objective', one's body or mind, for instance). Here to the contrary, the very notion of a sentient being is inherently and primarily objective. Buddha, therefore, figures in this situation as the *third person*, though in the passage itself He figures in the first person, and His words are addressed to all sentient beings (understood as actual or potential *objects of compassion*)[11] and are conveyed through the Arhats already exempt from the class of objects. That is why a little further on, when He turns again to precepts, He says to these Arhats (not to the sentient beings, of course): 'May he cultivate his mind in limitless compassion towards all animate beings' (*SN*, 149).

2.1.2.1. This objective situation gives us a very complicated picture of various gradations of objects, one example of which is shown in the category of 'animate beings' used as a sub-class of all sentient beings.

In *SN*, 146–147, we read:

> Whichever animate beings there are,
> shaking or strong, without exception,
> who [are] long or big,
> short, infinitesimal, massive,
> who [are] seen or unseen,
> [those] who live far [or] not far,
> those who [have] been or [still are] seeking for becoming
> may all sentient beings be happy.

2.1.2.2. The category of 'animate beings' (*pāṇabhūta*) is included in the broadest category of 'sentient beings' (*satta*) together with the very different and specific category of 'beings' or 'spirits' (*bhūta*).[12] The latter is, as it were, opposed to the even narrower sub-category of 'man', or, more exactly *genus humanum* (*manusiyapajā*) in 222–223 of *SN*, where all spirits are aroused, extolled and addressed in exactly the same manner as 'all sentient beings' in 146–147. The only difference is that the spirits are asked in addition to help and protect men because the latter bring them offerings:

> 222 Whatever beings have come together,
> whether earthly or those of the intermediate space,
> let all beings be glad.
> 223 Therefore, all spirits, all of you, take care of mankind,
> and be friendly [to them],
> who bring you offerings day and night;
> therefore, do protect them strenuously.

[I consider the last two verses to be of particular interest because the worship of spirits is not denied or rejected by Buddha here, but rather *neutralized*, ousted into the sphere of *cult*, of *natural religion*. And by this, the worship of spirits finds its place as a thing *naturally* appropriate to all sentient beings who have not yet realized the Calm State.][13]

The question, however, remains: What does it mean—'whatever animate beings (*pāṇabhūta*) there are, either those who have become (*bhūta*), or those still seeking for becoming (*sambhavesi*, *SN*, 147)'?

2.1.2.3. At the very foundation of this rather strange classification of all sentient beings (*sabbasatta*) is a very deep idea of the *tendency to transformation*. There is no *essence*,[14] but a mere tendency. On the one hand, it is a tendency to grow and grow grosser and thicker, and on the other hand, it is a counter-tendency to assume a *form*. In the course of development of this *counter-tendency*, we see the passing of some sentient beings to the dynamism of a quite different character and direction; they get thinner and thinner, subtler and subtler, until they become 'mere forms', 'forms only' (*rūpa*) and even 'formless ones' (*arūpa*) thereafter.[15] But out of what are these tendencies supposed to grow and dynamize? Out of nothing! And it is because of this that the third tendency arises, as it were, from nowhere, for it is not to be found either in nature or in counter-nature. It arises in a sentient being able to rid itself of the first two tendencies. Thus we have a tendency to dismiss the primary dualism of these two tendencies and to establish a new dualism of 'what is and what is not related to nature'. This new dualism can be detected in, or at least is deducible from, the beginning of *The Sutta of Turning the Wheel of Dhamma* (*Dhamma-cakka-pavattana-sutta*).

2.2.1.0. At this point we require a 'mechanism', an 'operator', through which this tendency towards transformation inherent in *all* sentient beings is brought into action. It is to be found in a very subtle notion of 'womb' (*gabbhaseyyā*) which serves as the main modifier of everything which is *externally* related to a sentient being conceived as possessing or not possessing form. Form is understood in *SN* as everything *formal* in relation to sentient beings, that is, in a much broader sense than that in which this term is technically used in Abhidhammic metaphysics. So, in the *SN*, 29 Buddha says: 'Like a bull having broken its bonds... I shall not enter again a womb'. And again later (*SN*, 152):

> He, disinclined (to embrace any) view,
> perfect in conduct, with accomplished vision,
> With greediness for sensual objects subdued,
> (He) will never again go to a womb.

2.2.1.1. In this sentence of Buddha, 'I shall not again enter into a womb', we have an example of objective causation (both in a positive and negative sense).[16] Having accomplished the rejection of His subjective psychical life, He found himself in a position where the very objectivity of *karma* (i.e., kamma, 'work', 'action' taken in its transmigrational aspect) had already ceased to exist. What we are dealing with here is not only the subjectivity of feelings, emotions, or attachments, but the whole of subjectivity already transformed mentally and intellectually into *conditions*. These conditions cause joy (*nandanā*) and sorrow (*socanā*) in a sentient being *subjectively*. But, if looked at *objectively*, these conditions participate in producing man's entry into a new womb. Thus, by becoming *subjectively unconditioned* (*nirupadhi*), a man on the one hand does not feel sorrow and joy (*na nandati na socati*), and on the other hand does not enter a new womb (*SN*, 33–34). To put it in a slightly different way, I would say that while a conditioned person thinks that he *feels* badly because the objective conditions are bad, an unconditioned person *knows* that *all* subjective conditions are bad because they make a sentient being subject to *objective* conditions of renewed existences which, in turn, are bad because they are the *conditions*.

2.2.1.2. The womb in *SN* figures as the very focus of all that is *natural*, and to cease entering a womb seems to have been in early Buddhism the most concrete and extreme case of *anti-naturality*.[17] The expression 'he will never again go to a womb' is coterminous with 'he is going to immortality', for the latter speaks of a *supernatural* state, while the former clearly refers to a pure negation of nature in its most essential process and function. On the other hand, the expression 'he will never again...', which is at the very end of *Mettasutta* of *SN*, can be interpreted as having its positive equivalent in the term 'Quiet Place' (or, 'Calm State')—*santapada* found at the very beginning.

2.2.1.3. These observations should not be taken to mean that the womb is necessarily and actually present in the existences of *all sentient beings* who, in their entirety, constitute nature. They mean only that every sentient being, irrespective of the time or place it finds itself in, and at this very moment of observation, is either born of a womb, or is going to enter it. If looked at from this angle, the womb can be conceived as if it were the centre of a field of certain 'natural forces' (that is, of those of 'becoming', 'being', 'growing') towards which all *separate* beings are oriented in one way or another, phylogenetically as well as ontogenetically.

2.2.2. The concept of nature set out here is purely dynamic, because it does not imply the idea of 'the whole of nature' in its unity. That is, nature exists only in completely *separate* beings, *all of them sentient*, which as such, have either emerged from the womb or are about to enter it (given of course, that there is no other direction for them). That is why we read of sentient beings who are 'seeking for becoming', that is, beings of whom nothing more can be said than that they are 'sentient' and directed towards the womb. Therefore, it can be suggested, as is shown in *SN*, 145–147, that the notion of 'sentient being' is the broadest category standing, as it were, on the very edge of the sphere of nature. Which in turn means, that this notion covers not only all 'beings', but also those 'animate beings' which have not yet become, that is, have not yet realized their 'centripetal' dynamism directed towards the womb. The last line of the passage thus implies that there are 'animate beings' who *are not* 'seeking for becoming', and it is because of that that they will never again go into a womb.

2.2.3. Psychologically speaking, the characterization of sentient beings as on 'the frontier of nature' is entirely negative, and hence insufficient to understand them: it needs a further explanation. The sentient beings, described so far by the Buddha in entirely negative terms, that is to say, as negatively oriented towards nature, must have been offered a positive *super-orientation.* In fact, this super-orientation is already contained in those lines where Buddha, speaking from (and obviously of) Himself, said: 'May all sentient beings be happy!' Immediately after this he advises everyone to 'cultivate an immeasurable mind of friendliness towards all beings', desiring to make their mind as it were *reoriented* in a completely positive way. This reorientation is expressed even more concretely in the following verses speaking of one 'whose mind is already disposed towards all beings'. It seems to me that what we have here is a subjective, positive, mental (that is, belonging to mind) factor, going hand-in-hand with a more objective, negative (that is, directed against nature) factor. The second factor exists as an alternative to the natural drive towards the womb, and both of them constitute this new super-orientation. But why 'super'? In my opinion we are dealing here with a situation in which one is clearly urged to cultivate such mental attitudes as will enable one to *contain* the whole phenomenal world within the grasp of a particular sort of Knowledge. The particularity of this Knowledge consists of its unique ability to grasp the positive (as 'mercifulness towards...') and negative ('away from... the womb') tendencies *as one*, thereby enabling a person who is endowed with such knowledge to stand, as it were, on the very margin between nature and non-nature. [Such knowledge, if taken in its *operational aspect*, assumes the term of 'Re-knowledge' (*prajñā, paññā*), while if taken in its purely *theoretical aspect*, it assumes the term of 'Further—or—meta-knowledge' (*abhijñā, abhiññā*). Both of them in turn find themselves complemented by the term and notion of 'recognition' (*aññā*), whereby they are referred to a concrete person as their bearer. And both types of knowledge are, as it were, opposed to a different and 'lower' sort of knowledge understood more as 'cognition of objects' and assuming the name of *saṃjñā*.]

2.2.4. There is another question left unanswered—can we call the womb a 'symbol of nature'? Or a symbol of something to be got rid of on the Way towards Nirvaṇa? And here, I am bound to say, the situation is ambiguous. Because, forgetting for the time being the context in which 'the womb' has been used, and passing to the broader contexts wherein it was and might have been used (it does not matter whether it was before or after this one), we shall come to a series of observations which can be summarized in the following way:

(1) The womb as a *notion*, reflecting two quite different and even contrary ideas: (A) that of the whole of nature to be dismissed, that is, an abstract and absolutely negative idea; and (B) that of the universal (and also 'natural') 'instrument of transformation', by means of which alone, a sentient being can be born as a man and thereafter become an *arhat*—in this case it is a more concrete and relatively positive idea. It is obvious that in the latter case we are dealing with the womb as a *conditio sine qua non* of Buddhahood too.

(2) The womb taken as a *visual image*, which evokes an idea of the 'universal container' or 'depository' where everything is included in a potential, hidden or not yet completely actualized state. However, as far as early Buddhism goes, nature itself is thought of as existing in the state of actualization, which means that this hidden potentiality might be referred to future Buddhas only, in which case we are dealing with a more abstract and purely positive idea.

(3) The womb as a *word*, used to provide pupils or beginners with a verbal instrument for their awareness both of their belonging to nature and of their possessing the hidden capacity to get rid of nature. In this there is a concrete and relatively positive idea.

If conceived in their connectedness, these three aspects of the 'womb' are to be understood as the three *forms*, that is mental, visual and word-forms *of the symbol*, the meaning of which cannot be defined otherwise than as 'everything which contains, or is being passed through'. Yet, and this is even more interesting, if we go a little deeper into the symbolic situation centred around the womb, we will clearly see that all tendencies (both centrifugal and centripetal) of all sentient beings are, in fact, attributed to their *sentience* rather than to their being. In other words, these tendencies are easily reducible to those of *thinking as such*. The womb then serves as an *object of thinking*, or as a symbolic objectification of the process wherein thought reflects its own tendencies *as they are*.

[2.2.5. There is one thing of overwhelming importance in Buddhist metaphysics too often omitted by epistemologically-minded Buddhologists, even by those of Stcherbatsky's rank—*the object of thinking*. In Buddhist metaphysics the object of thinking is apprehended as something totally different and completely divorced from the *object of knowledge* and, thereby lying in a dimension quite different from that subject to an epistemological analysis. First of all, the object of thinking is absolutely *unspecified:* theoretically at least,it might be anything excepting only what is *unthinkable* (*acintya*). This means that it is unthinkable not because we cannot think of it, but because it cannot be thought of by the nature of thinking itself (which, however, is nearly the same, empirically).]

2.2.6. However, these tendencies towards and away from the womb, that is, 'pro and contra nature', constitute only the *dynamic aspect* of the phenomenal existence of this humdrum world (*papañca*). In dealing with its *static aspect* we have to return to the notion of a 'sentient being' as such, that is, of a 'sentient being' viewed in its relative stability. What then is the most fundamental property of each and every sentient being, whether we take it in actuality or potentiality of its 'becoming' a sentient being? I think that this property may be defined as actual or potential possession of the six sensory organs (i.e., five plus mind or mentality). The sensory organs are regarded in *SN* not only as essential to all sentient beings, but also as those relatively stable elements which find their cosmic correlate in the relative stability of the world itself and serve as its main *support*.[18] The six senses are things by grasping at which the world acquires its 'origination' and its persistence together with the suffering and pain following from their dynamism. And this 'grasping' (*upādāna*) figures within this second (static) aspect of phenomenal existence as an instrumental category by which the consciously and ethically indifferent world assumes its conscious and ethical actuality. This actuality, in its turn, contains the possibility of choice between letting the world continue as it is, and getting rid of it together with its pain and suffering by throwing out all sensual graspings.

This 'process' is described in *SN*, 168–169, in a very clear way:

> In what is the world originated (*sampanna*)?...
> Having grasped at what, by what is the world afflicted?
> In the six the world is originated...
> And, thus, having grasped at the six, by the six the world is afflicted.

2.3.0. It is in connection with *form* that the concept of sentient being reveals itself in its most general features. Let us look at this passage from *SN*, 753–755: '[Those] who [are] formless, Oh Bhikkhus, are calmer than [those] with form'—this is one observation. 'Cessation is calmer than the formless'—this is the second observation... [and] the Master said this:

> The sentient beings who experience form, and [those] who [are] inhabiting the formless [state],
> Not apprehending [what] cessation [is]—they are going to be reborn.
> [Yet those] who, comprehending the forms, are stable in the formless,
> who liberated [themselves] in the cessation—these people [are] abandoning death'.

2.3.1. The problem of connectedness between the sentient being and form can be considered phenomenologically. Thus, form—or the absence of form—can be thought of as a condition *external* to the 'being sentient' of the sentient being. In this sense, for example, one or another sentient being is cognized as existing in the sphere of form—or of formlessness—at the moment of our thinking about this or that concrete sentient being. On the other hand, the form of a sentient being might also be cognized as a result of his inner properties, thought of in terms of the above-mentioned general tendencies, that is, as a *function of becoming* (or non-becoming) of sentient beings, if looked at as existing in the time previous to the present moment. But again, in so far as at each and every given moment we find ourselves in the universe where all results of all causes are present, we are able to think of form as necessarily connected with the existence of at least some sentient beings.[19] For it is they which are present all the time, being either endowed with form or devoid thereof. Of course, form itself cannot be thought of as an ontological category, though sharing in the quasi-ontological character of the sentient being with which it is connected, actually or potentially. If considered within the sattvic line of the Buddhist philosophical approach, form is interpreted in a way quite distinct from that used in the dhammic line where form is considered in the contexts of *rūpa-skandha* and *nāma-rūpa*.

2.3.2. Therefore, as we see in the passage cited above, it is in the degree of being 'calm' (*santa*) that form differs from the formless, and the formless from Cessation. Thus, the quality of calmness serves here, as if it were *fundamentum differentiae* in sentient beings, the very basis of their classification *into* these three states, while the *changes* in the degree of this quality may well serve as the main content of the notion of 'becoming'. Side by side with this quality of calmness we have in this passage another differentiating quality and perhaps even more important than the first—*the knowledge*, which is presented here as concrete knowledge of the state in which a sentient being finds himself, or his concrete knowledge of two other states, particularly that of Cessation. By this I suggest that knowledge here is a sort of 'modifier' of states, by means of which a sentient being can either progress from one state to another towards Cessation or, at least, be stable in the given state preventing thereby all possible degradations. It is in this sense that the term 'well-stabilized' (*susaṇṭhita*) is used here, but of course as a secondary quality of sentient beings that results from calmness—rather in the sense of a stabilizing factor which cannot be found either among the main mental states or among 'listed' states of consciousness. *Knowledge*, on the other hand, operates in sentient beings as the main dynamic factor which can exclude them from the *spontaneous* process of rebirth:

> ...(those) sentient beings who resort to knowledge, (they) do not go to a renewed existence.
>
> *SN*, 730.[20]

Looked at from this angle, 'calmness' and 'knowledge' may be presented as the static and dynamic (and thereby inner and outer) aspects respectively of the very 'being' of the sentient beings in its relation to form [a relation which might be quasi-symbolically marked by '+', '−', and '0' for 'form', 'the formless' and 'Cessation' respectively of sentient beings].

2.3.3. However, and I reiterate this point, *one cannot cognize sentient beings reflexively*. The old Kantian thought about the *impossibility of introspection* in the science of psychology is fully applicable to this case. One cannot think of oneself as a sentient being, using only the mentalist criteria.[21] That is to say, one has first to objectify the mentality as a whole, then to abstract oneself from this whole, and only then to consider oneself as a 'non-mental being', cognizing all sentient beings *as such*, i.e., apart from their mentality:

> Who beholds the vanishing and rise of sentient beings wholly – (Him), non-attached, Well-Gone, Awakened One, (I call a Brahman).
>
> *SN*, 643.[22]

The case is quite different when one has to objectify oneself, that is, to extricate one's personal mentality from oneself, and thus to be able to observe oneself as a sentient being, however superior to all other sentient beings One might be:

> He, the most excellent of sentient beings, the foremost person,
> The bull among men, the most excellent of (human progeny...).
>
> *SN*, 684.[23]

2.3.4. The matter is, however, more complicated. We have here the two objects of knowledge, which constitute a phenomenological dyad typical of the Buddhist philosophical approach as we see it in the early Suttas. The first object is a sentient being together with its form and/or formlessness, its rising and vanishing, and its becoming and non-becoming (as we have already seen in the passage referring to the sentient beings who have not yet become). [It is worth noting, that in this verse 'becoming' (instead of 'being') plays a role almost analogous to that of 'form'. That is, 'becoming' can be considered, from a certain viewpoint, as the focus of all natural tendencies of sentient beings related to 'womb' as their symbol. If looked at 'as such', becoming also reveals itself by degrees or gradations, as if it were a positive quality which, in fact, it is not.] The second object of knowledge is Cessation, known as the state (or perhaps more exactly, 'non-state') where 'form' and 'becoming' are not dismissed as non-existing (which we can see in the cases of non-becoming and formlessness), but simply as not relevant at all. Thus *the Knowledge of Cessation*, speaking objectively, consists in the nullifying of all possible objective contents of such objects as form and becoming. As a result, one and the same thing is known as one object, if considered in the sense of sentient beings, and quite another, if considered in the sense of Cessation. If we observe the passage cited above in *SN* 684, we can see the Buddha as *one* of the sentient beings, while from the point of view of the Knowledge of Cessation, He is not a sentient being, for His 'being sentient' is altogether unthinkable. And it is on the strength of being observed from the former point of view, that Buddha Himself can be thought of as one of the human progeny (*pajā*) which, in its turn, is considered as *a kind* of sentient being, or even a sort of synonym thereof.[24]

2.4.0. Philosophically perhaps the most important point to note here is that, once conceived of as a sentient being, Buddha, as a concept, remains *purely formal*, as formal as the concept of sentient being itself. That is why any similarity between a sentient being on the one hand, and a 'living soul' (*jīva*) in Jainism and a Leibnitzian monad on the other hand, is superficial and superfluous, however obvious it may seem. For, in so far as we are dealing with this concept in the context of *SN* and its commentaries, it is not endowed with anything like substance or even quasi-substance at all.

Therefore we see here the Buddha figuring in respect of sentient beings as (1) excluded from them on the strength of His *knowledge* of all of them as well as of Cessation, and (2) as one of them and thereby one of mankind, when *observed objectively*. Yet there is a third way in which He is again conceived as excluded from all sentient beings. This time it is achieved by means of His inner actions both of a reflexive and objective character, which is clearly seen in a particularly interesting passage where a Muni is directly opposed not only to all other people, but to the whole world of sentient beings.

> Considering ('counting') the objects and destroying the seed,
> He does not give way to lust for them;
> Such a Muni, seeing the birth extinct
> and leaving the reasoning behind, does not enter the number.

SN, **209.**

2.4.1. In this passage the whole content may be classified into two parts. One presents the facts which *exist as such*, while the other includes the actions by means of which a Muni does, or does not, relate Himself to the facts given on Table I.

Table I

Facts	Inner Actions
Objects	Considering ('counting')
Seed	Destroying
Lust	Not giving way to
Extinction of birth	Seeing
Reasoning	Leaving behind
Number	Not entering

[Note that negative actions here figure in a completely independent way and on one and the same level as positive ones. So, for instance, 'not entering' does not mean a pure negation of 'entering' but constitutes together with 'number' a separate semantic unit. It also means that 'not entering the number' and 'considering the objects' belong to the same level of abstraction.]

2.4.2. But what, after all, does all this mean?

(1) First of all, that He considers *everything as a thing* (*vatthu*), that is, as an object, or rather an unspecified object, of *His* thinking; He perceives it *as such*, without any connection with His subjectivity.[25]

(2) Secondly, *the seed* here (*bīja*) is a *symbolic term* corresponding to a certain *structure of consciousness*, where the natural tendency (which previously in this text was associated with 'womb') is already abolished, or more exactly, is present as already abolished together with 'lust for it'.[26]

(3) Thirdly, a Muni, in spite of his still having such mental states as 'considering', 'thinking', 'seeing', is already seeing the 'birth extinct'. That is, he is still acting as all who are 'born' act, but 'birth', as a structure of consciousness, no longer exists for him, 'the seer' (*dassin*). It means that birth here does not exist separately, but only as being together with 'extinction', constituting a new *structure* of consciousness which in turn finds in 'seeing' a corresponding *state* of consciousness (having nothing to do with that of ordinary or natural sight).

(4) Reasoning is left behind here in an unspecified way, because it figures mainly as a synonym of practically all natural or ordinary mental functions.

(5) And finally, we come to the most interesting category, that of the 'number'. The number of what? Obviously we are dealing here with *the number of all sentient beings.* That is, of all individual continuums of consciousness which have existed *all the time* in the sense that there was no time when they did not exist. And what is of particular importance, is that their number is a *definite* or *limited one.* This means that the quantity of all sentient beings is calculable, if not actually subject to a concrete calculation. This number *cannot grow*, although it is diminishing all the time on account of those sentient beings who were and are excluded therefrom by going out into Nirvana. Let me note, by the way, that it is those 'gone beyond' who were called in Mahayana-Sutras 'incalculable' and 'immeasurable' (skr. *asaṃkhyeya*, *aprameya*), while those 'left behind' were, in their totality, related to as 'the number'. However, there may also be another implication: that each concrete birth (or, at least each human birth) contains in an *objective* way a hidden possibility of being exempt from the number which serves, as it were indirectly, as the symbolic term corresponding to, or perhaps hinting at, a broader structure of consciousness. Perhaps this structure of consciousness can be conventionally called 'the totality of sentient beings understood as the definite or limited', in which case it will be opposed to 'the totality of Buddhas understood as the indefinite or unlimited'. In either case the 'number' symbolically corresponds to an everlasting cosmological duality of the conceivable universe.

2.4.3. We have arrived at a philosophical impasse. On the one hand we have a theory according to which an individual is an individual 'continuum of thought' (*cittasantāna*) or stream of states of consciousness (dhammas, that is). And, according to the same theory, the relative stability of the existence of a given individual continuum within one life-span is provided by, or rather manifested in, its 'name-form' (*nāma-rūpa*), while the even more relative persistence of this stream of consciousness throughout the whole chain of its existences might be understood as attributable to some hypothetical, let us say, *configurative principle.* This principle can be vaguely described as a persistent dynamic force due to which various states of consciousness, however many different configurations they may assume, have been configurated in such a way as to be recognizable in the case of the past, or predictable in the case of the future, as belonging to one and the same 'individual stream'.

On the other hand, we have the very comprehensive and factual, rather than theoretical, picture of the universe as consisting of sentient beings which are individuals par excellence, that is of beings whose individuality is already given in the *spatial separateness of their sentiences* and, therefore, does not require any further explanations as to their individual differences in terms of causes and effects. Moreover, if looked at from this point of view, all sentient beings appear not only as absolutely indivisible *facts* (that is, without any possibility of being subject to further analysis), but also as facts existing synchronically, that is to say, side by side with each other here and now. In which case both their previous history (in terms of karmic antecedents) and future changes (in terms of prediction) appear far more relative than their actual being.

Within the tenets of the texts of the Pali canon the gap between these *dhammic and sattvic lines* of individual existence seems to remain unbridged, if not unbridgeable, partly because each of these two lines is possessed of a symbolism and even mythology of its own. Speaking methodologically, this *dualism* in the understanding of one's individuality might, in a broader sense, become thought of as *the dualism of 'one' and 'individuality'*, where in the first term the notion of *separateness* (from, let me say, 'another one') is emphasized, while in the second term the notion of an *intrinsic uniqueness* is emphasized. All attempts to reduce one to the other remain futile, unless both of them have been reduced to a certain unifying principle which was later introduced in the theory of *Prajñāpāramitā*.

2.4.4. The very application of the word 'individualistic' or 'individual' to the earliest Buddhist teaching is justified only in so far as we use it in a strict terminological sense. It is so when Buddha spoke of the *different kinds of individuals*, or maybe more exactly, *different types*. There is, however, a deep conceptual difference between the Buddhist attitude and ours in this case. For when I say, for example, that 'John is the most irascible person I have ever met', I suggest that it is *a person* here to whom such an exceptional phenomenon of irascibility is ascribed. This in turn implies that this phenomenon does not exist otherwise than in being ascribed to him as a person. Contrary to this, in Buddhism it is not a person through whom a mental state or a characteristic is manifested and exemplified. Instead, we have here various mental states, the particular configurations of which *make an individual of a sentient being*. Or, more exactly, it is the configurations of mental states which make a sentient being belong to one or another kind or type of individuals. [It might be supposed that a kind of individual corresponds to a certain group of mental states assimilated thereby.] In practice, the number of types or kinds of individuals is infinite, and that is why it might well happen that some of them consist of no more than one individual, or even do not include anybody at all, remaining, as it were, as pure psychological potentialities awaiting their actualization.[27]

2.4.5. I know how tempting it is to be seduced into mythological parallels concerning the question of 'individuality' (given that the last is understood as succinctly distinct from 'personality'). Yet what we have to start with would be, in any event, not merely a simple mythology (I very much doubt the very existence of such a thing, for any mythology is given to us as already a phenomenon of our own *cultural* self-awareness), but rather some postulates of thinking, the origins of which could be sought for and unearthed somewhere else, in realms other than those, where that thinking itself was traced, detected and reformulated. And then 'mythology' would serve as no more than a manner of speaking or a purely conventional term by which the 'realms other than those' might be named.[28]

One fact, however, is very suggestive, that what *we* call 'individual' does correspond to two (at least) terms in the Suttas—*sakkāya* and *ajjhatta*. The first denotes, first of all, *objective* spatial separateness of a sentient being, the 'bodily space' of its sentience (wherefrom its literal meaning 'with body', 'possessing a body'). The latter stresses the *reflexive* character of a sentient being conceived mainly in the sense of self-observation. Both of them, however, seemed to have originated as secondary to, or perhaps, by way of predicates of, sentient being. But all the four terms—*sattva*, *sakkāya*, *ajjhatta* and *puggala*—taken together, may be regarded 'mythologically' as a nomenclature wherewith the disintegration or analysis (historically they are one and the same thing) of 'person' was marked. Or, one may even take risks in conjecturing that it was these terms in which was reflected the transition from 'personality' of Indo-Iranian mythology to 'impersonality' of Buddhism and, partly, Jainism.[29]

2.4.6. The only imaginable bridge between the dharmic line and the line of sentient beings is to be sought at the point where a static and synchronous thought of a sentient being, as it exists in the present, that is, at any present moment, is allied to a thought of *another* being possessed of the same *sentience*. That is, in this case we are dealing with a kind of analysis to which a sentient being is subjected, an analysis in which the whole sentience in its entirety is to be compressed and squeezed out as *one thought*. In this case, this thought is conceived of in its utmost 'heaviness' and 'solidity'. And it is its oneness which in this case excludes the possibility of thinking thereof in terms of states of consciousness (dhammas), because all states of consciousness belong to different groups and follow one another at momentary (*khaṇa*, 'moment') intervals.

2.4.7. Thus, a sentient being is presented in the passages above as a 'being' whose sentience does not possess any features obtainable or attainable by means of outer observation. In other words, a sentient being is observable as a whole only. Its thought remains unmarked, and that is why introspection is totally impossible here, for the very meaning of introspection implies the direction of observation from outwardly observable marks towards a totally unmarked thought. And I think that it could not be otherwise, for in the *Sutta-Nipāta* we are dealing with a specifically pragmatic religious situation conceived of as consisting of 'whole units' of inconceivable complexity, irreducible to the data deducted from the observation. The thinking of the sentient being cannot, for this reason, be interpreted otherwise than as a simple and non-analysable entity, in terms of which the whole world of religion was construed and realized as 'compound' and relatively existing.

[2.5. If we turn to the *Bhagavad-Gītā*, the text which in its extant form must have appeared considerably later than the oldest Suttas, we find there a theory of sentient being not altogether dissimilar from the Buddhist conception of sattva.

According to this theory, two basic entities are postulated. The first is the 'body' (*śarīra*) that comprises the bodily organism, the sensory faculties with their objects, the emotions, the mind and the intellect. This postulate is called 'the field' (*kṣetra*). The second is 'one who knows the field', 'knower of field' (*kṣetrajña*). His knowledge (*jñāna*) *discriminates* between that which is 'field' (body, mind, objects, etc.) and that which is 'no field', i.e., which is 'knower'. This knowledge is the inherent potential property of the knower, which may or may not be actualized.[30]

Then *sattva*, the sentient being, arises from, or is a result of, the 'conjunction' (*saṃyoga*) of 'field' and 'knower of field'. And the very phenomenon of *sattva*, as seen in the Bhagavadgita, can be reduced only to that combination of the potential discriminative knowledge and its objects. Which means that as a category sattva is entirely confined to the 'field-knower' aspect of the atmanic cosmology of the Bhagavadgita. And, indeed, if we look at the aspect of *puruṣa-prakṛti*, we will have seen in the purusha ('person') not a potential knower but a quite real 'experiencer' (*bhoktṛ*) of pleasure and pain produced by his contact with the three *guṇas* of prakriti. Moreover, in the context of the 'brahmic' aspect, it is *bhūta* ('a being') that figures in juxtaposition to the beginningless *brahman*, not sattva. The bhutas originate from the Great Brahman, their original womb; by him they are created, by him they are devoured, as the *creatures* do.[31]]

NOTES TO ESSAY 2

1 E. Conze called the theory of Dharma 'an ontological theory', and he was entirely right to do so, provided that his criteria of 'ontology' were basically theological and soteriological, and that his whole approach to the problem was that of *comparative* philosophy or religion. So when he says that 'dharma theory is unique', it means that it is unique as an ontological teaching. Speaking metaphilosophically, however, an ontology can be seen first of all as a *tendency* in the dynamism of philosophical thought and, therefore, cannot be seen as an 'equivalent' to any personal or impersonal 'objectivity' within a religion. See, E. Conze (1967, pp. 210–11). See also T.R.V. Murti (1973, p. 14.)

2 See K. H. Potter (1977, pp. 1–2, 14–15).

3 See E. Husserl (1950).

4 See O. Rosenberg (1924, pp. 67–8). I am fully aware of the strictly epistemological character of Rosenberg's approach to the problem, which I follow for the time being only to dismiss it entirely thereafter.

5 As for example: '... the body is not seen as it is', *SN*, 194.

6 'He knows it [i.e., the body] thoroughly, for He sees it as it is' *SN*, 202. But there is a difference, I think, between this passage and the following—'the departure from the world [has been] told to you as such', *SN*, 172. For in the latter case we have a metaphysical concept of *suchness* as already fixed and used in a more technical way.

7 I think that the classical formulation of this idea is contained in the well-trodden passage 'transient (are) composite dhammas', *Mahā-Parinibbāna Sutta* (p. 64). This place is not commented upon by Buddhaghosa as, evidently, too simple. My guess is that in the context of the Suttas and even in such supposedly late ones as *Mahā-Parinibbāna Sutta*, the term *saṅkhāra* (usually translated as 'composite' or 'compound') is not necessarily to be connected with the notion of *saṃskṛta-dharma* of later Abhidharmic classifications of dharmas (as in Th. Stcherbatsky, 1923, pp. 20–5, 95). I think that it cannot be argued that in the early Suttas a certain essential difference was felt between spontaneously working and consciously directed states of consciousness. As for instance, in *SN*, 731: 'Whichsoever suffering originates, it is all produced by composites (sankharas), yet by cessation of composites the suffering does not originate'. While in *SN*, 734 exactly the same *thing* is stated about consciousness (*viññāṇa*): 'Whichever suffering originates it is all produced by consciousness', etc.

8 Considering the problem of samskaras as far too difficult to be treated *en passant*, I will make only two remarks concerning its phenomenology. First, though dharmic, they cannot be thought of either as consciousness or as psychic (*cetasika*), or as form (*rūpa*) or as action itself (*karma*). Their *meaning* (not function) is to provide the cohesion of actions in space on the one hand, and their connectedness in a time sequence, on the other. Or as we say, that it is the fact of our *being conscious of* this cohesion and this connectedness that we call samskaras. That is, so to speak, we call by this name the very fact of our awareness of the complexity of things and actions. Secondly, samskaras figure as attributed or attributable to an *especial kind of complexity*, conventionally named 'a person'. Then the fact of their awareness assumes an entirely different and very ambiguous character, for it becomes more and more *separated* from a person itself, on the one hand (see below in Essay 6, note 17), though on the other this fact becomes more and more thought of as the main factor keeping a person together, i.e., making a person synchronically extant and diachronically extended. And it is in this last sense that samskaras can be thought of as a source of a pure and (see 6.0.6., note 13) abstract intentionality to which any volitional act could be reduced. But, of course, they do not belong to psychology, for they *cannot be explained subjectively* as a real and concrete volition. Therefore, our volitions might be seen as their realizations (in both conscious sense and that of actualization). For volition (or will) as such has never been singled out in Buddhism as a primary elementary state of consciousness, but remains all the time either a secondary effect of the composedness of all that is composite, or as a derivation of thought, a sort of 'volition of thought'. See W. F. Jayasurya (1963, pp. 16, 19, 229). We

may conclude these notes by saying that samskaras could be rendered as volitions only given their total previous desubjectivization. See, Anagarika Govinda (1973, pp. 95, 101) and C. Rhys Davids (1930, p. 85).

9 This term was used by L. Mäll (1968, pp. 54–62) in his paper read at a semiotical conference in Tartu in 1965 and purporting to stress the 'nullifying character' of the Buddhist concept of liberation.

10 The concept was introduced by the late David Zilberman in his *Approaching Discourses* (to be published) to denote a purely pragmatic situation in the context of which the central ontological idea should remain all the time undefined, and thereby it cannot be included in *the given* system of ideas.

11 The idea of 'sentient being' with respect to compassion, if looked at phenomenologically, would reveal two different aspects. The first aspect refers to *all* sentient beings taken together as *one* object of compassion, and regardless of any inner causal connection between their own state and that of the Buddha who displays this compassion. In other words, it does not matter why all sentient beings are the object of compassion, for the latter is displayed spontaneously. The second aspect takes into account specific conditions and facts pertaining to sentient beings. Specific in the sense more concrete than, for instance, the fact of their *suffering* or *ignorance*. If taken in this aspect, they would be depicted not simply as suffering, but suffering *because of* their previous deeds: 'Heirs take their wealth, but a sentient being goes in accordance with his action' (*Kamma*). See *Thera and Therī I*, v. 781, p. 76; *Thera tr.*, p. 75. Or else it is because of some *inner* conditions that sentient beings suffer: 'Sentient beings, deceived by thought (*citta*), delighting in Mara's realm...', *Thera and Therī*, v. 1141, p. 139; *Therī tr.*, p. 19.

12 Not for a moment do I consider these distinctions as possessing any real terminological or classificational value. However, if taken within certain and definite contexts, *satta, bhūta* and *pāṇa* may assume their specific terminological meanings. Although, of course, in most general contexts they are synonymous or at least, overlap each other all the time. See, for example, '... Sakka, the lord of beings (*Bhūtapati*)...' in *Thera and Therī II*, v. 365, p. 158; *Therī tr.*, p. 37. Or, 'Buddha, the Lord... has taught the Dhamma of the abolishing of all suffering to animate beings (*pāṇa*)' in *Thera and Therī II*, 306, 371, pp. 152, 154: *Therī tr.*, pp. 32, 33. It must be borne in mind, however, that *pāṅa* and *bhūta* may refer to *satta* as two subdivisions of the *whole class* of *satta*, whereas such terms as *puggala* and *jīva* represent two absolutely different *aspects of* individuality, figuring side by side with *satta*. See B. C. Law (1957, p. 42).

I think this passage is a clear example of what could be called a 'qualified pantheism', that is, when a religion is considered within another system of world-outlook (or another religion) not only as an *objective fact*, but also as, shall we say, a *separate phenomenon* acquiring its place, character, and *meaning* only *with relation to* this system. R. L. Patterson (1959, p. 166) very pertinently remarks: 'The Buddhists have shown us... how a system which is basically atheistic, can include a qualified pantheism in which the "gods" are merely selves which can rise to a superhuman level'.

13 I am not altogether sure whether or not there was a real 'cult of bhutas'. The two books on the subject (one pioneering and one quite recent) do not even mention it (J. Masson, 1942; M. M. J. Marasinghe, 1974). W. Kirfel (1959, p. 111) writes: 'Den Osten nimmt *Mahāsahasrapramardanī* ein. Sie ist schwarz von Farbe... Ihr Sitz ist die glühende Sonne, auf der sie in der Pose der Anmut sitzt, Bhūtas und Yaksas niedertretend'. Whereas A. G. S. Kariyawasam (1971, p. 87–8) attributes to bhutas a more abstract and symbolic representation: 'This seems to be the most general term used in Indian languages...to mean invisible spirit. ...Buddhaghosa explains the term "bhūta" as non-human (*amanussa*) ...and it implies that it signifies 'devas' in general...'

14 In *SN* 5, the essence (*sāra*) is a technical term: 'Who did not go after the essence in states of existence (*bhavesu*)...' In this case, however, 'being' itself is seen rather as *an individual* existence (and, to a certain degree as a *profane life*). This is so particularly in the 'ascetic contexts': 'Sumedha spoke: essenceless (*asāra*) is the way of existence (*bhavagata*)... either there will be going forth for me or death..,' *Thera and Therī II*, v. 465, p. 168; *Therī tr.*, pp. 46, 161–2, 165.

15 At the same time it could be suggested that the opposition 'form/formless' does not necessarily imply the idea of rebirth or time in general, and may well refer to the Buddha Himself. '(I) formless one (*arūpa*), travelling far, wandering alone..,' *Thera and Therī I*, v. 1122, p. 100; *Thera tr.*, p. 102.

16 We could say, though, that those who are going to the womb do so either on the strength of their ignorance, or because of their lack of the highest yogic knowledge: 'The fool comes to the womb (*gabbha*) again and again...,' *Thera and Therī I*, v. 101, p. 15; *Thera tr.*, p. 13. 'One comes to a womb and the next world, undergoing *saṃsāra* in succession; another with little wisdom (*appapañño*), who puts his faith in him, comes to a womb and the next world', *Thera and Therī I*, v. 785, p. 77; *Thera tr.*, p. 76.

17 'Naturality', of course, serves here as a term of *our* own meta-language, though a certain similarity could be seen in a Buddhist notion of *svabhāva*.

18 So, however paradoxical it might appear, it is 'thought' (*citta*) or mind (*manas*) which, if used as to what all psychical and mental life is reduced, constitutes and manifests the *static* aspect of sentient being: 'In "mind" we place ourselves in the "is"; in "will" [connected first of all with sankharas, see above, note 8] we place ourselves in the Becoming'. See C. Rhys Davids (1930, p. 73). All this is in sharp contrast with Jainism, where the idea of *inner* dynamism (as distinct from *outer* dynamism of *dharma*) manifests itself first of all in mind and the five senses. See P. S. Jaini (1974, p. 73).

19 I think that here we can see the common Indian idea of *objective causation by actions*, which in *SN*, 654 is manifested with no less clarity and wellnigh in the same words as it is manifested in the third chapter of the *Bhagavad-Gītā*.

20 '...(those) sentient beings who resorted to knowledge, that is who having known the Way of Arhats and rejected defilements, got rid of the influx', *SNC* II, 730.

21 This problem is one of utmost importance and difficulty, for a state, once objectified, ceases to be mental, as a person (*puggala*) once objectified, ceases to be a person. I agree with Ruegg (D. Seyfort Ruegg, 1974, p. 104) that '...in Buddhist psychology and soteriology it is the mental aspect that normally predominates, and the psychological types which Buddhism recognizes are then defined precisely with regard to their mental states'. The very word 'normally', however, I am inclined to regard as referring to a *static* (or *initial*) *condition* of a psychological observation (which, in turn, also ceases to be 'psychological' and becomes a phenomenological one).

22 '[He] who wholly knows the connection [with bodies] of [all] sentient beings, [as] manifestedly resulting from all [their] qualities', *SNC* II, 643.

23 In the commentary on this passage we read: 'The sentient beings comprise Gods, man, and so on; the progeny comprises the remaining states', *SNC* II, 684.

24 This is clearly expressed in *SNC* II, 654: 'The world, or mankind, or the sentient beings—the meaning [is] one, though [there is] a difference in expression'.

25 'Subjectivity' of an object here would mean its connectedness with emotional and motivational spheres: 'The recollection (*sati*) of one who thinks about a pleasant (*piya*) object (*nimitta*) is confused [when he sees (its) form]'. *Thera and Therī I*, vv. 794, 798, 800, 802, 804, pp. 77–8; *Thera tr.*, pp. 76–7. *Nimitta* in this passage is opposed both to *vatthu* and to *ārammaṇa* when the latter is used in a yogic context: 'I shall bind you [my thought] to the object (*ārammaṇa*) of recollection (*sati*) by force...,' *Thera and Therī I*, v. 1141, p. 103. *Thera tr.*, pp. 66, 200.

26 It is of an extreme significance that 'seed' is used here in the singular, i.e., as 'only the one seed left'. That is the seed, due to (or in connection with) which dharmas form the aggregates (*khandha*). A person (*puggala*) possessing one seed only, can be regarded as an 'extreme' or 'fringe' case, wherein the only thing he has in common with all sentient beings is 'structure (of consciousness) itself', i.e., taken irrespective of all its content. About 'single-seeders' (*ekabījin*) see *Puggala–Paññatti I*, p.p. 3, 16 (No. 39); *Designation of Human Types*, pp. 7, 24. Thus existence of such a person and even his 'person-ness' are seen to be merely *formal*.

27 On the whole, the problem of individuality is far more complex than that. Its very actualization is very ambiguous. On the one hand, it is a 'neutral' attainment: 'Through innumerable aeons they have attained inviduality (*sakkāya*)', *Thera and Therī I*, v. 202, p. 27; *Thera tr.*, p. 25. On the other, it is regarded as very much a negative factor: 'Seeing fear (*bhaya*) in

individuality...', *Thera and Therī II*, v. 339, p. 156; *Thera tr.*, p. 35. At the same time, it might assume a more *reflexive* character, as in: 'Having arisen (*samuṭṭhāya*) within me, my individuality (or, 'subjectivity'—*ajjhatta*) is quickly cooked...,' *Thera and Therī I*, v. 755, p. 74; *Thera tr.*, p. 73. See also *SN* 7, 174, where there can be seen something like a 'yogic' reflexion on 'subjectivity'.

28 I think that, for all its brilliance, the Lévi-Straussian approach to myths is as biased as it is elegant: 'Le mythe, c'est l'authenticité radicale. Je définissais cette authenticité par le caractère concret de la connaissance que les individus ont les uns des autres, mais rien n'est plus abstrait qu'un mythe, à l'inverse de ce qu'il peut sembler. Le mythe met en oeuvre des propositions qui, quand nous voulons les analyser, exigent de notre part un recours à la logique symbolique'. C. Lévi-Strauss and G. Charbonnier (1961, p. 59). I think that his bias, which reflects on the general methodological banality of the modern thinking *about* myths, is caused by the fact of confusion of (a) 'myth' as *our own cultural* abstraction, with (b) 'myths' as *their own concrete knowledge* (interpreted in the sense of and by means of our own cultural abstractions), and with (c) 'myths' as *their own symbolic apparatus* (which is *an instrument* of *their own* interpretation and transmission of their own knowledge) which unfortunately *cannot* be analysed by means and in terms of our own 'logique symbolique' (quel optimisme!). These three different notions of 'myth' can be investigated first of all separately, and only then a unifying phenomenology of myth may follow. I am aware, for instance, that 'individuality' itself is a term of *my* culture, and that I could apply it to an ancient Indian context only provided that it will be changed into a *meta-term* devoid of all my cultural characteristics (i.e., becoming thereby an absolutely abstract notion). And then, strangely enough, it so *happens* that in Vedic 'mythology' that what I call 'individuality' is opposed not to any sort of 'non-individuality' or 'impersonality', but to 'male entity' (*puruṣa*) and, at the same time, to a group of 'extra-individual entities', the individuality or non-individuality of which is irrelevant and not articulate. Nevertheless, I am inclined to think that 'personality' (as opposed to 'individuality' as well as to 'impersonality') played an extremely important role in the formulation of postulates of early Buddhism.

29 My rather vague surmise is that the 'Buddhist depersonalization' might have been brought about as a result, or consequence, of the synthesis of Indo-Iranian mythology where 'person' (of a deity) was present but relevant with some of the 'indigenous' mythologies, where 'person' was present but irrelevant. It seems to be possible also that the Vedic idea of a life-force or life-energy, not necessarily connected with a person, might have served on the one hand as one of preconditions for such a depersonalization and, on the other, as a 'phenomenological step' in the formation of what later became 'living soul' (*jīva* as distinct from *ātman*). See B. Heimann (1964, pp. 38–9).

30 *The Bhagavad-Gītā* (XIII, 1–6, 26–7, pp. 123–5).

31 Ibid., XIII, 15–6, 26, pp. 124–5; XIV, 3, p. 126–7. Zaehner entirely neglected this point in his commentaries, and his rendering of *sattva* as 'being' and of *bhūta* as 'contingent being' is as good as any other. However, he misses the point hopelessly in identifying *saṃyoga* of 'field' and 'knower' with the 'union of matter and spirit'. Because, as can clearly be seen from the context, 'field-knower' is only one out of seven (at least) aspects of the atmanic cosmological scheme. See *The Bhagavad-Gītā* (p. 347).

3. THE CONCEPT OF 'MIND—AND—THOUGHT' IN SOME OF ITS ASPECTS

Preliminary Meta-Philosophical Remarks

3.0.1. Before dealing with the *mentalist line* of Buddhist philosophy, I ought to introduce the reader to a broad meta-philosophical concept in terms of which both 'mind' (or 'mentality', *manas)* and 'thought' *(citta)* may be adequately interpreted. When taking such a concept into account, we have arrived at the following preliminary conclusions: (a) thought is cognized *(saññāta)* as generating all of its contents (or none of them); (b) thought is cognized as containing only *its own* mechanism of generation, which means, in turn, that it is not produced by any mechanism found outside it; (c) thought is, therefore, cognized as either 'thought as such', or as its own generative mechanism, formerly called 'mind' (or 'mentality'); and (d) the notion 'I' or 'self' *(atta)* appears as either no more than a particular content of thought [having thereby '*no meaning (attha)* of its own' *(anattā)*], or as a simple, formal attribute devoid of any properties other than those already contained in the given thought which produced it.

3.0.2.1. If we try to interpret the Buddhist concept of mind as presented in the Suttas (in the light of the insights generated by this metaphilosophical concept conventionally called 'Buddhistic'), we are able to single out certain distinctive features of mind. First of all, 'thought' and 'cognition' *(saṃjñā, saññā)* here are totally different from one another. They cannot be reduced to one another, nor can they be expanded to include anything broader than either of them taken singly. [I stress again, that this is the case only in the Pali Suttas, for in the Abhidhamma both terms be interpreted conjointly within *manoviññāṇadhātu.*] In the context of the present analysis, cognition cannot be regarded as thought, a type of thought, a type of 'thinking' or, least of all, as hierarchically superior to thought.

3.0.2.2. Secondly, mind is not to be understood as a product of 'individual mentality', for the mind's individuality is irrelevant. When we hear or read that '*one* speaks or acts with a corrupted mind', 'one' is simply a purely formal and illustrative attribute having none of the psychological depth of 'I'. Thus, mind presents no more than one dimension of what in *other* philosophical or psychological contexts is called 'I'. I dare state that, from *my own* Buddhistic, meta-philosophical point of view, an idea or belief might have existed in the apperceptional field of proto-Buddhism, according to which it is *impossible to observe the thought and 'I' at one and the same time.*[1]

To say that 'mind is individual' is inappropriate in the present context, for mind's individuality has no relevance whatsoever to the analysis of its states and functions.[2] For, *when distinguishing one mind from another, we deal with temporal changes more than with spatial differences.* However, to say that 'mind is not "I"' only means that 'I' is used thoroughly negatively and in a specifically Buddhistic sense, in contradistinction to the Upanishads, for instance, where 'self' is used quite positively and as the central concept. But taking into account this same statement (i.e., 'mind is not "I" ') there is also a strong implication that the very term 'mind' is used *as if it were instead of* 'I', that is, as if it were the psychological dimension of 'I', but without 'I's' ontological connections and inner religious correlates (i.e., when the individual potentiality of 'I' is linked with the non-individual absolute of Brahman). Therefore, the term 'mind' denotes a situation in which the psychological, mental dimension of 'I' is thought of as distinct from each and every 'being'.

3.0.3. When we dealt with 'thought' *(citta)* at the end of the second essay, we considered it to be the final result of our analysis of the concept of 'sentient beings'. And if looked at in such a way, that is, if looked at in anticipation of the future results as presented in later Buddhist schools (particularly in the *Vijñānavāda* and New Tantras), thinking would appear as an *object-concept*, and by no means as a *meta-concept*. Or speaking strictly methodologically, I would dare assert that thinking would still remain *a thing*, although an extremely indefinite one. It would be presented to us as the *core of sentientness of a sentient being taken in its dynamic aspect alone*. And like a 'being' *(satta)*, thinking would be understood in a purely formal way, which is why it would remain non-interpretable from the point of view of a broader meta-concept. I simply do not know of a concept by means of which it could be interpreted. For when I say—'I am thinking'—I cannot help but think that *this* thinking is *mine*. That is, it bears observable features of my mentality and is, therefore, not only mine, but *mental* too. It is mental in so far as it is psychologically interpretable, which, in turn, means that it is an act of thinking about such thought, and is therefore *marked* either subjectively, by my own personality, or objectively, by objectively observable results (in this case this very text of mine is a 'result' of the fact that 'I am thinking'). *And one cannot interpret what is unmarked in terms of what is marked—one can only do it the other way round.*

Hence thinking which is ascribed to a sentient being is broader as a concept than *any* meta-concept which can be thought of or invented (see 6.15).

3.0.4. Therefore, to get at what is *related to* thinking, we have to leave for the time being the 'line of sentient beings' and turn our attention to the Buddhist concept of mind or 'mentality', as it is treated in the Suttas. Mentality, in the framework of which thought appears, figures now as one of its components (i.e., as a mental state), now as the main content of thought, now as its object and now as a substitute of thought. Thought, as far as it is understood to be mental, ceases to be a formal concept and thereby turns into a compound notion endowed with content. This in turn, entails a completely different religious (i.e., pragmatic) role for thought than that which it played in the context of the sentient beings. This can be understood in the following way.

The sentientness of sentient beings fails to bear a mark of connectedness and relatedness to the state of Buddhahood or Nirvana, not to mention its belonging to one or another 'sphere', for example, that of 'form', of the 'formless' and so on.

For, if conceived of as *one's* sentientness, it is *individual*, but not personal. And this means that although separated totally from one another in space and in time, sentient beings have no individual or *personal* links with which their sentientness may be linked to the absolute. This is so because here the absolute refers to *non-sentientness*. That is why, in the *Sutta-Nipāta*, Buddha 'extols them all [all "beings", that is] to happiness', and produces, thereby, a *formal* religious connection between those who no longer belong to *the number* (collection, class) of sentient beings and those who still remain in that class (that is, who remain in what can be called a state of 'formal' or 'natural' religion). It is extremely interesting to note that a special term for such a notion of 'individuality' did not exist in early Buddhism because it was taken for granted that any manifestation of sentientness existed *individually only*, and, therefore, there was no need for denotation. Let us say that the idea of an individual instead of a man, and of an individual instead of a person, was perhaps introduced into the Indian philosophy of the pre-Buddhist period by Jainas (in the concept of 'living soul', *jīva* being conceived of as absolutely individual), and then partly adopted by *ājīvaka*, and finally treated in the Suttas as something totally self-evident. Using the word 'individual' as a metatheoretical term and applying it to the concept of sentient being, I am fully aware that it does not follow that thinking is individually marked—but that it simply cannot be thought of in any other way than as individual. For any mark or sign always indicates either directly or indirectly, that there is a condition by virtue of which a relation between two things is what it is. In so far as this condition changes, the relationship changes, in which case we find another different sign, or no sign at all. Hence, the individuality of thinking is totally unconditional in this context, which is why a sentient being assumes some *formal* features of the 'being' understood in a quasi-ontological way.

Within the *mentalist line* of Buddhist philosophy the sentient being disappears along with its 'thought-thinking' and its formal religious connections, and we are left with 'mind', a compound object. This object possesses not only an analysable inner complexity, but it possesses a complex *outer* capacity to change everything into itself as well. Or, speaking in terms of a meta-approach, *there is the capacity to interpret everything non-mental in terms of mentality* (as described in the Suttas). However, we cannot say that we are dealing with *one's* mentality, for 'one' is an individual having (as was mentioned in the second essay) 'one's' own mentality together with the five other senses, while by mentality we really refer to something which is, at least in principle, infinitely divisible and classifiable. And, even when it is an object of outer observation, it has the features and *marks* which can be only acquired as the result of a reflexive procedure. And this, in turn, means that in contrast to the previous case where we dealt with sentient beings, the mentality possesses some of the space-time characteristics of a *psychological object*, or speaking more exactly, of the only psychological object imaginable.

3.0.5. However, there is one basic distinction between our own understanding of what psychology is and the Buddhist understanding of it. To us, psychology was and still is a science which is *natural*, that is, which reflects the basic concepts of *human nature* and is, at the same time, a humanitarian discipline which reflects the basic concepts of *human culture* or of a *culture*. From the Buddhist point of view, a 'human' being is nothing more than an accidental case of the universal idea of a sentient being. The idea of a 'human' being is to be dismissed as soon as we deal with psychology (although it is relevant when we deal with strictly *Buddhological* problems). At the same time, it has nothing to do with culture, for the latter was simply never treated as an object of thinking by the Buddhists, let alone as an object of a mentalist analysis.

3.0.6. The *acultural* character of early Buddhist Teaching indicates that the meaning of one and the same notion changes, depending on whether it is used in the context of either a cultural or an acultural system of thinking. And this is why, for instance, the term *dharma* refers to very different states of affairs in the Upanishads (where culture is taken into account on the lower levels of the Teaching), in Jainism (where culture is irrelevant but still present), and in Buddhism (where culture simply *does not enter into the system at all)*. Yet it is not enough to say this. For I must also emphasize that the religious attitude of early Buddhists was consciously directed away from (though not against) Brahmanical religion and was therefore strongly acultural in its unspoken and initial postulates. Yet there is more to say: *the very conception of mentality in early historical Buddhism does not seem to be in any way connected with any religious experience whatsoever, except its own.* This might even give the impression that in early historical Buddhism some non-Buddhist yogic experiences were realized, analysed and reworked so that they could be used without their previous or actual religious contents. In this connection, such experiences were simply *taken as such*, and it was only *after* that, in the course of further developments, that Buddhist yoga assumed a specific religious content of its own.

3.0.7. It was, I suppose, in this pre-Buddhist (or proto-Buddhist) yogic experience, in which the cultural line of Vedic and partly Indo-Iranian mythology ceased to be reinterpreted, that we find the emergence of new objects of interpretation.[3] In effect, what might have occurred was that some yogis of the sixth century B.C. turned from symbolic interpretation of certain culturally-bound entities and events to inner-directed analysis of their own interpretative mechanisms. This might have happened in three ways (or stages). First, they left behind the idea of the 'Universal Male (or Androgynous Being) and developed the idea of an individual living soul (as in Jainism), an individual sentient being (as in proto-Buddhism) or an individual consciousness (as in Ajivika). Secondly, they forsook anthropologically contentful religious mythology in order to shift to the idea of *a* living being (regardless of the status of such a living being, i.e., either human, or divine, or animal status). Thus they dismissed the mythological concept of 'the universe as unity in space' (as well as that of its uniqueness in time) and adhered to a new idea of universal complexity and process. And one thing more must be added: this strange 'shift' was on no account achieved simply by changing from one type of mythology to another type, or by reinterpreting one type of mythology in terms of another one. What occurred was the dismissal of the most basic notion in hypothetical Indo-Iranian mythology, that is, the notion that *macro-anthropos is one event*. And those who consciously dismissed this basic notion (for I simply cannot believe that it was spontaneously forgotten or otherwise discarded) found themselves in an 'empty place' which, as it were, was waiting to be either filled by another mythology, or occupied by a different non-mythological type of consciousness.[4]

3.0.8. If looked at meta-philosophically—that is, from the point of view in which a certain concept or 'Gestalt' is considered *as such*, regardless of its place within a given body of concepts and regardless of whether this body of concepts is considered religious, mythological or purely conceptual (i.e., philosophical)—Indo-Iranian mythology is observed as consisting of elements having merely *objective* significance. This means that whatever concept we deal with would remain *the same* when observed from at least two points of view (not including the point of view furnished by my meta-approach). So, for instance, 'ritual action' *(yajña)* in the Vedas and Brahmanas would be considered as one and the same, this regardless of whether or not it is outwardly (physically) manifested, inwardly experienced, or symbolically interpreted. In an analogous way we may see in the concept of *Puruṣa* a type of consciousness, the content of which is 'the cosmic man', or 'the universe as man'. The idea of *ātman* might then appear as the result of a subsequent or simultaneous interpretation of this type of consciousness in the sense of *universal* predication. In this case, *ātman* serves as the only *real predicate* to all thinkable and conceivable subjects. That is why *ātman* not only acquires ontological status, but turns out to be independent of the above-mentioned anthropological type of mythological consciousness, and interpretable without any relation to this type, provided, of course, that all other predicates are suspended. By acquiring ontological status, *ātman* can be conceived of both subjectively and objectively, while *Puruṣa*, though it *can wish*, cannot be analysed as something which wishes and, at the same time, simply *is*, for it remains an *object only*. With regard to *ātman*, if it wishes or thinks, its wishes and thoughts may, from a certain point of view, be labelled 'objective', while from another point of view they may be labelled 'subjective'. The disappearance of *ātman* from the scene of yogic exploits (by the middle of the sixth century B.C.) produced a situation where mentality was explored as still *another*, *yet not absolute object*. At the same time, mentality was a 'place' where, incidentally, its meanings were to be fixed as a given mentality *ad hoc*. However, in principle at least, a 'person' could also figure in the context of mentalism, having already been deprived of the cultural characteristics of anthropological mythology, but waiting, as it were, to be endowed with the different characteristics or marks of the Great Person *(mahāpuruṣa)* as it is found in the early Suttas. And I think that it is in the concept of *pudgala* that we find the features of this 'transitional subject' of mentality. All this was the case, given that the objective mythological concept of Purusha was forgotten, given that the objective ontology of *ātman* was put aside, and given that the concept of a sentient being (too objective to serve as a 'bearer' of religion) was confined to its purely formal use. The notion of *pudgala* (or of the 'as it were a person') remained as a vague substitute for 'something mental'. It did not stand specifically for a 'human being', but for 'something' about which one can say nothing, unless there be a mentality already attributed thereto. Yet even then, it remains a secondary and derivative of 'a mentality'.

3.0.9. This process of 'de-anthropologization' (i.e., of the partial elimination of Indo-Iranian mythology) was carried out during the pre-Buddhist period. Hence, during the so-called proto-Buddhist period, mentality was analysed and attended to as 'one's' or 'anybody's', and not necessarily as 'human', or as 'his' or 'hers'. But there was another powerful tendency in this proto-Buddhist yogic movement, which, I suppose, was never singled out by yogis themselves. This was due, I think, to the simple fact that the very notion of 'culture' was totally absent there. Here I refer to the total disregard of *ethnocentric* features in proto-Buddhist philosophy. [May I emphasize that the notion of 'culture' is also absent from my meta-approach, and that I use it as no more than a meta-term designating an abstract European world-outlook, and only when it is confronted or contrasted with an Indian world-outlook.] I venture to submit that the *objective process of deculturization* (i.e., the neutralization of the notion of culture) in proto-Buddhism was carried out to such an extent, that the very possibility of returning to ethnical definiteness was eventually nullified. Nevertheless, in saying this, I stress that such a process can only be understood from the point of view of an external observer, and as such, it remains relevant only in the context of my meta-approach, where such notions as 'culture' and 'race' lack philosophical significance and are only used for the sake of comparison. I suggest that this process (whereby the concept of culture was emptied of its significance) was extremely important in facilitating the investigation of mentality by clearing it of all 'accidental' phenomena. Thus, the *manas* (or 'mind', 'mentality')—after having been entirely demythologized, deculturized, de-ethicized and, even dehumanized—is the main object of my investigation in this essay.[5]

3.0.10. When I spoke of the absolute objectivity of myth, I was bearing in mind that, if looked at from within a stream of tradition, a mythological structure cannot be *interpreted* in any way (least of all psychologically). And that if an outside observer viewed the same structure, he would, if necessary, come up against the same non-interpretability. The uniqueness and fixedness of a mythological event may permit a participant in a mythological situation to interpret his own mental states (in the terms of the given myth), but the opposite relation of interpretation is not possible. That is why one can talk about 'mythological thinking', but not about 'psychological mythology'. For the latter deals with the mental content of myths and presupposes thereby the possible existence of variables in the (subjective) interpretations of myth. This is so because of the fact that in a myth all mental contents are *non-mental*, and the process of demythologization begins exactly where the pragmatic level of mythology starts its own 'subjective' interpretation. So did yogis during the pre-Buddhist era, which did not prevent them from using some specifically mythological terms, plots and situations as *textual forms*—but their thinking was not moulded by these forms.

3.0.11. However, to say 'there is a myth', or 'it is a myth', one would not only have to point to a certain thing existing as an object of one's thinking, but one would also have to fix such an object *outside* one's own thinking. This would have to be done in order to be amply aware that one's thinking itself lies outside this object and all other such objects, constituting thereby a class of objects entirely different and clearly distinct from that of 'the things mythical'. By this procedure of thinking the other aspect of absolute objectivity of myth is established, where a myth is presented as a 'construct' or 'constructed object', comprising some specific traits and features of thinking (i.e., those directed outside, toward mythical objects). *It is the aspect of thinking which is not subject to the mythological (in this case) objectification, (i.e., it is the non-objectifiable core of thought) which starts being thought of as the absolute in relation to a mythology.* But, of course, such a formulation can preserve its integrity only provided that it is *mythology* which is objectified, for there are many other things subject to objectification, including thought itself. Yet as far as it is revealed in the Suttas, thought remains exempt from such objectification.

3.0.12. While adopting the term 'objectification' for use in the meta-philosophical approach, I have to note that there is need for another meta-concept which corresponds, partly at least, to the myth—that is, the concept of *empirical consciousness*. The notion of empirical consciousness, although it evokes certain European associations, might still be used to refer to certain types of thinkable objects and to the act of thought which refers to them. 'Absolute' thought might then correspond to the concept of *non-empirical consciousness*, that is, to a type of consciousness which does not deal with objects and which cannot be termed an object. This distinction is clearly drawn in the Suttas and is quite different, if not altogether different, from comparable Abhidharmic classifications.

3.1. *Mentality and Thought within the Context of an Objective Religious Situation*

3.1.0. The 'objective religious situation' is a meta-concept construed in the following way:

(1) Such a situation is called 'religious', for it is described in the text itself (*SN* 222—236) as an already established connection between men and the object of their worship, the ghosts (*bhūta*). This connection also contains various sacrificial acts, such as offerings, oblations, and so on.

(2) Such a situation is objective, for it is in no way related to the mental states or events of man (as opposed to those of ghosts or gods); all such states are objectively irrelevant.

(3) Such a situation is also objective in the sense that the Observer of this situation, the Buddha, does not identify with it in any way, though He may include it in the context of *His* situation (by including it, for instance, in *His* textual pronouncements). But this, in turn, might be thought of as 'religious', if looked at from another locus of observation (which is in our case, that of my own meta-philosophy).

(4) The Observer in this situation is on the level of Final Liberation or, speaking Buddhologically, is on the level of Complete and Perfect Awakening (*samyaksambodhi*) to which this religious situation if taken *as such*, has no relationship whatsoever. However, if considered as the natural *status quo* of one's (or anybody's) religiosity, this situation figures as a starting point or preliminary stage on the Path to Complete and Perfect Awakening. [I would like to suggest here that in the former case this situation is not marked, while in the latter case it is. But this is another matter which will be discussed latter.]

Now let us return to the passage in our text, in which ghosts are treated (*SN*, *SNT*).

222 Whatever ghosts have assembled there,
whether earthly or those of intermediate space,
may all ghosts be happy-minded,
and let them all listen zealously to what is said.
223 Therefore, all ghosts, do all of you pay attention
[and] show friendliness to human progeny
who day and night bring oblations [to you];
Therefore, do you protect them undistractedly.
225 The extinction, the getting rid of passion, the excellent immortality,
which Sakyamuni attained with composed [mind]—
there is nothing equal to that Dhamma.
This excellent jewel [is] in the Dhamma.
By this truth may there be Well-being.
226 The purity which the best of Buddhas extolled,
the concentration which they call uninterrupted—
there is no concentration equal to that...
227 The eight [kinds of?] persons praised by the True Ones,
[who] are [in] these four pairs;
they, the Hearers of the Well-Gone—
[what is] given to them will bear the great fruits.
228 [Those] who [are] with steady mind,
devoid of [desire for] sensual pleasure, [they] applied [themselves] well
to the Doctrine of Gotama [and] attained immortality...
230 [Those] who experience the Noble Truths
well-taught by the Profound Wisdom (of Buddha)—
they will not take the eighth existence,
even if they are strongly distracted.
231 Together with attainment of [this] outlook,
even one's three dhammas are left behind:
the view of reality [of one's] self, doubt,
and [the idea of] whatever moral prescription or observance is (accomplished).
He is also totally liberated from the four hells
and cannot commit [any of] the six crimes.
232 [And] even if he makes a sinful action
by body, speech or thought,
[it is] impossible for him to conceal [it],
[for it is] said (to be) impossible (for one who has) seen the State.

235 The old [is] extinct, the new is not to become;
those with thought averted from the future existence,
with seed extinct, without desires growing—
they, the stable ones go out like this lamp.
236 Whatever ghosts have assembled there,
whether earthly or those of intermediate space,
let us worship the Tathagata revered by gods and men,
may there be Well-Being.

3.1.1. The ghosts or spirits to whom this invocation is directed and who are described here as worshipped by men (human progeny—*manusiyapajā*) constitute the frame of a religious situation which, in turn, is included in another religious situation—that of invocation to the Three Jewels, that is, to the Buddha, the Dhamma and the Sangha. In fact, we have put three texts of situations, as it were, within one another in a rather whimsical way.

3.1.1.1. The first situation (A) comprises 'the eight (kinds of) persons' (*puggala*) the four of whom are those 'entering' (*paṭipanna*) upon the Path, and the other four are those already firmly established (*ṭhita*) on the Path and enjoying the fruits (*phala*) thereof. It contains a clear characterization of mentality and knowledge of these persons, some of whom are called the Hearers (*sāvaka*) of the Well-Gone (*sugata*), that is, the Buddha, and the Stable Ones (*dhīra*). The chief of these characterizations are: (1) steady mind; (2) absence of desire for sensual pleasure; (3) absence of distraction. Then follows non-accumulation of the three dhammas namely: (4) the view of one's self as real (*sakkāyadiṭṭhi*); (5) the doubt (*vicikicchā*), and (6) the idea of one's moral or religious achievements. The other five are: (7) inability (*abhabba*) of concealment of one's crimes; (8) seeing the State; (9) the thought averted (*viratta*) from future existence; (10) the seed (*bīja*) extinct; (11) no desires growing.

All these qualities but the tenth in one way or another reflect concrete states of one's mentality, although (8) may be conceived of as a *marginal* mental (or not altogether mental) state, the very being of which is conceivable only on account of the *objective* (and in this sense, not mental) State of Nirvana. But I will return to this a bit further on in connection with Situation C. (10) is of particular interest here because the notion of 'seed' sends us back to the concept of 'sentient being', while here seed is given in the mentalist context. Much later, especially in the treatises and commentaries of the Sautrantika school it assumed its full metaphysical and ethical meaning tied up with the 'rise of thought' (*cittotpāda*) in the individual continuum of thought (*cittasantāna*), and in the *Vaibhāṣika* School where it was denied an independent status. In *SN* (see 77 as quoted in the previous essay — '...with the seed annihilated...') 'seed' is still an intrinsic and, so to speak, *natural* tendency deeply implanted in one's mentality and underlying each and every thought, in so far, of course, as a thought produces either bad or good karmic effects. If we view the first line of *SN* 235 as if we were viewing the content of a thought, we can find in a 'seed' the inner capacity which, although it is not a thought, nevertheless predetermines the rise, continuation and repetition of thoughts, and which leads to certain effects in a future existence. That is why the event of extinguishing a seed is included in the context of the stanza beginning with 'the old is extinct, the new is not to become, those with thought averted from future existence...' For we are faced with a definite *content of thought* which in itself denies *the process of existing* in all of its phases. It causes the effect of 'reversal', whereby the seed becomes extinct or is annihilated. The direction of denial is in this case from *top to bottom.* This is so because the only thing which is empirically dealt with in this stanza is *thought*—not a person, or an 'I'—although in the end we do come to a point where we meet something which gives thought its karmic direction, and which might only be changed with the change of thought itself. So, the seed cannot be identified with a mental state, or even less with a non-mental state. But what is important is that the concept of seed stays in situation A apart from any connection with situations B or C.[6]

3.1.1.2. The second situation (B), which is called the 'objective religious situation', is marked by the invoking of ghosts. It implicitly includes *all kinds* of sentient beings, taken in their mutual relationship of 'worshipper—worship—worshipped'. It also includes all states, events and conditions which exist *objectively*, as for example (1) the endless cycles of existence; (2) *karma* as an automatic mechanism of retribution; (3) the four hells, and so on.

I think that it is impossible to find any other concept which is as misunderstood by European and modern Indian scholars as *karma.* To understand *karma* one ought to bear in mind that it is a specific type of force or energy which works spontaneously and in a *totally impersonal* way. And it is not 'persons', but certain *actions* that are subject to it, inasmuch as we are confined to situation B, where actions are not reinterpreted in the sense of *thought* (as we will see them reinterpreted in the next essay). As long as we remain in situation B, thought is to be considered as if it were an action, which preserves its role as a general karmic denominator. Nobody (and no thing) can change *karma* or reverse its course, which, however, does not preclude the possibility of one's being *exempt*, so to speak, from the 'field' or 'space' where *karma* works and where it will work regardless of one's presence or absence. If thought of in this latter manner, *karma* has nothing to do with future reincarnations ('wombs') or with persons who are to be reincarnated. For the only thing it really does is that it *connects* cause with effect. And by this we do not mean that it *produces* causes and effects. That is why I clearly distinguish between (1) existence, (2) *karma*, and (3) a particular case of existence, or 'hell'.

3.1.1.3. And finally, the third situation (C) contains the Buddha Sakiyamuni, the Teaching (*Dhamma*) and the Congregation (*Sangha*)—the Three Excellent Jewels (*ratana panīta*). A general cover term for this situation is 'the State' (*pada*) of Nibbana.

The 'super-mental' characteristics of the Buddha (as opposed to the *still-mental* ones described in (A) are: (1) purity (*suci*); (2) uninterrupted concentration of thought (*ānantarika samādhi*); (3) profound wisdom (*paññā*).

Situation C can be viewed in a two-fold manner. It can be identified with a concrete, historical Buddha as well as with other 'super-personal' Tathagatas,

Sugatas and Completely and Perfectly Awakened Ones. Or, it can be present as 'the State', which is completely impersonal. The double character of situation C becomes clearer when we pass to its effects on situations A and B.

First of all, C is related to A and B taken together, and in this relation it figures as the Universal Truth (*sacca*), whereby Universal Well-Being (*suvatthi*) is to be had. [Although, if referred specifically to A, it might be interpreted as 'Final Release' or 'Salvation'.]

However, if taken in its relationship to A only, the situation C presents *a new pattern of religious connections*, in which the Tathagata and His Pupils are objects to be worshipped by gods and men, whereby the fruits or results (*phala*) are to be had. The fruits and results are still understood 'karmically', that is, wholly in the sense of an *objective* religious situation.

Situation C establishes a *direct* connection with A (i.e., 'directly'—not through situation B). This connection may be viewed in three ways. The connection can be viewed, first of all, as a factor leading to immortality (*amata*) which might be interpreted here as standing in general opposition not to mortality, but to renewed existences (*bhava*). In this context it would be interesting to turn our attention to the initial line of Dhammapada, II—'Undistractedness is the path to immortality (*appamādo amatapadaṃ*)'—adding to this that in *SN* it is said that 'even if they were distracted (*pamatta*), they are to achieve...' The line from *SN* means that even such an important negative subjective factor as distraction (*pamāda*) gives way to the objective factors of C. Secondly, the connection can be viewed as a factor which, although it does entirely dismiss the Law of Karma, does nevertheless limit its effects (in this case—to seven rebirths for those who experience the Noble Truths). It is extremely important to note that the very mechanism of *karma* was conceived of as something which works in a very complex manner. It works in a *general* way, connecting bad and good *actions* (*kamma*) in one's current existence with bad and good actions in another (previous or future) existence. We have already seen how the general work of *karma* was limited with respect to those who were mentioned in the context of situation A. Now we see how situation C produces radical changes in the specific work of *karma* for those of situation A. We have seen that 'even if he makes a sinful action by body, speech or thought', he is no longer subject to bad karmic effects. And this is not because the Law of Karma is dismissed by or in situation C, but simply because he is, as it were, exempt from the 'karmic dimension' which, as such, remains unaffected by C.

At the same time, we can see here, that in contrast to the first stanza of Dhammapada (see the next section), priority is still given to *action*, not to the psyche (*cetas*). It is action which here covers anything made by 'thought, speech and body', for it is still the purely karmic aspect (though seen in a negative and positive way) which is stressed in this text.

Thirdly, the connection can be viewed in the following way. Situation C affects and influences the purely *subjective* aspects of behaviour and mind of those in situation A in such a way that they become 'unable' (*abhabba*), for instance, to hide their bad actions, words or thoughts. And it is very interesting to note that this inability itself is *objective*, for it is objectively consequent on and subsequent to 'their seeing the State'.

3.1.2. Now, summing up the whole content of this passage, we may put the main question in a rather different form: Is there a sign or indication by means of which the thought or mentality of those in situation A could be seen as distinct from the thought and mentality of those in situations B and C? Here I would risk the assertion that, if observed from our totally external, i.e., meta-philosophical, point of view, the thinking (and mentality) of those in B remains *unmarked*, the thinking of those in A, as related to or compared with that of C, seems to be *negatively marked*, and the thinking of those in C appeared to be *unmarked* (though for quite different reasons than the reasons for unmarked thought in B). Let me state, by the way, that even if thought is marked in situation C, its marks cannot be interpreted in direct relation to either B or A. Now I will back up this assertion.

Various mental qualities and properties of A are opposed to those of B in the form of either 'yes' or 'no'. So for instance, *SN* 226 implies that ordinary people (i.e., those in B) do not possess concentration (*samādhi*), those 'established on the Path' do possess it, while the Buddha possesses uninterrupted concentration which has no equal.[7] Or, passing to *SN*, 231, we find that those 'established on the Path' have left behind the three states of consciousness which are implied to have been preserved by ordinary people, while in the case of the Buddha, the possession or non-possession of any states of consciousness is, in principle, incapable of being determined (at least in the Suttas).[8] And it is even more important in *SN*, 235, where thoughts of ordinary people are objectively (from, say, the Buddha's point of view) directed toward future existences, thoughts of the 'Stable Ones' are averted from future existences, while the Buddha finds Himself *factually* outside any existences, let alone the thought of them. Here we are dealing with the *content of thought*, instead of thought understood in terms of mental states. Such a negative attitude towards practically all of the contents of ordinary thinking is typical in the Suttas. Thus, if we return to *SN* 5, we find that a real ascetic '. . . has not found any entity in beings', which implies that an ordinary man has, and so on.[9]

However, do these distinctions allow us to conclude with the idea that thinking differs with respect to whatever persons or types of persons we deal with in our observation? The answer is: definitely not. For only differences in *thought* make one person different from another, or 'non-persons' different from persons, and finally, persons different from Great Persons (*mahāpurisa*). It is here that we must seek for what can be named the *conception of objectivity of thought*, which, in turn, assumes a dualistic character in that it is understood to be something that simultaneously belongs and does not belong to 'its person'. It is dualistic because it is to be understood, at one and the same time, in a personal way as 'somebody's thought', and in an impersonal way as a state of consciousness.

3.2. *The Interpretation of Mentality (Mind)—and—Thought in a Passage from the Dhammapada*

3.2.0. In the beginning of the Dhammapada (*Dhp.*),[10] the most widely known anthology of the Buddha's sayings, we have a set of four verses which in itself, i.e., without any other 'outside' text, serves as a clear example of 'inner' interpretation. I think that its very composition contains the idea that one and the same thought can be presented in several segments of a given text in such a way that it assumes various degrees of *abstraction.* [When I say 'abstraction', I mean non-connectedness with a specific situation, a situation which can be empirically thought of and objectively described in terms of attributions concerning time, place or person.]

These are the lines of *Dhp.* to be interpreted:

(1) Preceded by mind [are] the dharmas, based on mind [and] mind-made;
(2) If one speaks or acts with a corrupted mind,
(3) Then suffering follows him as the wheel [follows] the hoof [of an ox].
(4) Preceded by mind [are] the dharmas, based on mind [and] mind-made;
(5) If one speaks of acts with a clear mind,
(6) Then happiness follows him like a shadow, not going away.
(7) He abused me, beat me, subdued me, robbed me—
(8) The hatred [of those] who stick to these (thoughts) is never ending.
(9) He abused me, beat me, subdued me, robbed me—
(10) The hatred [of those] who do not stick to these (thoughts) is extinguished.

3.2.1. Each of these ten lines is to be regarded as a *unit of text*, corresponding in its content to a certain *level of abstraction* of thinking. Lines (1) and (4) represent the highest level of abstraction—X; lines (2), (3), (5) and (6) represent level Y, and (7), (8), (9) and (10) represent level Z, the level of least abstraction. The units of each level constitute a text of interpretation. In this connection text X is considered as though it were interpreted in text Y; and text Y as interpreted in text Z. The very sequence of these lines shows us the direction of interpretation—that is, a direction in which we can observe the diminution of the abstractedness of content, or the emergence of concreteness. In Table II, these lines are grouped in three levels on the left, my summing up of the interpretations in the centre, and my own meta-philosophical interpretation is on the right.

3.2.2. I think that in 'one' who thinks we may see a certain reflection of the concept of a sentient being the sentientness of which is actualized in *an act of thinking*. This implies that one's thought (if observed synchronously and at this very moment) produces this unity of thought, speech and act which, in fact, constitutes the notion of 'one'. But if observed diachronically, that is, if separated by the event of rebirth, the two 'points of thinking' may be seen not only as two different *mental states* or two thoughts (various in their *contents*), but as two sources of a certain 'energy', the two poles of which form a 'field' of karmic force. And a thought, once it is in this field, is the cause of actions or events taking place at a different point, while a thought which is at a different point, causes an act or an event which is taking place in another field, and so on. So the very concept of karma seems to have been reformulated in early Buddhism. The new formulation was that thought is the source and cause of a certain force, the work of which is subject to its own laws (Law of Karma), not to be identified with thought itself. This is so, because the latter, if taken as such (i.e., as a single point of think-

Table II

Levels of Abstraction	Units of text	Texts of Interpretation		
		I	II	III
X	(1) (4)	'Preceded by Mind are the dharmas, based on mind and mind-made.'	The states of consciousness (dhammas) are mental.	Mentality or mind (manas) is *one*, if understood from the point of view of the states of consciousness (which, as such, are beyond the scope of our interpretation). Here the mind itself is nobody's.
Y	(2) (3) (5) (6)	'If one speaks or acts with a corrupted mind, then suffering follows him like the wheel follows the hoof of an ox'. 'If one speaks or acts with a clear mind, then happiness follows him like a shadow, not going away.'	The mind might be bad or good. One's speech and acts are connected with either suffering or pleasure only in so far as speech and acts are connected with either good or bad mind.	There are *two kinds of mind* here, There are *many minds* here, for it might be one's mind or another's. One's speech and acts have no intrinsic meaning of their own (with respect to suffering or happiness by which they are followed), but they acquire it with the mind only. [The term 'follow' does not imply that there is a period of time intervening between bad mind and suffering in one case, and good mind and happiness in the other.] Speech and acts are mental states. The bad mind and good mind are mental states too. [Speech and acts if abstracted from both good and bad mind, are also mental states, which, however, cannot be followed by either happiness or suffering.]

Z	(7)	'He abused me, beat me, subdued me, robbed me—	This is an example of thinking by those whose mind is corrupt—and this thinking of theirs is shown in hatred.	Here mind is interpreted as a type of thinking which is *concrete in its content*, and corresponds, respectively to 'hatred' (*vera*) and 'non-hatred' (*avera*). However, in both cases the content itself (i.e., 'he abused me, beat me, subdued me, robbed me') remains the same, serving, as it were, as a *mark* of
	(8) (9) (10)	The hatred of those who stick to these thoughts is never ending. 'He abused me, beat me, subdued me, robbed me— The hatred of those who do not stick to these thoughts is extinguished'.	This is an example of thinking by those whose mind is clear—and this thinking is shown by the absence of hatred in them.	either a negative, or a positive mental state (with 'hatred' and 'non-hatred' as their concretization). Yet, if taken as such, this content cannot be interpreted as a mental state, for it is a *pure content*, while the category 'mental state' remains a purely *formal* concept. But, of course, if one thinks that 'he abused me, etc.'—it can be interpreted as a mental state, and also the absence of such thought can be interpreted as another mental state. [However, there is no characterization of *a person who thinks* here; he remains as 'one' who speaks, acts and. . . thinks that 'he abused me. . .' etc. And unless one is present as a *definite* person who thinks, there can be no concrete situation at all.]

ing only), is not subject to anything other than itself. And it is here, I suppose, that we may indirectly glimpse the *absolute* aspect of thought.

3.2.3. To sum up the whole line of interpretation we can say that:

(1) Text X interprets the states of consciousness as 'mind', and in the sense of mind.

(2) Text Y interprets mind as either bad or good and as something that is working simultaneously with speech and acts and is connected with either suffering or happiness.

(3) Text Z interprets both bad and good mind in terms of the content of thought.

An *inner* interpretation is one in which the levels of abstraction are established by transposing the point of observation of an outside onlooker on to the text of *Dhp.* itself, and by shifting it from (1) to (10), following the diminishing abstractedness of the content. But this type of interpretation forbids one to 'ascend', for *it is dharmas which are interpreted in (1) in terms of mind* (i.e., as states of mind or as mental states), *and not mind which is interpreted in terms of dharmas.* The interpretation of mind in terms of dharmas can only occur in the metaphysical teaching of Abhidhamma, while we are now dealing with a simple, non-metaphysical catechistic text used by common people and understood in a common way, namely understood without an interpretation produced from the *outer* point of view. And indeed, a common believer places himself neither inside nor outside the text, for he first uses a religious text as a *thing*, and only afterwards does he view it as a thing possessing its own *content.* That is why the famous *Buddhist* interpretation of *Dhp.* found in Buddhaghasa's *Commentary* (*Dhp. C*)[11] serves as an example of *interpretation of an abstract thought in terms of a concrete situation*, and not in terms of a less-abstract thought, as was indicated in the above case.

3.3. *The Interpretation of Mentality (Mind)—and—Thought in the Commentary on the Dhammapada*

3.3.0. The very direction of our 'inner' interpretation of mind in the beginning of *Dhp.* (made by means of 'levels of abstraction') implied one extremely important fact, namely, that however far we might follow the line of diminishing abstractedness ('a state of consciousness as mind'—'mind as either bad or good, and as one's mind'—'mind as a thought of...'—'mind as hatred or non-hatred'), we would never come to a point at which 'one's mind' (bad or good) or 'one's thought of something...' has been changed into a *concrete thought* directed toward a certain object. We would not arrive at a point where 'one' is changed into a concrete person endowed with a name, whose actions, words and thoughts could be described definitely in terms of time and space. Hence, when we are dealing with a *situation of interpreting the non-situational text,* we might regard it as a 'zero-situation'. For we know that, while following the Commentary, we would sooner or later arrive at a point where the zero-situation can be interpreted as a more or less concrete situation. Or, in other words, as far as we *know* that the text is interpreted as a certain situation, it assumes the potentiality of being thought of *as a situation* regardless of its level of abstraction. And this is why the *segmentation of the text* into interpretable units is, in this case, quite different from what we dealt with earlier. We cannot segment the text deliberately, for it was already segmented by the Commentary.

So in this case, we treat the first three lines of *Dhp.* as a *single text* interpreted by *DhpC*. Then comes my own meta-philosophical interpretation which follows the interpretation given in *DhpC*.

3.3.1.1. *I. The text to be interpreted*

(1) Preceded by mind are the dharmas, based on mind and mind-made;
(2) If one speaks or acts with a corrupted mind,
(3) Then suffering follows him as the wheel follows the hoof of an ox.

3.3.1.2. *II. The interpretative text*[12]

One day ... the blind Elder (Chakkhupala), a man of outstanding energy (*viriya*), accustomed to walking, came down into the cloister in the last watch. Now, at that time many of the smallest insects came out upon the newly-wet earth and, as the Elder walked up and down, they perished in great numbers.

... When the almsmen (*bhikkhu*) ... saw the [dead] insects in the cloister, they asked: 'Who was it that walked in this cloister?' 'Our Master, reverend Sirs.' They were offended and said: 'See the deed of this ascetic. When he had the sight of his eyes, he lay down and slept and did not commit bad actions. But now, having lost his eyesight, he killed so very many insects.'

... So they went and reported the matter to the Tathagata, saying: 'Reverend Sir, the Elder Chakkupala, saying to himself, "I will go and walk", killed very many insects.'

[The Tathagata asked:] 'But did you see him killing them?' 'We did not, Reverend Sir.' 'Precisely as you did not see him, so he did not see these insects. Oh Bhikkhus, those devoid of the influxes (*āsava*) have no intention of thought (*cetanā*) of [causing] death (*māraṇa*).' 'But then, Reverend Sir, if he was predetermined to become an Arhat, how was it that he became blind?' 'It is because of his bad actions committed in a former life, Oh Bhikkhus.' 'But what bad actions, Reverend Sir, did he commit?' Well then, listen, Oh Bhikkhus.'

3.3.1.3. III. *The interpretative text*

Very long ago, when King Baranasiraja reigned in Baranasi, there was one physician who was wandering from village to village practising medicine. Seeing one woman with weak eyes, he asked: 'What is the trouble with you?' [She replied:] 'My eyes do not see.' [Then] 'I will make a prescription for you' [he said]. 'Make it, Oh master.' 'What will you give me?' [he asked]. 'If you will make my eyes well, then I together with sons and daughters will become your slaves.' 'Very well' [then], he said. So he prescribed a medicine, and after a single application of it her eyes were healed.

Then she thought: 'I promised that I together with my sons and daughters would become his slaves. But as he will not behave properly to me, I will deceive him.' When the physician came and asked 'Is it well?', she said: 'At first my eyes hurt only a little, now they are more painful than ever.' The physician thought: 'She is deceiving me, and would not give me anything... now I will make her blind.'

...And he compounded an ointment, went to her abode and ordered that she rub it into her eyes. Then her two eyes became extinguished, like the flame of a lamp. That physician was the Elder Chakkhupala.

3.3.1.4. IV. *The interpretative text*

'So, Oh Bhikkus, the evil action committed by my son joined him again and again, for a sinful action follows the evil doer just as a wheel follows after the hoof of an ox...'

And having told this story... the King of Dharma pronounced this stanza:

> Preceded by mind are the dharmas, based on mind and mind-made;
> If one speaks or acts with a corrupted mind,
> Then suffering follows him as the wheel follows the hoof of an ox.[13]

3.3.2. *The four texts if viewed as situations*

By summing up the contents of these four textual units, we may understand how the non-situational text I (regarded in the previous section as belonging to the highest level of abstraction) is interpreted by texts II–IV of the *DhpC.* in terms of various situations. And further, we may come to understand how these are interpreted in terms of one another. Let us try to follow this set of interpretations.

3.3.2.1. The zero-situation of I is included in the context of situation IV where *the entirety of text I* is attributed to the Buddha (the King of Dharma) when He was addressing the Bhikkhus. In this case we may suppose that there is a certain time (though it is not defined) which separates I from IV or, more exactly, which separates I as quoted in IV from I as it is in *Dhp.*

3.3.2.2. Situation II, which might be called 'the blindness of the Elder Chakkhupala', finds its interpretation in situation III, where (a) the blindness of the Elder is explained by the fact that the physician had intentionally deprived a woman of eyesight; where (b) this physician was identified as the Elder Chakkhupala; where (c) the time which elapsed between II and III is conceived of as definite, because it is the time between two rebirths (given that one rebirth does not necessarily immediately follow another one);[14] and where (d) situations II and III are described as *two rebirths*, provided that they are connected with one another by the *causal identification* of 'blindness' (in II) with the act of 'blinding' (in III).

3.3.2.3. Situations II and III when taken together and when viewed as attributed to Chakkhupala the physician, are interpreted in IV not only in the sense that 'Chakkhupala was the physician' (as in the end of III), but also in the sense that Chakkhupala and the physician are *one and the same person.* This is stressed by the fact that in IV the Buddha called this person 'my son' (*mama putta*).

3.3.2.4. Line (2) of I finds its positive explanation in situation III, where the physician was thinking (*cintitvā*): 'I will make her blind'. By this his thought (citta) can be identified as 'corrupt' (*paduṭṭha*) And line (2) of I finds its negative explanation in situation II, where the blind Elder killed many insects ('the smallest living beings', *pāṇaka*). The Bhikkhus thought that it was his *action* of killing that was bad. But the Buddha explained that since the Elder had not seen the insects (as the Bhikkhus did not see him killing them) his action was not bad. But of course, the Buddha did not say that it was good either, and it can be putatively stated that in this case we are dealing with a *neutral* or *indefinite* (*abyākata*) action which has *no karmic effect of its own.* We are dealing with an action which is followed neither by suffering nor by pleasure in another rebirth.[15] And it is stated quite unambiguously that an action, of whatever type, is, as such, neither good nor bad so long as it is not conjoint with intentionally good or bad *thinking* (*cetanā*).

3.3.2.5. Lines (2) and (3) of I are interpreted *by the situations* II–III. For here we see: (a) the corrupt thinking of the physician ('I will make her blind'), together with the following karmic effect, that is, Chakkhupala's blindness; and we see (b) that mind (*manas*) in I is concretized in II–III in terms of 'thinking', just as in the previous case suffering was concretized as blindness.

3.3.2.6. The very action of *reciting the stanza* (1–3) in IV by the Buddha places the whole zero-situation (I) within a pragmatic context in which this stanza might be interpreted as a sign of *Buddha's knowledge* about situations II and III, as well as of all other such situations.[16]

3.3.3. In order to sum up the content of both the *inner* and the *outer* interpretations of 'mind-and-thought' in *Dhp*, as looked at from the point of view of a meta-philosophical approach, I am going to make six observations.

3.3.3.1. *First observation:* concerning the comparison of these interpretations. In the inner interpretation, consciousness is present as the mind, or as something 'mental' (by no means the other way around!), while the mind exists as various *mental states* which are different both with respect to the degree of their abstractedness ('mind'—'one's mind'—'corrupt' and 'clear mind'—'hatred' and 'non-hatred'), and with respect to their quality ('mind as such', 'corrupted mind', 'clear mind', 'hatred', 'non-hatred'). In the outer interpretation the mind is described *in terms of content*, or as the process of *thinking about actions*, where it is related to certain objects and attributed to certain 'persons'. Actions, therefore, are included within the framework of thinking, and the whole situation is, in fact, one of thinking, not of action. And it is thinking that binds the situations together, or which binds one birth to another.

3.3.3.2. *Second observation.* The understanding of one situation in terms of another is possible only when there is a *third point* of observation from which an outer observer (the Buddha) can identify 'one person' as 'the other' person, and one fact as the consequence of another *thought*. However, understanding one situation as another was considered (in principle, at least) as achievable by the persons themselves (though the Bhikkhus in II happened to be unable to intuit that Chakkhupala did not kill the insects, because there was no 'thought of death' in him). But outer observation is possible only in the case of the Buddha (or the Buddhas), for He witnesses *all* situations, or all *thoughts*.

3.3.3.3. *Third observation.* Thus, *all situations are formed by the content of thought, and in the sense of 'content' of thought all situations are mental.* (It sounds as if we are speaking of the dharmas as when they are mentioned in the first line of *Dhp.*) So, if the content of thought is absent (as in the case of Chakkhupala's killing the insects), then there will be no situation at all.

3.3.3.4. *The fourth observation* to which we have just been led, is that *in the absence of a content* of thought, not only do actions lose their situational meaning or relevance, but *the thought itself takes on an absolute character.* It is here that we may conceive of a certain contrast between the *Bhagavad-Gītā* and *Dhp.* In the former the stress is placed upon *an action without any mental* (*intentional*) *context.* We have the idea of 'pure' or 'disinterested' action. But in the latter we do not yet have a clearly formulated idea of *pure thought.* The idea is still waiting to be worked out as the central concept of the 'thought-absolute' of Vijnanavadins and as the 'conscious principle' of the late Tantric schools.

3.3.3.5. *Fifth observation.* The most enigmatic point here (as in the Suttas on the whole) is that, apart from (a) the preaching of the *Dharma* (the Teaching), and (b) knowledge of the present, past and future of all situations, there is no indication of Buddha's specifically *religious* role. He is not described as possessing an ontological status of His own, a status to which all other sentient beings might have related as the *conscious* to the *extra-conscious*, regardless of the quality or degree of their consciousness. I think that such an ontological status, though not indicated directly, might have been inferred from the fact that the mere meeting with or being addressed by the Buddha, makes one an Arhat in this or the coming rebirth. It might be suggested that one's Arhatship is dependent on changes in one's own consciousness, though speaking Buddhologically, however deep the changes in one's consciousness might be, it would lead one no further than to a state of *maturity* preceding that of Arhatship. May I note, by the way, that Arhatship can be achieved (not in principle, but in fact) only after one has been included in a situation where the Buddha is *consciously* present.

3.3.3.6. *Sixth observation.* There is one strange thing in the Suttas, which is very difficult to formulate. I would risk naming it '*an extreme factuality of thought*'. Factuality is understood here in two senses. First, *each fact is thought of as a thought*, but likewise, *each thought is in itself a fact.* We may see a clear instance of such a factuality in II:

As the Elder Chakkhupala walked up and down, the insects perished in great numbers.	This is a description of the situation, made by the commentator as if he were a common person.
When the Bhikkhus saw the dead insects, they thought that he killed them. So they said to the Tathagata: 'Reverend Sir... the Elder... killed very many insects.'	This is a description of the situation, made by the Bhikkhus who were thinking as common persons.
Tathagata asked them: 'But did you see him killing them?' 'Certainly not.' 'Precisely. As you did not see him, so he did not see these insects.'	The Tathagata here equated the thinking of the Bhikkhus to 'not seeing', and He equated Chakkhupala's 'not seeing' to 'not thinking', and He equated Chakkhupala's 'not thinking' to 'not killing', stating thereby that the non-thought is the fact of not killing.
'Oh Bhikkhus, those devoid of influxes have no thought of death.'	This means that, while the physician might or might not have a bad thought, and that while the Bhikkhus might or might not have a wrong thought, the Elder Chakkhupala *cannot* have a thought of causing death. For such a thought simply cannot enter the *process* of his thinking.

3.3.4. The sixth observation requires further explanation. The thing is that when we are dealing with *one's mind or thinking* (given that it is 'one' who thinks, not a 'person'), our interpretation is confined to the *microcosm of mentality.* Our interpretation deals only with the microcosm which is limited by the time and space of one's life. And it is clearly implied throughout the *Dhp.C.* that one is free to think in one way or another within the framework of a given situation, even though the *whole* situation might arise as a karmic effect of one's thought in one's previous rebirth. So one's thinking might be considered, at one and the same time, either subjectively (i.e., from the point of view of freedom of choice), or objectively (i.e., from the point of view of the karmic predetermination). In cases where karmic predetermination is involved, the very category of freedom of choice is totally inapplicable. For in such cases there is neither freedom nor non-freedom, since thought is already *an undeniable fact.* And in the case where our interpretation covers the thoughts as ascribed to two or more of one's lives (i.e., when we deal with the macrocosmic mentality), we have to take into account the presence of the Buddha (or a Buddha) understood as *highest objectivity.* Objectivity which reveals *a person in 'one'*, and then, in the thinking of *this particular* person, is an objectivity that is higher than that connected with the karmic aspect of thought and mentality. So the final paragraph of the last observation is to be understood in the sense that since a person has become 'free of karmic influxes' (*anāsava*),[17] the thought of causing death cannot *objectively* penetrate his mentality, as if this thought possessed a negative will of its own. But this higher objectivity of thinking needs to be 'generated' and witnessed by the Buddha in order to acquire its factuality.

In the case of this factuality, it is the Buddha who retrospectively elucidates the connection between 'one' and 'another', that is, between Chakkhupala and the physician, thereby forming a person (of 'my son') out of the two existences taken together. It this case, the Buddha manifests a sort of *karmic memory* for those who are about to become Arhats, but who are unable to have such memory themselves.

3.4.1. From this it might be seen that the classical understanding of Buddhist philosophy as an analysis of thought (a type of understanding deeply implanted in the heads of the Buddhologists of this century) cannot be applied to that philosophy which can be educed from the Suttas. It is only in the Abhidhamma that, in effect, this analysis came into existence, probably as an outcome of the Buddhist yogis' *memorization practice* (*sati*, *saraṇa*). And once expounded, this philosophical analysis tried in all possible ways to make a restoration of pre-Buddhist mythological systems impossible. But I am not going to deal at length with this subject here. As for the Suttas, there is no analysis of thought, but instead an integral picture of the entirety of 'thought-mind'. The picture that exists on the strength of the observation of thought by the observer—an observation in which a sort of stereoscopic vision of all aspects of thought simultaneously present was achieved—'simultaneously' in the sense that there was no Abhidhamic 'sequence' and 'seriality'. In this picture, mythology was not included as an actual element of culture or religion. It figured instead as a natural *status quo*. Natural, that is, to those not yet transferred from the level of 'the observed' to that of 'the observers'.

3.4.2. Throughout the Suttas and commentaries, the Buddha figures as the Observer of all thoughts to which His attention is drawn within the context of a given situation. Thought or thinking is present in the *DhpC*, in the commentary on *Thera-and-Therī*, in the *Jātakas*, as well as in many other Pali texts, as the factor with which the Observer retrospectively connects one's one life with another, and thereby changes 'one' into 'a person'. The Observer, by identifying one's thought in one life with another's thought in another life, plays the role of, as it were, the person's '*superior thinking*', until such thinking has arisen in this person as his own (or until he himself becomes a Buddha). [And this is why, in the early historical Buddhism, the retrospective memory or recollection (*sati*) prevailed over prediction in the context of the mentalist line.] This superior 'objective thought' was conceived of as a *mental potentiality of thought itself* and not simply of *one's* thought. Therefore, we can infer that a 'person' assumes his personality either objectively, i.e., through the Observer's superior thought which recollects in various points or moments of thought, separated from one another, their oneness; or, subjectively, i.e., when one starts observing oneself as a point or moment where thought arises, and thus, by becoming an Observer, produces the Superior Thought for Oneself. Hence, the very notion of 'observation' is objective in its essence in both cases, though in the latter we call it subjective due to its 'personal' potentiality. This leads us to the strange idea that 'one' is, in Buddhism, a derivative of 'one's thought', 'a person' is a derivative of 'superior thought', and *the very concept of subjectivity, if understood Buddhistically, is nothing but a relative objectivity presented in self-observation* (that is, when one observes oneself as another). And in this connection, to make a terminological point, there is no object-subject opposition, in the sense that we used to find it in our psychological interpretations.

3.4.3. Now we are nearer to what might be called the 'results' of some specific yogic procedures—results which are expounded in the Suttas as initial postulates of yogic thinking and not as its final conclusions. The terminology used in the Suttas seems to have served the purpose of fastening together yogic thinking (during the period of its construction) and, at the same time, it might be considered as the *form* which is assumed by yogic thinking when it is already accomplished and when it is viewed retrospectively. But the specific character of the early Buddhist yoga is still a matter of conjecture, and the only thing we might say with any certainty is that from the very beginning the *objectification* of 'mind-thought' was emphasized. It is (a) objectification (still unknown to us), (b) its changes and shifts which resulted at first in the concept of 'sentient being' (not specifically Buddhist), (c) the concept of 'thought-mind', and finally, (d) the concept of a 'state of consciousness' (understood as distinct from 'mental state'). However, such an objectification would never have taken place had it not been for an 'objective religious situation' which was, in its own way, reworked and neutralized within the context of the other, specifically Buddhist, situation. And it is the latter which contributed so much to the working out of such modes of thinking which, if observed from a meta-philosophical position, can be regarded as being neither subjective nor objective.

NOTES TO ESSAY 3

1 Here I use the term 'proto-Buddhist' following Stanislaw Schayer (1938, p. 14).

2 I will explain that the *analysis* of thought took place no earlier than in the metaphysics of Abhidhamma, and that in the Suttas we are dealing with no more than the uses of terms which, only much later, were conceived of as resulting from such a metaphysical analysis.

3 See S. Schayer (1938, pp. 9–11). I am fully aware that to reduce religion to mythology is no less foolish than to reduce philosophy to epistemology. Nevertheless, I think that it is just at the point where a mythology begins to be demythologized that we can catch up with the moment when all living experience of a religion (as well as of the actual thinking in a philosophy) is immersed in the mythological text. Only later is it unearthed to acquire a 'new life' in the context of an absolutely new apperceptional structure.

4 May I hazard a guess that the 'emptiness' of the place is mainly due to the historical premonition of a coming *universalist* system of thought. So the very term 'pre-Buddhist' might be used analogously to the term 'pre-Socratic', when we deal with, say, Pythagorian philosophy, or Thales. If we retrospectively regard the philosophy of Jainism or Ajivika, we cannot help but feel that the need for a universalist philosophical system was very strong in *that place*, that this need was not satisfied by either Jainism or Ajivika, and that the apperceptional field of ancient Indian philosophy was still waiting for fulfilment. Or, as B. Barua (1921, pp. 194–5) put it, 'The end of philosophy was not realized'.

5 I would like to emphasize that the transformation of the notion of *manas* cannot be conceived of as psychological, that is, as technically belonging to the science of psychology. Because, were it so, we would have been turned back to the anthropocentrist meaning of this term. What we are really dealing with in the notion of *manas* is one of the dimensions of one's individuality, now coinciding with the dimension of 'thought' (*citta*), now overlapping it. It is only in the case of the *analysis* of 'I' that *manas* assumes its partly psychological meaning. However, such an analysis itself was intended to show that 'I' does not exist as an entirety, but only in its separately analysed elements and dimensions.

6 The parallelism of the notions of 'seed' and 'co-factor' (*saṅkhāra*) is also evident, particularly if we bear in mind the specifically dynamic implications of the latter as well as of some other terms derived from the root *kṛ* ('to do', 'to make', etc.). See B. Heimann (1964, pp. 52, 139).

7 When the Buddha said to the herdsman Dhaniya that his 'thought [was] subdued and freed', (*SN*, 23), He was figuring as if He were a perfect ascetic denying in *His* thought the *natural* qualities and propensities of the thought of a common man.

8 See *Dhp.*, 384: 'Gone beyond the two dhammas (i.e., "intuition" and "concentration"), where Brahman is said to be'.

9 See *Dhp.*, 383, where a Brahman 'knows that there is extinction of the impulses', while an ordinary man does not know this, and so on.

10 Quotations taken from the Sinhalese edition of *Dhp.*

11 *Dhp. C.*, pp. 19–21.

12 *Dhp. CT.*, pp. 157–8.

13 To give a complete picture we might now add the fourth 'interpretative text' epitomizing all that concerns Chakkhupala's blindness in his *last* rebirth (i.e., without any karmic references): 'I am blind, with eyes destroyed; I have entered this wilderness road. Even though I am prostrate, I shall go on, but not with a sinful companion'. See, *Thera-and-Therī* I, v. 35, p. 14, *Thera tr.*, p. 12.

14 I doubt if this type of time is identical with karmic time.

15 Perhaps Chakkhupala, as an Arhat to be, simply *could not* commit any non-neutral action, for that rebirth was his last one.

16 See *SN*, 80, where it is suggested by the Buddha Himself that 'reciting the stanzas' is a particular pragmatic *action* not to be confounded with the Tathagata's 'ontological status'.

17 Just as in very many other Suttas, this particular term is often used in the *Thera-and-Therī* [see vv. 47, 99, 100, 116, 289 (*Thera tr.*, pp. 7, 13, 15, 33, with detailed commentary on pp. 133–4)].

4. TOWARDS UNDERSTANDING THE BUDDHIST CONCEPT OF 'THOUGHT AS RELATED TO A PERSON'

Preliminary Remarks

4.1. *The Rise of Thought*

4.1.0. The 'rise of thought' (*cittuppāda*) appears in the *Dhammasaṅgaṇi* (*Dhs.*),[1] the first book of the *Abhidhamma-Piṭaka*, as the starting point and the axis in the description of all *thinkable* situations. That is why, I dare suppose, the term itself is so rarely and scarcely commented upon or explained.[2] Moreover, the very term 'thought' (*citta*) when figuring in the context of 'rise of thought', seems to assume such an abstract and universal meaning, that it would hardly be possible to reduce it to anything more abstract and universal. One could even say that its actual or potential qualities and conditions, whichever they might be, become thinkable and describable only provided that the very fact of its 'rise' has already taken place. *Citta* is the 'fact of thought' which, in itself, is to be regarded as totally *neutral* and *simple* (or 'elementary') until it has become connected with these qualities and conditions. Given, of course, that the latter have no existence of their own, and do not come into a kind of relative existence until they have become connected with a 'fact of thought'.

In accordance with a meta-philosophical approach, tentatively used here, one may single out the three distinctly different aspects in the 'rise of thought'. [This approach, among other things, implies that my own philosophical standpoint serves as no more than an instrument neutralizing the oppositions in the philosophies observed (including those of my own philosophy). As for this particular case, it serves to neutralize the oppositions between, say, anthropology and philosophy, or philosophy and psychology.]

4.1.1. If interpreted in its first aspect, the 'thought arisen' is seen[3] in its *absolute connectedness* with *an object*. So, in the beginning of the chapter on 'the rise of thought' of Dhs. 'a thought arisen' is described as 'having such and such an object (*ārammaṇa*)...'[4] The corresponding place in *Aṭṭhasālinī* (As.),[5] the main commentary on *Dhs.*, gives the following definition: 'thought is what thinks of [its] object'.[6] Which is further elaborated thus: 'Whatever might be an object in connection with which a thought is arisen,[7]... it is arisen with all objects'.[8] So, a thought arises not being connected *specifically* with one object or another, and is, as it were, opposed to all of them (although to each one of them only at the given 'moment of rise').

4.1.2. At the same time, its absolute connectedness with an object does not mean that thought figures as 'a subject' with respect to an object. And here we are coming to the second aspect of 'the rise of thought'. The thought, if observed strictly Abhidhammically and in the context of its rise, cannot, even formally, be imputed to an 'empirical I' (the last term is used here as the 'formal subject' of such expressions as 'I think', 'I observe', etc.). There are no psychological implications in this case. [For if observed meta-philosophically, the psychology of thought would appear as an epiphenomenon of culture, or of philosophy, etc. (given, of course, that we observe 'thought' here and now as if it had already been 'transformed' in or by, the Buddhist philosophy).]

Moreover, the thought here is ascribed to a 'person' (*puggala*) in a manner quite analogous to that in which it was connected with an object. The following Abhidhammic formula shows it very clearly: 'In one occurrence (*samaya*) the thought arises in connection with one object, in another case with another; in one occurrence it arises in one person, in another occurrence in another; in one occurrence it arises with one object in one person, in another occurrence it arises with another object in another person', etc.[9] I would even assert that the rise of thought can be presented as a certain 'class of occurrences', each of which consists of, at least, *three components: a thought, an object, a person.* But they cannot be regarded as equivalent, for a person is reduced (or, reducible) here (i.e., in the context of a given occurrence) to 'a thought of an object', and 'an object' to 'a thought', not the other way around. So it would even be possible to say that a thought, when arisen, is 'objective' and a person is not a 'subject of thought'. For the last is not a *predicate* in any Cartesian sense: it is 'thought itself' that thinks, not a person. In saying that there is no psychology in persons here, I mean that a *person*, if observed with respect to and in the context of, rise of thought, seems to be no more than a 'flat place' devoid of any psychological depth, whereas an *object* seems to imply time of thought rather than place or space of it.[10] Yet I have to admit that this last consideration is very questionable.

4.1.3. In tackling the third aspect of rise of thought we find ourselves confronted with the problem which was so important when the concept of 'sentient being' was investigated (see Essay 2): is a thought arisen simple or complex? And the answer is by no means an easy one, for whichever context we take, a thought arises in its connection with and in relation to very many other things and factors. The simplest occurrence (*samaya*) of such a connection might be seen in the abovementioned combinations of 'thought plus object' (the 'zero-combination') and 'thought plus object' plus 'person', to which all other occurrences might be reduced as to the most general case. The very beginning of the chapter on 'rise of thought' of *Dhs.* gives us an example of a far more complex case when a thought arises connected with very many factors, conditions and circumstances, such as states of consciousness (dhammas), karma (*kamma*), mental states, spheres of existence, objects, etc. Among all of them, dhammas stand, as it were, apart, for they figure in the context of all Abhidhammic classifications as their main content, and in the context of connection with thought they stand as its *main classificational correlate.* One thing, however, ought to be stated here as a methodological postulate: if we regard the dhammas as purely *relational* categories (i.e., not as phenomena), then the rise of thought has to be regarded as *the fact* to which all dhammas could be related in one way or the other. The inclusion of this fact into any classificatory unit of Abhidhamma as well as identifying it with any complex context where it stays as a component, does not make it complex itself. The stream of thought (*cittasantāna*) remains all the time only abstractedly postulated metaphysical *potentiality* until it assumes its *actualization* in the momentary and totally *discrete* fact of the rise of thought. That is why, I suppose, this category is commented upon, if anything, in a very oblique way (i.e., as if there were nothing on which to comment). We read, for example, in the *Abhidhammattha-Saṅgaha*[11] of Anuruddha (*Abh.S.*, V, 31), that '... if discerned from the point of view of rise of thought, there are twelve kinds of unwholesome (*akusala*) karma.'[12] However, when we deal with *rebirth* of (an individual) consciousness in one or another karmically-determined plane of existence, then this category does not enter the scene,[13] for it refers mainly to the *ontogenesis* of thought, not to its phylogenesis. Yet the moment—'the thought is arisen (*uppannaṃ hoti*) in the sensuous sphere (*kāmāvacara*)'[14]—is thought of or meditated upon as the appearance of a simple and single *object* totally devoid of any *inner* complexity (i.e., as an object which is not a composite one) as well as devoid of any *personal* characteristics ('personal' here means also 'complex').[15] And then it can be considered as *the universal object* (or 'object of all objects') for, terminologically speaking, the karmic forces are not accountable for the 'rise of thought' itself, but only for its *coincidences* with objects, spheres of existence, etc., that is, for all 'cases' (*samaya*) in which it happens to occur. The very mechanism of 'rise', however, *cannot* be reduced to karmic factors as far, at least, as we speak of a single, given thought, not of a stream of thought as the whole.[16]

4.2. *The Rise or Generation of the Thought of Awakening*

4.2.0. The Thought of Awakening (*bodhicitta*) can be regarded as the central concept of Mahayana philosophy, or perhaps it would be better to say, as the main entry into the system of Mahayanist philosophizing, irrespective of all possible doctrinal dogmatic and metaphysical differences between various schools and sections. The simple cataloguing of all meanings, connotations and contextual uses of this term would constitute a volume of several thousand pages.[17] However, given that my aim here is no more than to show some metaphysical connections of this concept with the concept of 'thought' (*citta*) in the Abhidhamma, I would confine myself to an extremely short and abstract exposition of the three main philosophical aspects of *bodhicitta*, or speaking more exactly, the three moments to which it could become reduced phenomenologically.

4.2.1. First is a *quasi-ontological aspect*, in the sense of which the Thought of Awakening represents the *potential*, *latent* and, to some extent, *unconscious* Bodhisattvahood, spread all over the beginningless universe of sentient beings. The term 'quasi' here is used in order to show that on the one hand, both *Prajñāpāramitā* and *Śūnyavāda* approaches, if used, would make this concept unavoidably *relative* (or 'relativistic'). On the other hand, it still remains uncertain whether, if taken as an ontological category, *bodhicitta* would figure on the plane of separate and individual sentient beings or on the plane of the whole dharmic universe. Or, one can even say, particularly in the light of the late developments of this idea in

Tantric Buddhism, that it is *mind* itself (i.e., each and every mind whatsoever) which is latently and potentially *bodhicitta*—i.e., 'mind as potentially awakened'. However, even provided that the individuality of *bodhicitta* is uncertain (in the sense exactly analogous to that in which individuality of a Bodhisattva is uncertain) its *non-psychologism* is absolutely certain. That is, it is totally devoid of any capacity to form the *complex* mental phenomena or to figure as an elementary, formative and basic principle to which they could be reduced.[18] Moreover, if understood in the Abhidhammic (and even Abhidharmic) sense, i.e., in the sense of states of consciousness, dharmas cannot be thought or conceived of as psychologically correlated to *bodhicitta*. For they belong to two absolutely different *dimensions* which neither coincide with nor overlap one another. That is to say, that *bodhicitta* cannot even be considered as belonging to a stream, on the strength of the latter's belonging to the level of the Abhidharma. It seems as if there were several philosophies existing in parallel where the very term 'citta' was used simultaneously in several different ways.

4.2.2. The second aspect might be called 'soteriological' or 'yogic', for it is in the sense of this aspect that *bodhicitta* is thought of or meditated on as having already risen, been acquired or produced *consciously*, i.e., in the sense of *individual* awareness (or self-awareness). That is, *after* having become actualized, changed from the state of potentiality into that of realization, it is described in its gradual development: 'After its production, the Bodhicitta proceeds on in an upward march through ten... stages of Bodhisattvahood (*bodhisattvabhūmi*)'.[19] The concept of time is invariably involved here, for however short this process might be, it still remains a process including the series of psychologically (or 'yogically') significant moments not identical with or equivalent to each other. Yet there is no real psychology there, because, figuratively speaking, the Thought of Awakening is referred to 'thought' in the same manner as a Being of Awakening (*bodhisattva*) is referred to a 'sentient being' (*sattva*). That is, the process of *bodhicitta* can be conceived only, so to speak, from the point of view of a Bodhisattva, who, by definition, cannot have any point of view whatsoever, and whose mentality is neither structured nor functions on different levels.

The literature devoted to 'development' of *bodhicitta* is, indeed, immense, and I would not concentrate any longer on this aspect, but to note one thing. A Bodhisattva of, for example, the tenth stage of the realization of *bodhicitta*, cannot be viewed as a *personal* manifestation of the Thought of Awakening understood in the sense of the first aspect. Or, we may say, that a personal Bodhisattva (named so-and-so) cannot be reduced to an impersonal principle of *bodhicitta*, for the reason that each *individually named* Bodhisattva can be thought of as a 'place' where this or that series of quasi-psychologically different moments has happened, but not as the 'cause' or 'agent' which produced these moments. Thus, the purely nominal individualism of a Bodhisattva (reminding us of the purely nominal individualism of a sattva) can only in the abstract be traced 'back' to the *bodhicitta* understood in its quasi-ontological aspect.[20] In other words, one may even say that neither *bodhicitta* (taken 'as such') nor *bodhisattva* (regarded at the final stage of development of *bodhicitta*) can be thought of as a phenomenon, while development itself of *bodhicitta* can.[21] Yet this phenomenal development of *bodhicitta* is all the time separated from the non-phenomenal quasi-being of *bodhicitta* by an extremely enigmatic fact of the rise, or production, of *bodhicitta*, which constitutes the third aspect, the most significant for our purpose.

4.2.3. The Rise of Thought of Awakening (*bodhicittotpāda*) can be phenomenologically compared with the 'rise of thought' (*cittotpāda*), for both may be interpreted as the *conscious* phenomena serving as the metaphysical point of departure in the respective philosophies of Mahayana and the Abhidhamma. Given, of course, that in the second case a thought emerges from 'nowhere' of a previous dhammic moment of 'non-thought', while in the first, the Thought of Awakening appears as an actualization of the uninterrupted state of its own latent being. However, in both cases we have the *conscious fixation of a fact, the very existence of which at another (i.e., previous or future) time or in a different place (e.g., in a different sentient being), though metaphysically postulated, is beyond the pale of any subjective awareness.*

So, for instance, saying that Thought of Awakening is always and everywhere latently present, does not imply the 'logical' necessity of its rise, although the fact of the rise can be 'soteriologically' reduced to the timeless potentiality of the Thought of Awakening. Likewise, one's becoming a Bodhisattva of the tenth stage cannot be deduced from one's previous experiencing of the 'rise', but one's already achieved Bodhisattvahood can be reduced retrospectively to this rise. The 'rise' remains, therefore, the *central* fact in the genesis (i.e., both phylo-and-ontogenetically) of a Bodhisattva.

4.2.3.1. The content of *bodhicitta*, if 'caught' at the moment of its rise, presents in itself another very complicated problem. For, speaking dogmatically, it comprises Emptiness (*śūnyatā*) and Compassion (*karuṇā*) thought of *as one*.[22] The point is, however, that the notion itself of *śūnyatā* is here referring, first of all, to all *sentient beings* (*sattva*) which, with respect to Emptiness, are non-beings. While the notion of *karuṇā* refers, quite explicitly, to *all* sentient beings taken as *one object* (however multiple and diversified it might be), for the sake of which a Bodhisattva-to-be, the one in whom the rise of the Thought of Awakening has taken place, is to give himself up as a sattva ('being'). So that his re-awareness of all sattvas as empty, and of himself as a mere *sattva* (or very often, as even 'a mere body' viewed as totally 'disposable of'), would bring him on a different level of 'being'. And it is in his re-awareness of the Thought of Awakening, that this thought referring to itself, becomes *non-reflexive*, and relatedness to other sattvas becomes entirely objective in the rise of *bodhicitta*, and therewith sattva becomes 'the object of content' in *bodhicitta*, or the focus in its rise. [Given, of course, that it may also include the re-awareness of itself as the all-pervading potential state of *bodhicitta* in the whole universe (metaphorically depicted as 'the ocean of *bodhicittas*') i.e., some return to the quasi-ontological aspect of *bodhicitta* may take place *within* the 'rise'.] All psychological characteristics of the Rise of the Thought of Awakening would then be appearing as merely formal, for instance, as 'decision', 'resolve', 'resolution', etc.[23] Because, this thought is only formally 'a thought', that is, if understood at the moment of its rise, this understanding itself becomes devoid of all formal psychological modalities.[24]

4.2.3.2. What is particularly interesting to note, is that a Bodhisattva-to-be is related to *bodhicitta* in the same way as a sentient being, *sattva*, is related to its 'sentientness'. That means that both are metaphysically postulated (the first explicitly, the second implicitly) as *pre-existent* with respect to their awareness (or self-awareness) in a human being in the case of *citta*, and in a future Bodhisattva in the case of *bodhicitta*. So, *citta* becomes *actually* aware of itself in a man and *bodhicitta* in a future Bodhisattva. That is, a real phenomenology of thought starts not with an act of its being experienced *by* one, but with an act of its becoming aware of itself *in* one.[25] [And of course, this awareness cannot be characterized as 'reflexive', because it is referred to anything but itself.] Therefore, it might be said, that the very *place* in which the rise of the Thought of Awakening occurs,[26] is a person (*puruṣa*). Then the previous or other states of this very place can be conceived as *an individual*, whereas the state of the already consumed Bodhisattvahood would be seen again as the Realization of Non-person, assuming the name of a Great Person (*mahāpuruṣa*). It is, therefore, the moment of self-awareness in thought, which makes an individual a person, but it cannot be stated thereby that a thought itself is personal, for as such, it is impersonal.

4.2.3.3. The moment of the rise of the Thought of Awakening is not a moment in a strictly temporal sense, for its occurrence can be ascribed to a *place only*. It cannot even be thought of in terms of *duration*, for the latter implies a series of moments (as *bodhicitta* in the second aspect does), whereas here we deal with a simultaneous 'concurrence' of the Thought and its being aware of itself.[27] I think that there is no time 'between' these two, for in the sense of *bodhicittotpāda* they are *one* thought.

4.2.3.4. The term *utpāda* itself seems to be very ambiguous. It can be thought of as either 'rise' or 'generation' (or even 'production'). The latter implies the cases (*samaya*), when the volitional moment is described and, particularly, when some other agents or agencies enter the scene and figure as consciously and non-spontaneously generating *bodhicitta* in future Bodhisattvas.[28] One can only guess if the opposition 'spontaneous—non-spontaneous' would be any more relevant in this case than it was in the case of rise of thought, for were it even a Bodhisattva or Buddha who produced or induced *bodhicitta* in a Bodhisattva-to-be, it remains quite uncertain whether it was one and the same 'entity' of *bodhicitta* actualizing itself in both of them (i. e., *bodhicitta* taken in its first aspect), or it were two different 'states' actualizing one another. However, one thing remains quite clear: the notion of 'person' might be used here only with relation to this 'point-moment' of *bodhicittotpāda*, and it is in this way only, that the notion of person could be interpreted as *coinciding with* that of thought.[29]

4.2.4.1. All this, however, would not lead us to any somewhat comprehensible phenomenology of the person of a Bodhisattva. We are bound, therefore, to return to 'a person in general' as the *place* where 'a thought' may happen, and it is with respect to this happening that some crucially important implications reveal themselves, to which the very concept of 'person' is reduced, or, more exactly, without which such a reduction would be virtually impossible. Firstly, a person implies a certain *diachronical finiteness*. And this is not necessarily to be understood in terms of strictly temporal calculation as opposed to the timelessness of the beginningless universe, but rather in terms of the *landmarks* in which or by means of which a Buddha or a Bodhisattva *can* see his own or anybody else's 'trans-reincarnational' existence up to the very moment of this seeing. [Personally, I doubt very much whether such an existence could ever be thought or conceived of apart from this 'act' of seeing.] The landmarks are: (1) the appearance of *bodhicitta*; (2) the prediction, made by a Buddha, by which one's future Buddhahood is predetermined (*niyata*), and (3) the stage in the course of the Bodhisattva's career (usually it is the eighth *bhūmi*) whereupon no reversal is possible. [I omit here the tenth stage of *dharma-megha*, as automatically entailed by (3), or by (2) through (3).] So, the person of a Bodhisattva here could be conceived 'diachronically' in the following way: from 0 (in the beginningless universe of sentient beings) to (1), or (1) and (2) together—*infinite* and *indefinite;* from (1) or (1) and (2) together to (3)—*infinite* and *definite;* from (3) to 0 of *Nirvana*—*finite* (in Mahayana) and *definite*. And it is an *infinitude* of the interval (1)–(3) that makes a Buddha himself an *infinite person* or, shall we say, a 'non-person', whereas in the case of a *śrāvaka* or *pratyeka-buddha*, this interval (where, of course, we will have the beginning of one's *path* and/or the meeting with a Buddha instead of *bodhicitta*, and a 'provisional arhatship' instead of the *acalā bhūmi*) is quite *finite* and easily calculable.[30] Moreover, this interval may have become so indefinitely large (either in terms of 'kalpas' or in terms of 'reincarnation', or both) in the case of a Buddha, that his personal 'biography' or 'onto-genesis' would be made a negligible quantity if compared with a phylogenesis of his Buddhahood. Whereas the *śrāvakas* and *pratyeka-buddhas* seem to be (in principle, at least), much nearer to the rest of sentient beings with respect to the definitiveness of their biography.

4.2.4.2. Secondly, as regards the 'place', the very idea of the body of a Buddha or a Bodhisattva is far more fluid and indefinite (in view, probably, of an extreme transformability of their bodies) with respect to its 'physical' limits, so that in no way can it be taken as a criterion or even a symptom for an identification of his personality.[31] Since a Bodhisattva cannot be identified as *one* other than through *bodhicitta*, and since this identification cannot be realized other than from the point of view of a Buddha or a Bodhisattva of the Tenth Stage (who themselves are no longer the sattvas), the body with its deeds, speech and thoughts would inevitably be reduced to a *topos* of thought (not 'thoughts'!).[32] And it is this thought which would serve as the only factor of identification of several sattvas as *one* (as in the case of Chakkhupala in Essay 3) or of innumerable (*asaṃkhyeya*) rebirths as those of one and the same Buddha.[33]

However, what is particularly important to note with respect to both 'temporal' and 'spatial' implications of the idea of person, is that here we do not deal with the general or logical reasons, but exclusively with the concrete *retrospective observations* made by the Buddhas and Bodhisattvas, or with no less concrete *predictions* made by the Buddhas.[34]

4.3. *The Transfer of Thought*

4.3.0. So, it is clearly seen that in the case of the Rise of the Thought of Awakening in a future Bodhisattva, his person can be 'detected' solely at the very moment of this rise, or generation, wherefrom it starts its development to non-personality (or Great Personality) of Bodhisattvahood. Yet one most enigmatic thing still remains an undeniable fact: *there cannot be anybody* (*or anything*) *who might have existed* as 'a sattva only', or even as 'a Bodhisattva only', as far as it goes. There must always be in someone something 'left', not covered by such concepts as 'thought', 'stream of thought', 'mind' (*manas*) or even 'the Thought of Awakening'. This is something which is hardly perceptible in the purely 'impersonal' enumerations and formulations of the Abhidhamma, but which is quite 'personally' expressed in *Bodhicaryāvatāra* by Shantideva as well as in very many Tantrist texts, something which, in effect, is ascribed to thought (or any other of the concepts mentioned above) as a 'personal', non-ontological force or energy operating with and generating, this thought.[35] And it is this same force, the constant 'remainder' uncovered and uncoverable by any thinkable term or notion (such as *puruṣa*, or *jīva*, or *sattva*, or *pudgala*, etc.), which, *though not being relational* itself (unlike the karmic force, for instance), can, none the less, be *indirectly indicated* when various operations with thought are described, as the *source* of these (mainly yogic) operations.

4.3.1. When we read—'Thou, having generated the Thought of Awakening out of desire of happiness for all sentient beings...'[36]—we may suppose, that something *happens* in the 'space' between the Thought of Awakening (and 'desire', *iccha*, for this thing) and 'thou', and that this 'happening' cannot be ascribed either to 'thou' (i.e., the author's empirical 'I') or to the Thought of Awakening. Yet, speaking strictly Buddhistically, such an interpretation may have taken place only in the cases when we deal with totally conscious and specifically yogic procedures by means of which 'thought', or 'mind', or 'consciousness' is fixed, posited by a Bodhisattva or a yogi, as an *absolute object*. Moreover, the objectification here goes as far as to enable Shantideva to liken the mind to an inanimate thing, magically constructed (*nimitta*) and entirely obedient to him or another sentient being.[37] And I think that it was in its relatedness to this active quasi-personal force that thought assumed the meaning and term of 'consciousness' (*vijñāna*), irrespective of however synonymously they might have been used previously. I could even go so far as to assert that it was in the very context and process of such a 'yogic' objectification, where the thought itself (or 'as such') could have acquired the aspect of its 'objective being' related to and correlated with this 'force'.

4.3.2. *The yogācāra* posulate about the thought being 'self-conscious' (or 'self-illuminating', *svaprakāśa*) must by no means be understood in the sense of its being 'reflexive'. On the contrary, it is quite evident that it implies neither the subject (a person) nor an object (an idea) of thought. In its aspect of self-consciousness, the thought mirrors itself without producing any 'objectification' at all, while, if looked at in the aspect of its relatedness, the thought can be interpreted as reflexing the modifications and changes in this 'personal' force.[38] Which means that its quasi-personal character itself can be established only through thought and by means of a secondary interpretation of thought as related to this force. And, if interpreted in this way, this quasi-personal force would seem to be a 'naturalistic formation' rather than a metaphysical entity, whereas its counterpart, i.e., thought itself, would be seen as totally 'unnatural 'or 'nature-less' (*asvabhāvika*).[39] And then, what I consider as particularly important, the various instances of 'empirical I' might be regarded as merely illusory modifications of this quasi-personal force, as modifications possibly induced by another force.[40]

4.3.3.0. This two-aspectedness of thought, implicitly contained in the *yogācāra*, found its explicit description in the texts of the so-called New Tantra in Tibet where the second aspect related to this quasi-personal force, assumed the name of 'conscious principle', (*vijñāna*, tib. *rnam-shes*), whereas the first aspect started being merged with the concept of mind (*manas*, tib. *yid*).[41]

Three conceptual features mark this extremely powerful movement of Buddhist Yoga which began around the eleventh century A.D. These are:

(1) the idea that the mind (or thought), as such (i.e., by its own nature), is as supernaturally hard, solid and immutable as the *Vajra* (the symbol of the highest solidity) and possessing such a nature that it cannot be treated in terms of either subjectivity or objectivity;[42]

(2) the idea of transformation (and transformability) of all natural bodily and mental functions of a yogi into their supernatural correlates (also called the Vajra-correlates—this idea was particularly strongly stressed in the teaching of the *Guhya-Samāja-Tantra*);

(3) the idea that the individual conscious principle of a man could be deliberately and consciously transferred from one body to another, from one place to another, from one time to another.

[It is necessary to emphasize here that the very term 'idea' as it was understood throughout the Buddhist Tantras means, first of all, the capacity to do 'it' rather than think 'it'.]

The last feature is particularly characteristic of the Karmapa Sect, and that is why I would like to concentrate here on the facts and events related to its past and present as they are described in the recently published book devoted to its present reincarnated Head and his holy predecessors.[43]

4.3.3.1. This book gives us the description of the lives of the sixteen Karmapas based upon a few Tibetan sources, the chief of which is the *Blue Annals*, orally commented on by the present Karmapa himself.[44] Yet, to put it more exactly, we have here the history of *one* life of one Bearer of Consciousness, whose limits of existence are rather difficult to ascertain because, dogmatically speaking, we can hardly imagine a time when he was not existing. I will try to explain this point.

'Karmapa' (*las-can*) literally means 'the Possessor of Karma', which in its turn, signifies that he is not subject to the Law of Karma but, on the contrary, he masters it, and goes from reincarnation to reincarnation choosing the place and time where and when to be reincarnated. The present Karmapa is said to have been an Emanation *(sprul-pa)* of the Bodhisattva Avalokiteshvara, the highest spiritual patron of Tibet. The *Blue Annals* state that previous to becoming the Karmapa he was a Bodhisattva of the Blessed Period (*bskal-bzang*). Then after achieving the Highest Complete Awakening, he underwent five reincarnations, in one of which he became a disciple of the greatest Buddhist philosopher and yogi, Nagarjuna (c. second century A.D.), until in his sixth rebirth he became reincarnated as the first Karmapa under the name of 'the Knower of the Three Times' (1110–93). Until recently (he died in 1981) he was living as the sixteenth Karmapa at Rumtek in Sikkim and according to the Prediction in due time he will become one of the Buddhas of the Future, namely, Buddha Lion (*seng-ge*), the Buddha listed after Maitreya (*BA*, 412–13); in the *Bhadra-kalpa-sūtra.*[45]

4.3.3.2. But how did he continue his existence from the time when there was no time up to the time when it will be quite distinct from ours? This Yogic process of the Transference *(grong'jug, 'pho-ba)* of one's conscious principle (*rnam-shes*) into another body is described in the book and corresponding sources with a great deal of clarity, though without too many technical details. So, we read that the second Karmapa (1204–83) performed the action of 'transferring his conscious principle into another body' (the term corresponding to Skt. *parakāya-praveśa*) of a boy who had just passed the point of death (i.e., whose own conscious principle had already left him, but whose life-principle was not altogether extinct). However, when the boy's parents saw him returning to life again, being terribly afraid therewith, they pierced the child's eye with a needle so that the conditions were not suitable. And after that, the second Karmapa withdrew his conscious principle from the boy's dead body and, after assuming the form of a Being of the Intermediate State (one that is between death and rebirth, *bar-do-ba*), entered the womb of his future mother.[46]

4.3.3.3. In almost all cases of the sixteen Karmapas, including the present one, we have one and the same 'pattern of becoming': (a) the Karmapa predicts, either by sealed letter or, much less often, orally, where his conscious principle is going to be transferred; (b) he performs such a transference; (c) the child born thereafter is recognized, usually by Reincarnated Lamas of some other Tantrist lineages, as *the same* Karmapa. It does not mean, however, that we have literally the same 'man' (not to speak about 'person' or 'I') but rather, the *individual structure of consciousness* (primarily emanated from the timeless Bodhisattva). This idea, if regarded phenomenologically, could have led us to the triple (if not trinitarian) interpretation of the conscious principle: (a) as a quasi-ontological category related to that of Buddhahood; (b) as the psychical fact or event related to the conception of the Body of Transformation (*sprul-pai sku, nirmāṇa kāya*), according to which each conscious principle *is* individual (yet from which nothing could be deduced about individuality thought of as a person); (c) a mental entity of 'thought' (*sems-nyid*) to be yogically meditated upon and concentrated on. The last one is referred to as one of the main objects of yogic activity but by no means affected or changed by it or by any other act, fact, or event.[47]

4.3.3.4. Seeing that, we can speak of all sixteen Karmapas living from 1110 up till now as *one* in the sense of one *consciousness*, but not in the sense of one *man*. This might be confirmed by many passages in the *Blue Annals* and many other sources. So the second Karmapa was said to have seen the appearance of the first Karmapa (*BA*, 423) and quite obviously, they were different men whose conscious identity was maintained by an especial yogic recollection (*dran-pa*) permitting all of them to see in each other one and the same conscious core (*BA*, 284).[48]

So, we may ponder, there must be one and the same consciousness, or conscious principle thought of (or meditated on) as *achronic continuity* of thought. If taken in its synchronic slices, it would be opposed to various men or other sentient beings (*sattva*) as an individual conscious principle to its individual bearers. Yet if taken dïachronically, it would be opposed to something which is neither consciousness nor an individual, neither a sentient being nor its sentientness, but which can see itself (or recollect itself) as *one consciousness*. That is, it can recognize itself in many (in fact in innumerable numbers of) individuals with *one* consciousness, but it is not *one with* this consciousness. This 'it' appears, as in the previous example, as something operating with thought, or recollecting consciousness, or transferring the conscious principle, that is, as something which could be interpreted in the sense of consciousness (or thought, or mind) only—not the other way around. And in such an interpretation only this 'something' becomes 'something personal', and thus consciousness assumes its *relative ontological status*.

4.4.0. It is very interesting to note that to modern exponents of Mahayanist Buddhism (and especially in its tantric form) the person very often assumes the features of the subject of *awareness* rather than of the subject of consciousness, thinking, or mind. The very classification of persons becomes a kind of hierarchy in *understanding*, which could be, though no more than indirectly, deduced from the Abhidhamma. One of these exponents, Dhargyey, writes: 'There are three ways of apprehending the *distinction between* the self and the personality. A person with understanding of *śūnyatā* holds the view that the self does not have an independent existence. Others believe the contrary... There are also those who... have no view on the nature of the self, yet they see and understand the conventional existence of phenomena and apply this likewise to themselves...'[49] This passage alone clearly shows that its author does not see the 'understanding' of non-existence of independent self as if this understanding were figuring *instead* of the self—for it is the five skandhas which figure 'instead'. The notion of personality seems to be possible here only as a result of a *reduction* of the 'situation' of understanding to a threefold structure, viz. the understanding of *śūnyatā*, and non-existing self, and the five relatively existing dharmic complexes (skandhas). This situation seems to be far more complex than the situation of the 'rise of thought', with which this essay starts. Because, as Guenther and Kawamura rightly point out, the understanding itself (or 'awareness', *rig-pa*) is nothing else but thought or consciousness (or 'mind' according to Guenther's terminology) 'as such', while in the triad of rise of thought ['thought+objects (including dharmas)+subject'], thought (*citta*) acquires a quasi-absolute character in the sense that it is what it is and as it is, and cannot be anything else, at a given moment at least.[50] And of course, in the 'rise of thought' a person is a mere 'subject of thought', whereas in the 'situation of awareness'—and it entirely applies to the above-cited passage from Dhargyey—*a person is the subject of awareness, and not of thought.*

So, the person understood as a 'carrier' of awareness (if not as 'awareness itself' taken in its space-and-time definiteness), and awareness understood as thought as such (*sems-nyid*), and all mental functions (including 'thought' observably functioning and memory), understood as modifications of thought [or 'mental events' (*sems-byung*, in Guenther's terminology)]—that is what constitutes, as it were, the hypothetic 'situation of a person' as maintained by the Tibetan New Tantra and its latest exponents Eastern and Western alike. This indeed is absolutely congruent with the oldest Abhidhammic standpoint that the subject of thought is not a person unless and until he has become a Great Person (i.e., not a *puggala*, but a Maha-Purisa) as well as with the doctrine of Thought of Awakening, where one becomes a Noble Person (*aryapudgala*) because of the transformation of his thought (or mind) into the highest awareness of Awakening. And is it not crystal-clear that, in the context of this consideration, neither awareness nor thought-as-mind can be regarded in terms of a psychological approach?

Thus, returning to the end of 4.3.3.4 (and alas, we have not gone much further from where we started) we, in a partial agreement with Guenther, can say that this *one consciousness* is, in effect, one for many individuals in succession, only provided that there is its 'as-such-ness' figuring now as a hidden potentiality of consciousness, now as its understanding or awareness able to describe itself in terms of 'as-if-it-were memory' of other rebirths.

4.4.1. In its Indian form the theory of reincarnation seems to be utterly distinct from any other transformation of 'one' ('self', 'soul', etc.), and it is in the sense of just this distinction that one's death (rather than birth) is regarded as the point of departure. This means that one's individual line of existence is not simply divided between different bodies, but that there must be death as the main factor delimitating the one existence from the other. [Not even 're-incarnation' itself, i.e., insertion into a womb, for there are cases when after one's death one acquires a 'form-less' existence (*arūpa-dhātu* in Buddhism), or attains the state of final liberation from all existence.]

Particularly important here is that, after the moment of death, all events that befall a soul, self or consciousness are described in a purely *objective* way, that is, as it were by a 'third person' (and almost always *in the third person*). It might even seem that the very fact of a *direct* experiencing of one's reincarnation may have annulled reincarnation itself, which by the way, would, though indirectly, follow from the early Buddhist doctrine of Karma. However, taken in a context broader than Buddhist or even Indian, *reincarnation could be seen as directly complementary to any consciousness which is aware of itself.* Moreover, it can be asserted that, as a phenomenon of consciousness, reincarnation could have appeared on the surface of texts only because there had already been the idea of an external observer objectively watching the whole situation. [When I say 'external observer' or 'third person', I mean that the 'first person' is one told or otherwise informed of one's *other* reincarnation, with which 'the second' could be, conventionally, identified.][51] Probably, this idea could be regarded as but one necessary element in the structure of consciousness, of which reincarnation is another necessary element.

4.4.2. The referring to oneself in the third person boils down to a possibility of quite another explanation. When one looks at oneself in the past (or even, in the present) one sees a *mental mechanism* (*manas*) responsible for thoughts, words and actions leading to *one's* (and not this mechanism's) *perpetuation* (in the karmic sense)—namely of *one* who cannot be identified with one mental mechanism or another. Such a mental mechanism, however, cannot be ascribed to *one;* on the contrary, it is one who may or may not ascribe a certain mental mechanism to oneself, not the other way around, because no mental mechanism could do such an ascription. [By this I mean, that a mental mechanism can do it only in an abstract, general way, and not in a concrete and individual way.] When the mental mechanism is a past one, this does not mean that it existed *really* in a certain past. Quite the contrary: it is this ascription, made in one's actual present, that *forms* the past itself, the past which simply does not exist out of or apart from, this ascription. We cannot say that this or that mental mechanism really preceded that which we call 'one' taken at the time prior to the very 'act' (or, more exactly speaking,'thought') of such an ascription. So, the past appears to exist as no more than a function of one's ascribing to oneself a mental mechanism—the past is *mental*, so to speak, and momentarily actualized by one *from* the present moment.

4.4.3. There is, however, one more aspect to this ascription. In thinking of its mental mechanisms one, as it were, relegates to them all one's conscious modalities (memory, intentions, motivations, ratiocination, etc.). In doing this one *estranges* onself from all that which is mental, and endows a mentality with such reflexive *conscious* capacities as self-consciousness, self-awareness, self-observation, etc. Once relegated and ascribed to a mental mechanism, they all become *mentalized*, i.e., become interpretable and interpreted as *naturally* mental or mental by their *own nature* (*svabhāvataḥ*). And then only one's 'dementalized' thought (or, consciousness—for, taken in this function, they are terminologically *one*) may think of them as non-natural because of their not partaking of *its* own nature, or even may think of them as artificial, mind-made, etc.

We can even go so far in our purely conjectural considerations as to suppose that, at least in Buddhism alone, the very idea of rebirth might have appeared as subsequent and consecutive to the idea of triplicity 'thought/consciousness/mind', where thought is thought of as putting the conscious reflex *over* mind.

4.4.4. Returning to Essay 3 we may deem that, when the Buddha said in his tale about a previous rebirth of the Elder Chakkhupala that 'Chakkhupala was that physician', this did not mean *literally* that the physician *was* Chakkhupala. Because it was the position of Chakkhupala the Arhat, from the point of view of which the *partial* identification of Chakkhupala with the physician could have been possible at all. That is, the Chakkhupala's Arhatship made it *objectively* possible to have identified his *then* 'present' mentality (understood, of course, in the broadest sense) with the already past mentality of the physician. Or, more technically speaking, the Buddha, acting as an external observer of mental mechanisms of the others, identified Chakkhupala with the physician *through* the identification of a certain mental structure of Chakkhupala—namely his blindness combined with the absence of thinking of killing—with a certain mental structure of the physician (namely, the latter's thought of killing combined with the action). So my conjecture here is that the very situation of identification here became possible only by virtue of Chakkhupala's becoming an Arhat, which in turn *separated* his 'identifiable' mentality from the unidentifiable conscious 'reflex' *over* mentality. The last could be seen as a capacity restricted to Arhats and their like only, and at the same time, as an *objective condition* producing the 'recollection' of one's previous rebirths, if not the previous rebirths themselves.

4.4.5. This, of course, is a commonplace in the *Jātakas* as well as the Dhammapala's commentaries on the *Therī-and-Thera-Gāthās*. A similar commonplace occurs when the Buddha identifies himself with a Bodhisattva—the latter term used not only in the sense of 'the Buddha in one of his previous rebirths', but also in the sense of a Being of Awakening or, at least, a Being who gave the Bodhisattva Vow or experienced the Thought of Awakening. In this case, when the Buddha said (*The Sūtra of Golden Light*, XVIII, pp. 92–7), 'this prince [who had given his body to a tigress dying of hunger] was the Tathagata'—it was clearly meant to demonstrate (to Shariputra and others) that he indeed was, because the Vow (or Thought) of Awakening in the prince could be thought of as a real and absolute basis of identification which, in this case, is not partial for it refers to the unanalysable *conscious* (i.e., not mental) core of the Bodhisattvahood in them both. That is, in a way directly opposite to the previous case, the Bodhisattva here could be identified with the Tathagata or Buddha not only retrospectively and from the point of view of the Complete and Perfect Awakening of the latter, but also from quite another point of view—that of, as it were, impersonal Bodhisattvahood. This last can be, conjecturally of course, considered as not only non-mental, but also non-conscious in the sense of its being devoid of all *modalities* of consciousness. Then, returning to our 'standard' situation where the Buddha by his supernatural power (*anubhāva*) unearthed the *stūpa* with the bone relics of 'his own' body (i.e., that of the Bodhisattva-prince devoured by a tigress), we may surmise both the Buddha and the prince to be identical as the two instances of one and the same *Awakened* Consciousness. Therefore, we may even go so far as to present this whole case as if it were that *consciousness* which recognized *itself* in the prince and the Buddha, but did it (in *this* case) through the Buddha. But here, unlike the previous case, we cannot say that without that act (or *thought*) of recognition by the Buddha, there would be no 'prince-rebirth', for their *one* Bodhisattvahood was already there—it could be 'detected' at the very moment of the prince's decision to give his body to the tigress. This hypothesis can be summarized in the following way: not only the memory of one's past rebirths, but one's past rebirths themselves could happen solely through a *present thought* which actualizes them, so that they *do not exist* apart from or without, this actualization. I may surmise that two other factors (i.e., besides thought itself) are necessary for bringing about this actualization. *Subjectively*, there must be an *intention* (which, however, may have been *objectively* motivated or caused by a situation, circumstances, etc.) coinciding with or ascribed to an actualizing thought. *Objectively*, such an actualization could take place *only when one was* (the use of 'was' is merely conventional!) *conscious of what was happening*. In other words, one's thought in the present can actualize only that which was one's (or another one's) thought in the past. Thus a *phenomenal* character of the *whole* situation of actualization is evident: only that can be recollected or thought of what was or, at least, could have been, conscious of itself. Then a rather dubious corollary may follow: one cannot actualize in one's thinking that which is a *mere object*. [For mere objects alone could be thought of as 'others', or 'equally others', or 'equidistant others'—which S. Collins (1982, p. 190) has so vividly failed to understand. Or else it can be said that by *objectification* alone one can change a (*conscious*) *phenomenon* into *another* consciousness. But this is too difficult to go on with!]

4.4.6. Now, one observation could be made concerning the means of identification or recognition of one's previous rebirth. Obviously, only in a metaphorical way can one call it a 'memory', and only if we understand memory as an *epiphenomenon* or a particular case of the modalities of consciousness. But even then we must see it, however vaguely and imperfectly, as conventionally more reducible (or, reductible) to some initial *phenomenal conditions* of our own thinking than of that which we may conjecturally attribute to the 'subjects' of these cases. When, in the first case, the Buddha told the bhikkhus of a previous rebirth of the Elder Chakkhupala, he produced this identification in a merely objective way, as if he were identifying with one another the two absolutely objective facts—the fact of Chakkhupala's being blind with the fact of the blindness caused by the physician and, thereby (but not the other way around), identifying the Elder Chakkhupala himself with the physician. I call the character of this identification objective not only because it is directed to a person other than Buddha himself (it could have been directed to himself too), but because it was directed at the facts the connection between which is conceived as purely objective (in this case it is *karma*). The very objectivity of this connection, however, has nothing to do with the concept of memory understood in the sense of an objective psychological method. For in the latter, the most essential thing is that some fact becomes an object of the objectively verifiable *process of remembering*, whereas in our case it is the *act of recollection* which can be neither deduced from remembering, nor can remembering be inferred from it. Such a 'karmic recollection' is also frequently mentioned in the Dhammapala's commentaries. In these commentaries various bhikkhus and bhikkhunīs recollect their previous rebirths, which serves, probably, as an indirect symptom of their impending Arhatship, whereas two other symptoms were regarded as direct and sufficient: Buddha's sending to them his Body of Enjoyment (*sambhoga-kāya*) and their own producing the *sign* (*aññā*). But there is no memory in the psychological sense of the term there, for that which we are treating now is memory not as a psychological phenomenon but as an *epiphenomenon* of consciousness, or perhaps more exactly, of thought. But can we then qualify 'thought that recollects' as subjective with respect to an object of recollection even if this object is identified by the recollecting thought as 'the same person'?

4.4.6.1. There is something utterly inconclusive about the objective memory. That is why prior to answering this question we have to emphasize that what the notion of epiphenomenality of memory amounts to is not the memory as an *object* of thinking, but *thinking* of memory or even, perhaps, *our* thinking of memory. The Buddha's recollection of his previous rebirths, if seen from this point of view, would seem as definitely *non-subjective*, for the Buddha can be identified neither with any previous rebirth of his (for the reasons referred to in the beginning of this section) nor, least of all, with his recollection. And as it also was remarked above, it still remains uncertain what it is that is recollected, whether it is *produced* rather than reproduced by recollection? In which case, of course, the term 'objective' simply would not apply!

4.4.6.2. So, returning to what we have called phenomenal conditions of memory understood as an epiphenomenon of consciousness or as our thinking of memory, and singling out the notion of recollection as one of the most essential modalities of such thinking, we may come to the conclusion, however inconclusive it may be, that 'objective' and 'subjective' are not in opposition to one another here. On the contrary, if we still stick to these two terms, they would appear as constantly shifting from one *thought* to another, now leaving one thought for another, now coinciding in one and the same thought, now not being applied to any thought at all, though never being applied to anything other than thought. This non-fixedness of the epiphenomenon of memory in terms of 'object-subject' I regard as a most obvious phenomenal condition.[52]

4.4.6.3. Of course, I cannot but admit in this connection that the very relegation of conscious modalities in the case of one's identifying oneself with one of the previous rebirths could be seen as a *conscious act* (or fact) to which the epiphenomenon of memory might be reduced. That is, in this case memory (even in the sense of recollection) would be apprehended as no more than a term of interpretation of consciousness or, more exactly, as a way in which consciousness interprets its modalities. But while our everyday and commonsensical understanding of memory is the placing of connected events in the 'objective past', the notion underlying the Buddhist understanding of recollection is that it is the act of this 'placing', that produces what we call 'the past time'—that is, the past itself appears then as 'a mere subjective derivative' from this placing (which, then, would be seen as merely objective). Moreover, would not the time itself—that is 'past plus future', but not the discrete moments of present states of consciousness—appear as a product (if not a by-product) of one's *retrospective* thinking of one's previous rebirths? [Albeit I am fully aware here that, if looked at from the point of view of the present states of consciousness (i.e., present dharmas), the interpretation of time would be very different.]

4.4.7. The conscious reflex that establishes the above said partial identity of *one's* present subjective instance of consciousness to one's past subjective instance of consciousness cannot itself, be thought of as 'one's' or 'another's'. And it is more than evident that such conscious reflex does not operate with the binary opposition 'one/another' or, one may say, when it works, this opposition is eliminated. But without this opposition the very notion of *subjective* memory loses its sense entirely. This is extremely important for our understanding of memory in general as of one of the *structures* of consciousness, the structure that is simply unfathomable in the absence of this opposition. That is why we can conjecture that, in the case of all Karmapas, the 'remembering consciousness' was neither 'one's' nor 'another's', neither 'subjective' nor 'objective', neither 'remembering' nor 'remembered'.

The whole history of all Karmapas (together with their 'pre-kalpic' antecedents and 'post-kalpic' aftermaths) could be pondered on as an extreme case of 'pure' reincarnation. Pure because we have no *karma* here; nor have we any (metaphysically, at least) 'beginning', i.e., the absolute instance from which one's recognition of one's previous rebirths actually began. So that knowledge of the fact merges here with its objective factuality. This may give us a reason to reduce the notion of reincarnation to a series of conscious recognitions by the conscious reflex which witnesses itself, its very *presence* in the endless series of minds, each bearing either an individual name, or a class name of a sentient being. When I say 'endless', I mean that this witnessing always starts at a given *present* moment and stretches back towards the endless past. And the only name that could be (conventionally, of course) applied to the whole series is the name of a 'person' in whom such a reflex started working and who, thereby, has no future of a sentient being any more.

That all Karmapa rebirths are 'non-karmic' by definition clearly indicates an essential difference between reincarnation and *karma*. In its simplest form the postulate of reincarnation ['...never was there a time when I did not exist, or you...' said Krishna to Arjuna in the *Bhagavad-Gītā*, II, 12, pp. 74–5,] could, as we have already seen, be reduced to a certain type (or types) of conscious operations or, shall we say, to a kind of awareness. Not being itself a phenomenon, reincarnation, nevertheless, can be phenomenologically approached, because these conscious operations in spite of their 'neither-objective-nor-subjective character' deal with concrete objects and subjects (such as 'lifespan', 'body', 'womb', 'condition of birth', etc.). Karma, on the contrary, does not presuppose any thinkable conscious operation as a part or component of its content—for entirely non-contentful it seems to be. Karma can be thought of neither as a thing, nor as an object for, at least in the universe where reincarnation takes place, it operates non-personally, indiscriminately and—one may conjecture—non-discretely (in relation to thought which is discrete par excellence). That is, when we think of *karma* in a strictly Buddhological way, it appears as one of the *explanations* concerning the *being* of the *saṃsāra* and our own perception and knowledge of the *saṃsāra*. To say that *karma* is a fact would be as sheer a nonsense as to say that space is a fact. For *karma* cannot be regarded as on the level of facts, while reincarnation can.[53]

4.5. Returning to the questions discussed in 4.3, I would like to add one more point concerning the Buddhological understanding of 'consciousness as personal or/and non-personal'. The problem of 'something conscious-and-personal' can be connected neither with the ontological 'self'—because of its non-existence, nor with the psychological 'I'—because of its irrelevance. Probably it is in a 'space' between *anattā* and *pudgala*—where the subject of *non-empirical consciousness* could be sought for, even if not found. My surmise is that this 'subject' can be traced in situations where he identifies himself with some other 'person' whose state is either that of empirical consciousness or of a fringe character (i.e., 'between' empirical and non-empirical). This identification, itself of a 'fringe' nature, does not cover *the whole* subject of non-empirical consciousness, but only his 'subject-component'.

This is probably why, apart from all possible linguistic and stylistic considerations, the Buddha refers to himself in the third person when speaking of himself as a Bodhisattva or a *sattva* in one of 'his' previous rebirths. In fact, He does not say 'I was he', but 'He (or the Tathagata) was at that time such-and-such person'. This, indirectly of course, shows the partial and incomplete character of such like 'reincarnational' identifications in Buddhism. All this induces me to ponder over the possibility that, *in any retrospective identification we have a residue left unidentified (and probably unidentifiable), and that it is this residue due to which, because of which and by means of which such an identification may become possible*.

4.6.0. Now, one may well start doubting whether the whole philosophy of Thought in Buddhism would disappear, giving place to purely naturalistic considerations concerning the Thought's 'real nature', and having nothing to do with the thinking about thought. The point is, however, that none of the Buddhist Yogis, from the great masters of the Abhidhamma of old up to the great masters of the Abhidharma of the Yogacara-Vaibhashika School, and from the ancient ascetics of the primary *Saṅgha* up to the modern Tibetan recluses—none of them have been *philosophizing only*. Their philosophizing is all the time merged with and melted into their meditational practice, and what we are actually doing here is no more than another futile attempt to realize the yogic processes through the terms and notions given to us as either results of these processes or as postulates preceding them. And when I say that my approach to these terms and notions is *meta-philosophical*, I do not mean the Wittgensteinian investigation of the uses of these terms and notions, but their understanding in the sense of *other* terms and notions—other than Buddhist ones as well as my own.

Moreover, the yogic procedure of thinking about (or contemplating on) thought could be meta-philosophically interpreted as one which does not establish the meaning of thought (for it is void of any meaning), but which makes the thought a 'natural' object, not a 'naturalistic concept'. And all we have been dealing with is a conceptualized (or conceptualizing) description of the yogic procedures related to thought, not a conceptualization of thought itself. Then, that very 'something' to which these yogic procedures are indirectly ascribed, would be seen as the non-naturalized and persistent 'quasi-person' of a yogi. However strange though it might seem, such 'quasi-personness' cannot be thought of outside the yogic procedures and, thereby, attributed to non-yogis.

4.6.1. There is one thing more that I want to add to the previous considerations. I think, and the *history* of Buddhist thinking on thought confirms it, that the Buddhist analysis of 'empirical I' (together with the Buddhist analysis of reflexive procedures understood in the sense of empirical consciousness) practically abolishes any possibility of one's *real biography*.[54] The focus of the philosophical thinking has been removed in Buddhism from the ontogenesis to the phylogenesis of thought, from one's *bios* to one's karmic pre-history (for everything in the sense of *karma* remains pre-history, while the history is always just about to start its course at each given present moment). And this is so, because the Buddhist analysis of empirical consciousness aims to detect thought in its *present* moment. Or, rather, the very character of such an analysis makes each moment of thought present, whereas the European tradition of philosophical psychology (from Kant to von Hartman and Wundt) tended to turn all instances of thought into the past. And the very fact that the Buddhist analysis of the present empirical consciousness has been performed in terms of a non-empirical category of *dharma* entails the fact that one's individual existence has been ousted into the *interpersonal* space of one's previous (and, in principle, the future ones too) reincarnations to get its interpretation in terms of a non-empirical category of karma.[55] For the 'psychological present' plus the 'combined past' are not enough to constitute what *we* call 'a person' in any system of thought.

4.7. The notion of *bhavaṅga-citta*, though it stays on the remote periphery of the Buddhist philosophy of thought, is of great interest and enigmaticity. My very hazardous rendering of this term is 'thought-factor of existence', which means, or rather implies, two quite different ideas. The first is, that there is something in thought which persists during the interval between one's death and one's next rebirth (and which, therefore, could be reduced to one's 'last thought' before death). The second is, that each individual stream of thought (when thought is taken in its *ontogenesis*, of course) contains a certain component or components (*aṅga*) which, as such, cannot be reduced to, or explained in terms of, the laws of causality regulating the composition and serial sequency of an empirical consciousness. Unfortunately, there are no hints in the early Abhidhamma concerning the character and content of *bhavaṅga*. So one can only surmise as to what extent (if any) it includes the idea of its individuality (not that of a person, of course), or to what extent it is self-conscious.

There is, however, some reason to believe (according to later Abhidhammic commentaries) that this notion might have been associated with the consciousness or thought of a Tathagata, to which such 'psychological' oppositions as 'conscious/

self-conscious', 'conscious/subconscious', 'conscious/unconscious', 'individual consciousness/non-individual consciousness'—cannot be applied. And all attempts to reduce it to 'subconscious flux' are ridiculous.[56]

4.8. The concept of *dhātu* (see 5.7.4.1) seems to be, in some respects at least, quite analogous to that of *bhavaṅga-citta* in the religious metaphysics of Buddhism. I use the term 'metaphysics' here to stress the non-relational character of *dhātu*, if compared with *dharma* or, even, with *citta*, for that matter. Once again, this term, not infrequently used in the Abhidhamma, appears on the surface of suttas, sūtras, commentaries and votive inscriptions to remind one of some deep undercurrents of Buddhist thought, undercurrents wherefrom some dim variety of ontology emerges, which can be neither discerned in nor reconstructed from the Abhidhamma itself. Here I will limit myself by singling out only some of the most obvious features of this rather mysterious concept.

(1) Figuring in such composite terms as *nirvāṇa-dhātu* and *tathāgata-dhātu*, dhatu denotes, more or less definitely, a certain *persistence* of one's conscious being.[57]

(2) When referred *to the past*, it is very often connected with bodily relics of a Buddha whereby the very idea of *dhātu* as understood as 'element', assumed its *solid* or even 'material', meaning. This, in turn, cannot help evoking very often-mentioned parallels and affinities between Nirvana and *rūpa* ('form', 'organism' and, to some extent only, 'body'—*śarīra*). Although, one may conjecture, the word 'body' itself [particularly in such a composite term as *śarīra-dhātu* ('bodily relics')] might have been used as a merely *symbolic* term. So, we may say that what persists after Tathagata's death is *an element* (to render *dhātu* as 'element' is an arbitrary affair though) which bears in itself something of Nirvana as *already achieved*, and which is present in his body's relics.

(3) When referred to *the future*, it seems to exist in all sentient beings (in principle) as a *latent* possibility or potency to become a Tathagata and to achieve Nirvana. This potency is, on the one hand, present unmanifestly in any *thing* and can be, as such, regarded as 'Tathagata's embryo' (*tathāgatagarbha*).[58] On the other hand, however, a still living bodily structure can also be seen as, at least partly, responsible for perpetuation of this 'element of Nirvana yet to be achieved' (i.e., *Nirvāṇa-dhātu*), or even identified with this element in a more than symbolic way. But I cannot help stressing here one thing, metaphysically exceedingly important: taken in the last sense, *dhātu* does not perpetuate anything but one's potency of becoming a Tathagata (as we have seen the Bodhicitta *in one*—as *one's* potency to become a Bodhisattva, not a *sattva* and, least of all, *the same sattva*). It does not, therefore, perpetuate oneself. It is also worth mentioning here that this 'structure', so to speak, that is, '*dhātu* as/or/in a body' (for undoubtedly it is a structure of consciousness, not a simple concept) cannot be seen in its *actuality*, but only either in its projection from the past to the future, or in its 'retrospection', as in the case of 'relics'.

(4) However, a possibility still remains that in some not yet known common proto-Buddhist-and-Jainist milieu, *dhātu* might have been not a 'universal element' present in all sentient beings, but something by means of which only Tathagatas

(and their like) persisted. This, however historically uncertain and dubious, does not contradict in any way the main soteriological postulates of the Canonical literature and, least of all, those of the Abhidhamma. This is to say, that what we deal with in the case of Tathagata's relics too, is a sort of indication of the existence of an especial *cult* of Tathagatas. [One may, of course, ask oneself: Can we deduce from the worship of pacceka-buddhas, as described in the commentaries of Buddhaghosa and Dhammapala, the actual existence of the *cult* of pacceka-buddhas at a 'pre-canonical' time?] Even if it were so, it looks as if *tathāgata-dhātu* were not the 'essence' (*sāra*) of one's being a Tathagata, but rather a 'bearer' of something due to which one could have become a Tathagata.

(5) There is, however, yet one problem which cannot be avoided while we study the Abhidhamma. In the Abhidhamma *dhātu* has very many analytical meanings. Even if we confine our observation to *Dhs.*, this text alone would show us at least 31 of them, not to speak of so-called 'variants' of these meanings (see Essay 5, Table III, T. 8,9; Table VI, △2, MS5; △3, MS12; △4, MS15; △5, MS27; also MS321–337 and 343–350). Their comparison with, as well as relation to, the dharmas, will show, *comparatively* and *relatively* speaking, the more 'subjective' character of dhatu than that of dharmas. 'Subjective' does not mean 'essentialist' here but it involves what can be called 'psychological modalities' of an individual. So, by saying 'element of mind' (*manodhātu*) I mean a certain fact (or, group of facts) underlying the mind (*manas*) *specifically*—that is, not in the sense that 'all is mental' in one way or another, but that there is something specifically and technically mental which, for example, cannot be said about or ascribed to 'consciousness in general' (*viññāṇa*), but only to 'consciousness in the sense of mind'—i.e., *manoviññāṇadhātu* (that is probably why, there is no *viññāṇadhātu* in *Dhs.*). Likewise, in a more or less analogous way, it can be said that the term *dharmadhātu* denotes something which is specific with respect to dharmas taken in their ontological aspect, i.e., aspect of *dharmatā*. [That is, we may argue that while *cakkhudhātu* ('element of sight') implies a psychological (i.e., partly at least, 'subjective') character of sight, the 'element' of Tathagata implies a 'specific ontologism' of the Tathagata.]

NOTES TO ESSAY 4

1 There is some reason to believe that this book might have remained an *oral* text for a longer time than other books of the *Abhidhamma-Piṭaka.*

2 As a system of metaphysics the Abhidhamma has not one but several 'entries', that is, several 'central' concepts each of which might figure as a starting point as well as a focus of investigation of the whole system. So, according to *Dhs.*, the two main concepts are 'dhammas' ('states of consciousness') and 'kammas' (the kinds of karma). In the *Abhidhammattha—Saṅgaha* (one of the chief abhidhammic compendia) Anuruddha singles out the four 'main entities' (*paramatthato*—'in the ultimate sense'): 'thought' or 'consciousness' (*citta*), 'conscious' (or 'mental') properties (*cetasika*), 'form' (*rūpa*) and Nirvana (see below n. 11). To Stcherbatsky it is *dharma* in its entirety and classificational plurality, which serves as the central concept, while Nyanatiloka reduces the 'manifold phenomena' of Abhidhamma again to the triad of 'thought—the physical—the psychical'. See Nyanatiloka (1971, p. XIV). See also A. Govinda (1973.)

3 'Seen' means that its own 'thinkability' was considered in the Abhidhamma itself as *objectively visual.* That is, not only in the sense that all possible objects of thought were *primarily* thought of (or meditated upon) in their visuality, but also in the sense, that the very character of abhidhammic *oral* tradition was stressedly visual (the latter idea was clearly expressed by Lance Cousins in his paper for the International Symposium on Buddhology at the School of Oriental and African Studies, University of London, November 1979).

4 *Dhs.*, p. 18.

5 *Aṭṭhasālinī* can be seen as the final result of the interpretational work performed by the School of Buddhagosa.

6 *As.*, p. 73.

7 *As.*, p. 87.

8 *As.*, p. 88.

9 *As.*, p. 87. An absolutely 'subjective' attitude of the European psychology to consciousness is splendidly summarized by C. G. Jung (1976, p. 10): 'The important fact about consciousness is that nothing can be conscious without an *ego* to which it refers'.

10 But of course, the time here is understood not in the sense of *duration*, but in the sense of *occurrence* (i.e., as one *samaya* or another).

11 I used the text of the *Abhidharmārtha-Saṅgrahaya* here. Also see *Abhidhammattha-Saṅgaha* (*Compendium of Philosophy*), p. 146, and *Abhidhammattha-Saṅgaha*, p. 8. To Shwe Zan Aung, *cittuppāda* is 'a complex (i.e., consisting of many factors and components) state of consciousness' (*Compendium of Philosophy*, p. 234) or 'separate state of consciousness' (pp. 25, 94), or 'a class of thought' (p. 98), while Narada renders it as 'thought'. He writes: '*Citta, Ceto, Cittupāda, Nāma, Mano, Viññāṇa,* are all used as synonymous terms in Abhidhamma...no distinction is made between mind and consciousness', *Abhidhammattha-Saṅgaha*, pp. 8–9.

12 *Abh. S.*, p. 132.

13 *Abh. S.*, pp. 120–1.

14 *Dhs.*, p. 18; As., p. 87.

15 '*Citta* is much more frequently placed as object of activities and conceived as "outside" the speaker (it should e.g., be restrained). But as we have found, identification is also frequently implied.' See Rune E. A. Johansson (1965, p. 179). I think that there Johansson lost sight of the fact that it is one thing to identify a thought (*citta*) with *my* thought, but quite another one to identify a thought with *a person.* The latter would undoubtedly involve some 'karmic' moments.

16 In general this conclusion coincides with Dharmakirti's views on the subject.

17 An excellent summary of the subject is given by S. K. Nanayakkara (1971, p. 184–9). The main source of our information remains, of course, Shantideva's poem, *Bodhicaryāvatāra.*

18 'The earlier (Mahayanist) sense of Bodhicitta is the realization of the essencelessness of the dharmas, while in *Śrī-guhya-samāja-tāntra* it is described as... the unity of Śūnyatā (emptiness)

and *Karuṇā* (compassion)." In the Sekoddeśatīkā, Vairocana Tathagata explains: "My citta is devoid of all existence, it is dissociated from any skandha, dhatu, ayatana—or from subjectivity and objectivity—it is without origination..." ' S. N. Dasgupta (1950, p. 98–9).

19 S. N. Dagupta (1950, p. 10).

20 And again in a manner more or less analogous to that in which a 'sentient being' (*sattva*) can be reduced to the 'sentientness' (*citta*).

21 A very audacious attempt to produce a specifically phenomenological analysis of the yogic thought was made by Guenther who classified the thought (Tib. *bsam-pa, sems*) into several levels. Each level corresponds to a certain stage of yogic realization of thought by thought itself, so that the whole classification seems to be a result of the observation produced by the thought of the highest level, from the viewpoint of which the lowest level would appear as 'minus yoga' (but not as 'absence of yoga'). See H. Guenther (1966).

22 S. N. Dasgupta (1950, p. 98).

23 So Emmerick renders *bodhicitta* (Tib. *byang-chub-tu sems*) as 'resolve', which seems to be only partly justified by the context. See *Khotanese Sūrangama-samādhi-sūtra* (p. 98).

24 Though, of course, when described, this re-awareness assumed some *outer* features and, first of all, those of volition, will or volitional impulse (*vega*).

25 This was, in fact, overlooked by Nyanaponika Thera (1965, pp. 18–19) when he treats any mental experience as a phenomenon.

26 'Occurs' here is used strictly in the sense of 'an occurrence' or 'occasion' (*samaya*!), see Nyanaponika (1965, p. 6).

27 Thus it can even be said that there is no time in the *bodhicitta* understood in its first aspect, though there is the time in the sense of 'inner duration' in the second aspect (so-called 'psychological time'), and there is a 'timeless moment' in the fact of *bodhicittopāda*. The idea that time is no more than a term in the description of thought, is very tempting but hardly applicable to 'the time' (*kāla*), though quite applicable to 'a time of...' (i.e., *samaya* understood in the sense of a 'concurrence', *samūha*) See Nyanaponika, 1965, pp. 104–6.

28 See, for example, the place referred to in n. 23.

29 One may suppose that in this case 'generation' is not an equivalent of 'creation'. It seems that the meaning of generation here is much nearer to that of manifestation, whereby a symbolical character of the term is stressed. There are tantrist texts where it is suggested that *bodhicitta* (called 'the best thought') is all the time *there*, and that an adept must 'make the best thought'.

30 See E. Lamotte (1974, pp. 97–8).

31 It is stressed that a Bodhisattva of the tenth stage provides himself with an especial body made of the dharma elements (*dharmādhatu-kāya*), that he transforms at will. [I doubt whether it is the same as 'mindmade body' (*manomaya-kāya*), see below n. 37.

32 See E. Lamotte (1974, p. 100).

33 An attempt, though infinitely less enlightening than that of Dharmakirti, to identify a person through 'bodily actions' was recently made by T. Penelhum (1980). The core of his methodology is expressed in the following very Wittgensteinian way: 'In a general discussion of self-identity it is not possible to avoid epistemological considerations, since in outlining the rules of application for an expression like "the same persons" one is bound to ask in what circumstances users (and learners) of our language are able to tell whether to apply it or withhold it, and this is, in the broadest sense, an epistemological question' (pp. 57–8). And what is particularly amusing about this Wittgensteinianism (apply it or withold it please!) is that 'the same person' is clearly though perhaps, without the author's noticing, opposed to 'a person' just as an 'expression' (in the sense of uses of language) is opposed to a 'thing'. Or, as epistemology is opposed to psychology. Thus, survival is, to Penelhum, a very strange operation—logical of course—by means of which what is known as one person (and this is a *fact*, not an expression) would be recognized as 'the same person'. This does not mean that *two* persons could be recognized as 'one and the same person', for this would entail quite another operation having nothing to do with logic. So we have here two essentially different situations. But Penelhum is not aware of this difference and goes with the logical analysis of the uses of his own language, not having noticed that his two criteria of personal identity—bodily identity and self-identifying memory—are logically inconsistent and arbitrary. The first criterion is

that, if the two persons have one and the same body they are one and the same person. The second is that if one person remembers his experiencing the actions done by another, they are also one and the same person. Using the first criterion, the author passively postulates that where there is a body, there must be a person while for the second criterion, he implies that each *fact* of remembrance contains, as a possibility at least, 'a person who remembers', though not necessarily 'a person who is remembered'. The first postulation, however, cannot be accepted for merely logical reasons because the very *idea* of survival presupposes a sort of transformation (even in the heads of those who accept it) where one simply cannot operate with the thought of 'this same body' or even 'this same mentality' for that matter. The second postulation isolates, and quite artibratily so, 'actions' taken as such, from what can be seen as mental or, more specifically, reflexive actions (including those of memory and remembrance). It is the Buddhist scholars of Dharmakirtean lineage who for the first time ventured to regard an *act* of thinking as an (outer) action, side by side with other *bodily* actions, and then reduced it to thought as such (also together with other bodily actions).

34 The general and philosophical approach to this problem implies a certain 'quasi-logical' position (*koṭi*) such, for instance, as 'whether or not a Tathagata exists after death?' See D. Seyfort Ruegg (1977, pp. 1–2).

35 In some cases thought or mind is as operable or even manipulable as one's body. When Shantideva 'gives up' his body for being disposed of by and for the sake of all sentient beings, it seems to be separated from 'him' as the Thought of Awakening is separated from 'them'.

36 *Śāntideva*, 1960, VI, 80, p. 102.

37 *Śāntideva*, V, 57, p. 63. De la Vallée Poussin (1907, p. 38) wrote in the footnotes about such a construction (*nirmāṇa*) of a thing or body: 'It has no consciousness'. The generation of construction of various things, be it a tree, palace, a Bodhisattva, or even a Buddha, is a common case in both Mahayana and Theravada literature. I refer particularly to the introductory chapter in Buddhaghosa's *Aṭṭhasālinī*, where the Buddha creates his 'double', and where it is stated that some could discern which Buddha (not the body of the Buddha, but Buddha!) is 'genuine' (*samma*) and which is 'constructed' (*nimitta*). There is also a passage in the *Vimalakīrti-Nirdeśa* (X, pp. 103–4), where a messenger-Bodhisattva is created, etc. At the same time, even in the Suttas such a 'creation' or 'construction' of a body is described as *mental* in the first place, and brought about by the supernatural power (*iddhi*) in the second. We read that the Buddha '. . . by His supernatural power approached me with body made of mind. . .,' *Thera and Therī* I, v. 901, p. 83; *Thera tr.*, pp. 85, 250. Being itself quite a commonplace in Buddhist literature, this power of mind making the bodies is often ascribed to Mara, etc.

38 This, however, does not imply *the absolute* of consciousness. On the contrary, that very reflexing of the 'modifications' by the thought means that consciousness (or thought) is reflexed upon *by us* (or somebody else) in its aspect of modification or transformation (*pariṇāma*), though in this case the 'dichotomising' work of consciousness makes the consciousness think of itself as an object (or rather, the object). See in I. Yamada (1977, pp. 159, 166, 167).

39 The admission of such a force as a naturalistic concept was made for the first time by Charlie Broad and, most interestingly, it was made in the sense of a *process* the temporal characteristics of which are provided by the consciousness observing it. See C. Broad (1959, pp. 44, 130, 155–6, 171).

40 This other force might be that of karma (*vāsanā*) according to the teaching of late yogacarins.

41 The nomenclature of thought is particularly complex in Tibetan Buddhism, where it contains some strong elements of pre-Buddhist religious life. R. Stein (1962, pp. 150–5), very often explains 'the conscious principle' or 'consciousness' in the sense of 'spirit'. It is highly appropriate here to be reminded of Tucci's words that '(some) Tibetan words are symbols, which can evoke living experiences which the word as such can only suggest, but not define. . . To give an example, the word *sems*, a pillar of the Lamaist Doctrinal edifice. . .', G. Tucci (1980, p. VIII).

42 It is emphatically said in the *Jñāna-siddhi* that our Bodhi-mind, which is of the nature of the Vajra, is itself the Buddhahood; so Buddhahood should be realized through conceiving all things as the self (*bodhicitta idaṃ vajraṃ sarva-buddhatvaṃ ātmanaḥ*). S. N. Dasgupta (1950, p. 92).

43 See *Karmapa* (1976). I am rather doubtful about whether it is really necessary to connect the name of Karmapa tradition with the concept of *karma*. All Karmapa reincarnations have nothing to do with *karma* because of their not being subject to its law and, in this sense, even the term 'reincarnation' sounds rather conventional. Besides that, we have many suggestions that the name they had assumed was that of a monastery in Khams region, founded in 1147 by the first Karmapa. See H. E. Richardson (1958, p. 139). All things considered, the traditional interpretation of the term as 'the activity (*phrin-las*) of Buddhahood' is far more acceptable. See Karma Thinley (1980, pp. 21, 36, 43, 67).

44 See *Blue Annals* and *Blue Annals* tr.

45 See *Bhadra Kalpa Sūtra* (The Sixth Buddha).

46 *Blue Annals*, 425. It is particularly interesting to note that the most general and trivial rendering of the term *'pho-ba* is 'a stream' (*srotas*), 'dynamism' (in the *Tibetan-Sanskrit-Mongolian Triglotte* edited by Anton Franz Schiefner). Evans-Wentz translated *'pho* as 'the transference of the sum total of karmic propensities (of "personal" consciousness)'. See *Bardo* (1960, pp. 85–6). *'Pho-bo* is a priest performing the death ceremonies connected with *bar-do*, for he is an 'extractor of conscious principle' (p. 18). The first Evans-Wentz's interpretation of conscious principle as 'karmic' and personal does, quite certainly, contradict the yogic postulate of its non-karmic and non-personal character. Otherwise, who transfers what? A totally different, and obviously pre-Buddhist interpretation of *'pho-ba* is given in Stein's book (1962, pp. 151–2): '...if one makes the transfer (from one body to another, or to a paradise) untimely, he commits the crime of killing the Gods'—so Milarepa was told, because our body with all its senses is inseparable from Gods. Though further it was stated (in connection with Naropa), that 'it (le transfer de l'ésprit) was meant to get a new body after having chosen a fresh corpse' (p. 154). Very often, however, this 'act' is described in a quite casual and matter-of-fact way: '...having taken twice of tea, he committed the transference (of his conscious principle)', *Blue Annals*, 280; *Blue Annals* trans., p. 316. Sometimes, it is depicted as a mere 'shifting' in space: 'Then he changed the place of (his) bodily life from (the spot) on the border of Nepal and Tibet, (where he had) practised the severe austerities', *Blue Annals*, 455; *Blue Annals* trans., p. 521. A more general interpretation of the transfer is given in S. Beyer (1973, p. 135).

F. Fremantle and Ch. Trungpa (*Bardo*, 1975, p. 33) translate *'pho-ba* as 'ejection of consciousness', and qualify the means of ejection as 'thinking' ['...(the dying person)... should effect the ejection of consciousness, which liberates spontaneously as soon as it is thought of'], whereas Evans-Wentz renders it as 'remembering' (*dran-pa*). No attention, however, in either of these translations is paid to the fact that in the situation of transference (or ejection) thinking (or remembering) is *that which establishes a reflex over that which is to be transferred* (i.e., over 'conscious principle', *rnam-shes*). Moreover, even in the texts where consciousness, or conscious principle, is mentioned as being identical with the Seed of Thought of Awakening, this reflex is neither commented upon, nor does it lead to any additional considerations concerning its nature and its relation to consciousness which 'thinks of' or 'recollects' within the context of Bardo. When we read in Dhargyey (1978, pp. 24–5), for example, that '...because of previous meditational experience a person is able to control his consciousness throughout this death process', or that 'after (the decomposition of our body begins)... we perceive our mind in its purest form'—the only conclusion one may arrive at is that there can be one phenomenology for 'control' and 'perceiving' and quite another for 'consciousness' and 'mind' here. In this connection, also see D. I. Lauf (1977, pp. 45–6), D. M. Back (1979, pp. 19–23), and G. Tucci (1980, pp. 36, 98–101).

47 See *Blue Annals* (422). This idea, particularly in the case of Karmapas, resulted in that which could be seen as ontological pre-temporal 'before-being' of consciousness or thought: '...the underlying reality of both samsara and nirvana is the thread of mind's primordial purity...' See Karma Thinley (1980, p. 35).

48 '(The Fourth Karmapa)... replied that he was not able to recall his life as the first Karmapa very clearly and that he could only remember a little of his life as the Third Karmapa. However, he... recalled his life as the Second Karmapa perfectly'. Karma Thinley (1980, p. 63).

49 G. N. Dhargyey (1978, p. 168).

50 See H. Guenther and L. Kawamura (1975, pp. XV–XVI, XXV–XXVIII).

51 In various texts of Bardo (see note 46) this external observer is an especial Lama who may well instruct a dying man (or *bar-do-ba*) in the second person.

52 This gives rise to three essentially different *concepts* of memory in Tantrist Buddhism. If seen as no more than one of the mental events or modalities of consciousness [(*sems-byung*). See H. Guenther and L. Kawamura (1975, Introduction and particularly p. 10)], memory (*dran-pa*) is utterly ambiguous. Because, belonging to the general category of the non-awakened mind [*sems* = *ma-rig-pa* (*avidyā*—'ignorance')] here, memory figures in a negative sense, whereas constituting one of the specific *psychological* functions of mind (e.g., fixating the mind on an object, or reproducing an object for the mind), it may figure in a positive or neutral sense. If seen as a state of consciousness or *dharma* (see Essay 5, Table VI, △△ 13, 22, 26, etc.), it may be positive, negative, or neutral. And finally, if looked at in its direct opposition to the Absolute of 'thought-as-such', memory stands as an absolutely negative phenomenon. In the last case, the Awakened thought is equalled with 'non-memory' (*ma-dran-pa*), and memory finds its symbolic form as thinking of Death. See for instance, in Eli (1978? pp. 30–1, 200) memory is connected with *karma* causally, which is utterly naive, for memory is subjective, while *karma* is objective (though not an object!).

53 This remark does not apply, of course, to Jainism where the notion of *karma* is entirely and unambiguously realistic and naturalistic. But in Buddhism *karma* is *not an entity*, which of course does not mean that it is 'non-entity' (*asāra*) like 'self' (*atta*). Not-entity here stresses karma's *relational* character, its non-substantiality, not its non-existence. That is why it is so difficult to operate with *karma* as a *specific* notion, and J. Bennett (1976, p. 175) is absolutely right when he says that '...(karmic) connection of (the previous individuality) with a new totality is real, but not yet realized. We have no means of verifying that the connection is made at the moment of conception, but *on systematic grounds* this appears to be likely'. On the other hand, too often the substantiality of *karma* has been wrongly inferred from purely *symbolic* meanings of the term. See G. Obeyesekere (1980, pp. 143–55). Referring to the last book, I may remark that it is *theoretically* impossible to construct 'a purely theoretical model' (W. D. O'Flaherty, 1980, p. XII) of that which is in itself a very complex theoretical construction. This also holds true in respect of the problem of so-called 'collective karma'—that is, can we say that 'transference' of *karma* in time could be postulated as existing in place too? See Dhargyey (1978, p. 176). Jung, unfortunately, used the term *karma* now in a concrete, now in a metaphoric way, and tends to isolate it from its genuine relational meaning. ['It often seems as if there were an *impersonal* (i.e., collective) karma'], and too often confuses it with reincarnation. ['The question of karma is obscure to me, as is also the problem of personal rebirth...']. See C. G. Jung (1980, pp. 260, 350–1).

54 In saying this I mean that a consistent analysis of empirical 'I' would leave one with utterly abstract and depsychologized elements of 'I' on the one hand, and with the *types* of persons, on the other. While what a *real* biography is about is an objectification of *a person*, not of his type nor, least of all, of his psychology. Here, of course, this objectification has been conceived as a yogic process, though in the context of a different culture it may manifest itself in quite another kind of human activity or variety of texts. M. Bachtin writes (1979, p. 132): 'A biography or autobiography is, so we understand it, that nearest transgredient form in which I can objectify myself and my life artistically. We will consider the form of biography only to the extent it would serve our auto-objectification...' The notion of 'personality' would then emerge in the context of late Mahayana Buddhism, not as a result of the self-objectification by a yogi, but as a result of an *external* objectification of this very yogi by another person. Or, rather, as a result of a *secondary* analysis of this yogi's life into the objective and the subjective, which, of course, cannot be done in the context of any specifically yogic procedure. In connection with this question of 'biography-personality' I would permit myself a rather too-long quotation from a recent article of mine: 'There is a long way between "I" and "personality" in the history of texts, in literature and sometimes even in the life of an individual man, but very seldom during the course of one and the same novel. There cannot be a recipe for how to convert "I" into personality. Reflexion and introspection—whether by the author or by his heroes—can exist as no more than an additional feature of such a conversion. In the history of philosophy the transition from "I" to personality was sometimes achieved by direct negation of "I" (as in the early Buddhism), or by identification

of 'I' with one of the states of consciousness in the stream of conscious life (as in William James, Paul Carus and, though in a completely different context, in Edmund Husserl). In the new European literature the transition from 'I' to personality was achieved during the 200 years from Rousseau to the experiments with anti-novels of the 60s and the films of Antonioni and Bergman. And in such a (astronomically) short time the European literature repeated the essential stages of the development of more than 2,500 years' history of philosophy, the history of philosophizing about personality, the essence of which can be summarized into two short sentences: reflexion still is not 'I'; 'I' still is not personality.

This movement towards personality was not unilinear, for personality did not always remain in the focus of the universal thought. On the contrary, it was very often the case that after being directed towards personality the literature returned to 'I' again. Also, I do not think that this movement can be traced in the whole literature; it exists only when the very problem of personality exists, though there are many writers in whose work personality arises without any problem at all, that is, as something naturally given. This was the case with Joyce, Proust and Faulkner who have one thing in common in spite of all the differences in their artistic world-outlook; at the very moment when the writer took up his pen, or was about to do so, the personality of his heroes already existed—without the existence of the heroes these authors simply could not have written at all. The personality already existed from the very origin in the embryo, in the ancestors, in the pre-consciousness of the concrete lives of their heroes as a sort of initially given existence in the continuum of which the author included himself, and continued to think and write having been therein.' A. Piatigorsky (1979, p. 14).

55 The term *diṭṭhadhamma* (lit., 'seen dharma') means in Abhidhamma 'the present *dharma*', that is, so to speak, that if taken in terms of time, all conditions of one's thinking are to be reduced to the dharmas of the present only. This notion figures in the context of one of the highest states of consciousness, almost synonymous to Nirvana and is connected with the 'indeterminate states of consciousness' (*dhammā abyākatā*). See Dhs., pp. 145–6.

56 And one may only guess whether or not *bhavaṅga-citta* could be regarded as 'original' [in the sense of 'pristine', 'primordial' (*pakati, prakṛti*)]—that is, exempt from any temporal order and existing 'at all times' in one way or another. See, Upali Karunaratna (1971, pp. 17–20). It figures as '. . .abstruse and obscure concept' in the Max Hoppe preface to George Grimm's book (1958, p. 12) The idea of *bhavanga* as 'being of consciousness' (i.e. not as an 'individual being' alone), practically leaves unanswered the question of its processuality. What we probably deal with in this case is an extreme (or 'extremal') state of consciousness needed when the last is to be transposed or transferred (see L. Cousins, 1981, pp. 21–5, 27–30).

57 John Bennett says (1976, pp. 175–6): 'The (Personal) Individuality is not in space and time. It is not even in the unperceived dimensions of eternity and hyparxis. It can best be described as a state of essential potency... we must understand... that the (Personal) Individuality is the spirit of man only as a possibility to be realized. The stage is set—but the action has not started'.

58 The absolute or ontological aspect of *dhātu* in connection with *tathāgatagarbha* is amply treated by D.S. Ruegg (1969: particularly important are pp. 97–100). In accordance with Vasubandhu, *dhātu* is interpreted in the sense of ultimate *natural* causality. This, partly, at least, may have confirmed the conjecture that in the Abhidhamma *dhātu* figures as a notion (or, even, 'a thing') which might have had a great vogue in pre-canonical times. Further investigations may have revealed its meaning as a 'primary substance' (not an essence!) to which some other abhidhammic notions could be reduced, such notions as 'mind', 'thought' and even—who knows?—'the dhammas'. The 'material' aspect of *dhātu* is excellently shown in a recent article by H. W. Bailey (1980).

5. RISE OF THOUGHT AS PHENOMENON AND SYSTEM

5.0.1. We have already seen here, in 4.1, that the rise of thought (*cittuppāda*) is the most essential thing in the abhidhammic theory of consciousness. Moreover, it is the rise of thought alone that makes of the Abhidhamma a theory of consciousness, for it is the absolutely necessary *initial phase* both in the *objective process* of consciousness itself and in the *subjective process* of our awareness thereof. And it is so, because in the context of rise of thought only can all other elements of this theory find their place and acquire their concrete phenomenal meaning.

The rise of thought is postulated in the *Dhammasaṅgaṇi* as an event[1] wherein the thought (named as *citta* or some other term substituting it) arises in such-and-such sphere (*avacara*) with such-and-such qualities and properties, associated with such-and-such mental states, having such-and-such objects, possessing such-and-such composition of its content, and connected with such-and-such states of consciousness or dharmas (or, more exactly, *sets* of dharmas).[2]

5.0.2. In order to show how the rise of thought is structured in a particular case, let us look at the case No. 162 of Book I (*cittuppāda kaṇḍa*) of *Dhs.*:

> Which are the indeterminate (*abyākata*) dharmas (in that case)? When the element of mind (*manodhātu*) has arisen (*uppannaṃ hoti*), accompanied by indifference (*upekkhā*), resulting from the ripening (*vipāka*) of the wholesome (*kusala*) action (*kamma*) wrought and accumulated in the sensuous sphere (*kāmāvacara*), and having as (its) objects (*ārammaṇa*) form-objects, sound-objects, smell-objects, taste-objects, tactile objects, dharmic objects or whatever other (object), then, in that case there is: touch, sensation, cognition, volition, thought, reasoning, reflexion, one-pointedness of thought, faculty of mind, faculty of living, indifference, and faculty of indifference – these are [in that case] indeterminate dharmas.[3]

What in that case is touch? In that case it is touch, touching, contact, being contacted—this is the touch in that case. [Then follow the analogous questions about the other 19 dharmas, and the answers containing their respective explanations.]

5.0.3. The text of this case (*samaya*) of rise of thought seems to be very easily and succinctly segmented in the following way:

I.	*Nomenclature of Thought* (T) i.e., one of 9 terms denoting thought and/or used instead of 'thought' (*citta*).	— In this particular case (No. 162)—'element of mind' (T–8 *manodhātu*).

II. *Sphere of Thought* (*S*)
i.e., one of 13 combinations of one of four spheres (*avacara*) with one of three general qualities of thought and dharmas.

— In this particular case (No. 162)—'sensuous sphere with indeterminate dharmas' (S.6 *kāmāvacara abyākata*)

III. *Composition of the Content of Thought* (*C*)
i.e., one of 22 variants (0–22) of content (divided into subvariants marked by letter), or one of their combinations.

— In this particular case (No. 162)—'has arisen' (C.O—*uppannaṃhoti*) + 'resulting from wholesome action wrought and stored up in the sensuous sphere' (C.16—*kāmāvacarassa kusalassa kammassa katattā upacitattā vipākaṃ*).

IV. *Trancic Variables* (TV)
i.e., one of 16 characteristics (1–16) which may be applied to or connected with the dhyanic (trancic) content of thought. Or one of their combinations.

— In this particular case (No. 162)—none.

V. *Objects of Thought* (0)
i.e., one of 6 objects of senses (1–6) or all of them, or 5 of them (i.e., without 0.6 which is 'dharmic objects') or one of 22 specifically dhyānic objects marked by brackets [(1)–(22)].

— In this particular case (No. 162)—0.1–5.

VI. *Mental Variables* (MV)
i.e., one of 15 general characteristics of mind (1–15) or one of their combinations ascribed to thought in a given case.

— In this particular case (No. 162)—'indifference' (MV5, *upekkhā*).

VII. *Set of Dharmas* (D)
i.e., one of 26 sets of dharmas (1–26) varying in number (from 10 to 61 in one set) and in assortment of dharmas. There are 83 kinds of dharmas (△△1–83) and 65 variants of some of them (marked by letters).

— In this particular case (No. 162)—D22 [△△1, 2^{h}, 3^{f}, 4^{f}, 5^{f}, 6^{c}, 7, 10^{c}, 16^{f}, 18, 57, 58 (12)].

VIII. *Mental States* (MS)
To each of 83 dharmas and their 65 variants there corresponds one set of mental states (varying in number from 1 to 33 for one dharma). There are 355 mental states for all dharmas taken together (1–355).

— In this particular case, (No. 162)—for example, △1 (*phassa*—'touch') connotes the four mental states (see above, 5.0.2.) i.e., MS1–4.

5.0.4. Thus, by using the above demonstrated system of conventional denotations, each of 234 cases of rise of thought in *Dhs.* could be described by a corresponding formula. The case No. 162 quoted in 5.0.2 would then be present as: T.8; S.6; C.16.0; 0.1–5; MV.5; D.22.

In Tables III–VI all variants of all segments of rise of thought are listed with relation to the case of rise, where they appear for the first time, and following the order of their appearance in the First Book of *Dhs.*

Table III. Nomenclature of Thought

No. of Term	Term and its Translation	Nos. of Cases
1	citta—'thought'	1–8, 111–112, 145–146
2	jhāna—'trance'	9–144, 166–220, 229–234.
3	cakkhuviññāṇa—'eye-consciousness'	157, 221
4	sotaviññāṇa—'ear-consciousness'	158, 222
5	ghānaviññāṇa—'smell-consciousness'	159, 222[a]
6	jivhāviññāṇa—'taste-consciousness'	160, 222[b]
7	kāyaviññāṇa—'body-consciousness'	161, 222[c]
8	manodhātu—'element of mind'	162, 223, 225
9	manoviññāṇadhātu—'element of mind—consciousness'	163–165, 224, 226–228

Table IV. Sphere of Thought[4]

No. of Sphere	Sphere and Character of Thought	Character of Dharmas	Nos. of Cases
1	kāmāvacaraṃ kusalaṃ—'the sensous sphere (and) wholesome (thought)'	A. kusalā—'wholesome'	1–8, 111–112
2	rūpāvacaraṃ kusalaṃ—'the sphere of form (and) wholesome (thought)'	do.	9–106, 113–114
3	arūpāvacaraṃ kusalaṃ—'the sphere of formlessness (and) wholesome (thought)'	do.	107–110, 115–118
4	lokuttaraṃ kusalaṃ—'the supramundane sphere (and) wholesome (thought)'	do.	119–144
5	akusalaṃ cittaṃ—'unwholesome thought (in the sensuous sphere)'	B. akusalā—'unwholseome'	145–156
6	kāmāvacaraṃ kusalaṃ—'the sensuous sphere (and) wholesome (action)'	C. abyākatā—'indeterminate'	157–165
7	rūpāvacaraṃ kusalaṃ—'the sphere of form (and) wholesome (action)'	do.	166–167
8	arūpāvacaram kusalaṃ—'the sphere of formlessness (and) wholesome (action)'	do.	168–171
9	lokuttaraṃ kusalaṃ—'the supramundane sphere (and) wholesome (thought)'	do.	172–220
10	akusalaṃ kammaṃ—'unwholesome action (in the sensuous sphere)'	do.	221–224
11	neva kusalā nākusalā—'of (act which is) neither wholesome nor unwholesome'	do.	225–228
12	rūpāvacaraṃ jhānaṃ—'the trance in the sphere of form'	do.	229–230
13	arūpāvacaraṃ jhānaṃ—'the trance in the sphere of formlessness'	do.	231–234

Table V. Variants of Content

No. of Case	Nomenclature of Thought	Sphere of Thought	Variants of Content No.	Variants of Content	Trancic Variables No.	Objects of Thought No.	Mental Variables No.
1	cittaṃ (thought)	kāmāvacaraṃ kusalaṃ—(pertaining to the sensuous sphere (and) wholesome)	0	uppannaṃ hoti—'has arisen'		1 form-objects 2 sound-objects 3 objects of smell 4 objects of taste 5 tangible objects 6 dharma-objects	1 somanassa-sahagataṃ—'accompanied by mental gladness' 2 ñāṇa sampayuttaṃ—'associated with knowledge'
2	do.	do.	0	do.		1–6	1,2 3 sa-saṃkhārena—'with synergies'
3	do.	do.	0	do.		1–6	1 4 ñāṇa-vipayuttaṃ—'dissociated from knowledge'
4	do.	do.	0	do.		1–6	1,4,3
5	do.	do.	0	do.		1–6	5 upekkhā—sahagataṃ—'associated with indifference' 2
6	do.	do.	0	do.		1–6	5,2,3

7	do.	do.	0 do.		1–6	5,4
8	do.	do.	0 do.		1–6	5,4,3
9	jhānaṃ (the first trance)	rūpūpapattiyā maggaṃ bhāveti—'he cultivates the way of attainment of form'	1 vivicceva kāmehi vivicca akusalehi dhammehi—'separated from sensuous things (and) separated from unwholesome dharmas' 1ª savitakkaṃ—'with reasoning' 1ᵇ savicāraṃ—'with reflexion' 1ᶜ vivekajaṃ—'born of separation' 1ᵈ pītisukhaṃ—'(full) of joy and pleasure' 0⁽¹⁾ paṭhamaṃ jhānaṃ upasampajja viharati—'(he) abides in the attainment of the first trance'		[1] paṭhavīkasiṇaṃ—'earth-device'	
10	jhānaṃ (the second trance)	do.	2 vitakkavicārānaṃ vūpasamā ajjhattaṃ sampasadanaṃ cetaso ekodibhāvaṃ—'suppressing the reasonings and reflexions (together with) tranquillization and fixation of the psyche' 2ª avitakkaṃ—'without reasoning' 2ᵇ avicāraṃ—'without reflexion' 2ᶜ samādhijaṃ—'born of concentration' 2ᵈ — 0⁽²⁾ dutiyaṃ jhānaṃ upasampajja viharati—'(he) abides in the attainment of the second trance'		[1]	

(*Cont.*)

No. of Case	Nomenclature of Thought	Sphere of Thought	No.	Variants of Content	Trancic Variables No.	Objects of Thought No.	Mental Variables No.
11	jhānaṃ (the third trance)	do.	3 0(3)	pītiyāca virāgā upekkhako ca viharati satoca sampajāno sukhaṃ ca kāyena paṭisamvedeti yaṃ taṃ ariyā ācikkhanti—'upekkhako satimā sukhaviharati'—'dispassionate for joy and indifferent (he) abides; recollectful and self-conscious (he) experiences by body the pleasure of which the Noble Ones declare: "Indifferent and recollectful, he abides in pleasure..." tatiyaṃ jhānaṃ upasampajja viharati—'(he) abides in the attainment of the third trance'		[1]	
12	jhānaṃ (the fourth trance)	do.	4 4a 4b 0(4)	sukhassa ca pahānā dukkhassa ca pahānā pubbeva somanassadomanassānaṃ atthaṅgamā—'by the avoiding of pleasure and by the avoiding of suffering, (and with) previous mental gladness and mental sorrow gone away...' adukkhamasukhaṃ—'without suffering and pleasure' upekkhāsatiparisuddhiṃ—'of utter purity (attained) by recollection and indifference' catutthaṃ jhānaṃ upasampajja viharati—'(he) abides in the attainment of the fourth trance'		[1]	

14	jhānaṃ(2)* 5	do.	2a 1b 2c 1d 0(2)*		[1]	
15	jhānaṃ(3)*	do.	2 2a 2b 2c 0(3)*		[1]	
16	jhānaṃ(4)*	do.	As in No. 11 0(4)*		[1]	
17	jhānaṃ(5)*	do.	As in No. 12 0(5)* pañcamaṃ jhānaṃ upasampajja viharati—'(he) abides in the attainment of the fifth trance'		[1]	
18	jhānaṃ(1)	do.	1 1a 1b 1c 1d 0(1)	1 dukkhapaṭipadaṃ—'(With) process painful' 2 dandhābhiññaṃ–'(with) special knowledge slow'	[1]	
19	do.	do.	do.	1 3 khippābhiññaṃ—'(with) special knowledge rapid'	[1]	
20	do.	do.	do.	4 sukhapaṭipadaṃ–'(with) process pleasant' 2	[1]	

(*Cont.*)

No. of Case	Nomenclature of Thought	Sphere of Thought	Variants of Content No.	Trancic Variables No.	Objects of Thought No.	Mental Variables No.
23	do.	do.	do.	5 parittaṃ—'(thought) limited 6 parittārammaṇaṃ—'(with) object limited'	[1]	
24	do.	do.	do.	7 appamāṇārammaṇaṃ—'(with) object immeasurable'	[1]	
25	do.	do.	do.	8 appamāṇaṃ—'(thought) immeasurable'	[1]	
45	do.	do.	do.		[2] āpokasiṇaṃ—'water-device'	
45[a]	do.	do.	do.		[3] tejokasiṇaṃ—'flame-device'	
45[b]	do.	do.	do.		[4] vāyokasiṇaṃ—'air device'	
45[c]	do.	do.	do.		[5] nīlakasiṇaṃ—'black—blue device'	
45[d]	do.	do.	do.		[6] pītakasiṇaṃ—'yellow device'	
45[e]	do.	do.	do.		[7] lohitakasiṇaṃ—'red device'	

45[f]	do.	do.	do.		[8] odātakasiṇaṃ—'white device'	
46	do.	do.	5 ajjhattaṃ arūpasaññī bahiddhā rūpāni passati—'not consicous of himself (as)form, he sees external forms...' 5[a] parittāni—'(as) limited' 5[b] tāni abhibhuyya jānāmi passamī ti—'having them mastered, and saying "I know, I see", he...' 1		[1]	
65	do.	do.	5 5[a] 5[c] suvaṇṇadubbaṇṇāni—'(as) beautiful and ugly...' 5[b] 1		[1]	
67	do.	do.	5 5[d] appamāṇāni—'(as) infinite...' 5[b] 1		[1]	
88	do.	do.	5 5[e] nīlāni nīlavaṇṇāni nīlānidassanānī nīlanibhāsāni—'black-blue, of black-blue colour, black-blue-spaced, of black-blue luminosity...' 5[b] 1		[1]	

(*Cont.*)

No. of Case	Nomenclature of Thought	Sphere of Thought	Variants of Content No.	Trancic Variables No.	Objects of Thought No.	Mental Variables No.
89	do.	do.	5 5^f pītani pītavaṇṇāni pītānidassanānī pītanibhāsāni—'yellow, of yellow colour, yellow-spaced, of yellow luminosity...' 5^b 1		[1]	
89^a	do.	do.	5 5^g lohitakāni lohitakavaṇṇāni lohitakānidassanāni lohitakanibhāsāni—'red, of red colour, red-spaced, of red luminosity...' 5^b 1		[1]	
89^b	do.	do.	5 5^h odātāni odātavaṇṇāni odātānidassanāni odātanibhāsāni—'White, of white colour, white-spaced, of white luminosity...' 5^b 1		[1]	
90	do.	do.	6 rūpī rūpāni passati—'possessed of form, he sees forms...' 1		[1]	

91	do.	*v*do.	5 1		[1]	
92	do.	do.	7 subhaṃ ti—'saying "How beautiful!" he...' 1		[1]	
93	do.	do.	1 1[a] 1[b] 1[c] 1[d] 0[(1)]		[1]	6 mettāsahagataṃ—'accompanied by friendliness'
100	do.	do.	do.		[1]	7 karuṇāsahaga-taṃ—'accompa-nied by mercy'
102	do.	do.	do.		[1]	8 muditāsahaga—taṃ—'accompa-nied by sympathy'
104	jhānaṃ[(4)]	do.	4 4[a] 4[b] 0[(4)]		[1]	5
105	jhānaṃ[(1)]	do.	1 1[a] 1[b] 1[c] 1[d] 0[(1)]		[9] uddhumātaka-saññā sahaga-taṃ—'accompa-nied by the no-tion of a swollen corpse'	

(*Cont.*)

No. of Case	Nomenclature of Thought	Sphere of Thought	Variants of Content No.	Trancic Variables No.	Objects of Thought No.	Mental Variables No.
106	do.	do.	do.		[10] vinīlakasaññā-sahagataṃ—'accompanied by the notion of a discoloured corpse'	
106[a]	do.	do.	do.		[11] vipubbakasañ-ñāsahagataṃ—'accompanied by the notion of a festering corpse'	
106[b]	do.	do.	do.		[12] vicchiddakas-aññāsahaga-taṃ—'accompa-nied by the no-tion of a corpse with cracked skin'	
106[c]	do.	do.	do.		13 vikkhāyitakasañ-ñāsahagataṃ—'accompanied by the notion of a corpse gnawed and mangled'	
106[d]	do.	do.	do.		14 vikkhattakasañ-ñāsahagataṃ—'accompanied by the notion of a corpse cut to pieces'	

106[e]	do.	do.	do.		15 hatavikkhittaka-saññāsahagatam—'accompanied with the notion of a mutilated corpse'	
106[f]	do.	do.	do.		16 lohitakasaññā-sahagataṃ—'accompanied with the notion of a bloody corpse'	
106[g]	do.	do.	do.		17 puḷuvakasaññā-sahagataṃ—'accompanied with the notion of a corpse with worms'	
106[h]	do.	do.	do.		18 aṭṭhikasaññā-sahagataṃ—'accompanied by the notion of a skeleton'	
107	jhānaṃ(4)	arūpapattiyā maggaṃ bhāveti—'(one) cultivates the way of attainment of the formless'	8 sabbaso rūpasaññānaṃ samatikkamā paṭighasaññānaṃ atthaṅgamā nānāsaññānaṃ amanasikārā—'by wholly transcending the notions of form, with (all) reflexes gone away, (and totally) mindless of the notions of the manifold...' 4		19 ākāsānañcāyatanasaññāsahagataṃ—'accompanied by the notion of the basis of unbounded space'	5

(*Cont.*)

No. of Case	Nomenclature of Thought	Sphere of Thought	Variants of Content No.	Trancic Variables No.	Objects of Thought No.	Mental Variables No.
108	do.	do.	9 sabbaso ākāsānañcāyatanaṃ samatikkammā—'by wholly transcending the basis of unbounded space...' 4		20 viññāṇānañcāyatanasaññāsahagataṃ— 'accompanied by the notion of the basis of unbounded consciousness'	5
109	do.	do.	10 sabbaso viññāṇānañcāyatanaṃ samatikkammā—'by wholly transcending the basis of unbounded consciousness' 4		21 ākiñcaññāyatanasaññāsahagataṃ— 'accompanied by the notion of the basis of nothingness'	5
110	do.	do.	11 sabbaso ākiñcaññāyatanaṃ samatikkammā—'by wholly transcending the basis of nothingness...' 4		22 nevasaññānāsaññāyatanasaññāsahagataṃ—'accompanied by the notion of the basis of what is neither notion nor nonnotion'	5
111	cittaṃ	kāmāvacaraṃ kusalaṃ	0	9 chandādhipateyyaṃ—'dominated by desire' 10 hīnaṃ—'inferior'		1 2
111[a]	do.	do.	0	11 viriyādhipateyyaṃ—'dominated by energy' 12 majjhimaṃ—'medium'		1 2

111[b]	do.	do.	0	13 cittādhipateyyaṃ—'dominated by thought' 14 paṇītaṃ—'superior'		1 2
113	jhānaṃ(1)	rūpūpapattiyā maggaṃ bhāveti	1 1[a] 1[b] 1[c] 1[d] 0(1)	9 14	[1]	
115	jhānaṃ(4)	arūpūpapattiyā maggaṃ bhāveti	8 4	9 14	[19]	5
119	jhānaṃ(1)	lokuttaraṃ jhānaṃ bhāveti—'when he cultivates the trance of the supramundane...'	12 niyyānikaṃ apacayagāmiṃ—'leading out (and) unmaking...' 12[a] diṭṭhigatānaṃ pahānāya paṭhamāya bhūmiyā pattiyā—'(and) avoiding of (all) views and opinions in order to attain at the first stage' 1		[1]	
124	do.	do.	do.	15 suññataṃ—'empty'	[1]	
131	do.	do.	do.	16 appaṇihitaṃ—'aimless'	[1]	
138	jhānaṃ(1)	lokuttaram maggaṃ bhāveti—'(when) he cultivates the supramundane way'	12 12[a] 1	1 2	[1]	

(*Cont.*)

No. of Case	Nomenclature of Thought	Sphere of Thought	Variants of Content No.	Trancic Variables No.	Objects of Thought No.	Mental Variables No.
138[a]	do.	lokuttaraṃ satipaṭṭhānaṃ bhāveti—'(when) he cultivates the supramundane advance in recollection'	do.	do.	do.	
138[b]	do.	lokuttaram sammapadhānaṃ bhāveti—'(when) he cultivates the supramundane right efforts'	do.	do.	do.	
138[c]	do.	lokuttaraṃ iddhipādaṃ bhāveti—'(when) he cultivates the course of supramundane power'	do.	do.	do.	
138[d]	do.	lokkutaraṃ indriyaṃ bhāveti—'(when) he cultivates the supramundane faculty'	do.	do.	do.	
138[e]	do.	lokuttaraṃ balaṃ bhāveti—'(when) he cultivates the supramundane power'	do.	do.	do.	

138[f]	do.	lokuttaraṃ bojjhaṅgaṃ bhāveti—'(when) he cultivates the supramundane component of (complete) awakening'	do.	do.	do.	
138[g]	do.	lokuttaraṃ saccaṃ bhāveti—'(when) he cultivates the supramundane truth'	do.	do.	do.	
138[h]	jhānaṃ[1]	lokuttaraṃ samathaṃ bhāveti—'(when) he cultivates the supramundane quietude'	12 12[a] 1	1 2	[1]	
138[i]	do.	lokuttaraṃ dhammaṃ bhāveti—'(when) he cultivates the supramundane dharma'	do.	do.	do.	
138[j]	do.	lokuttaraṃ khandhaṃ bhāveti—'(when) he cultivates the supramundane aggregate'	do.	do.	do.	
138[k]	do.	lokuttaraṃ āyatanaṃ bhāveti—'(when) he cultivates the supramundane basis'	do.	do.	do.	

(*Cont.*)

No. of Case	Nomenclature of Thought	Sphere of Thought	Variants of Content No.	Trancic Variables No.	Objects of Thought No.	Mental Variables No.
138l	do.	lokuttaraṃ dhātu bhāveti—'(when) he cultivates the supramundane element'	do.	do.	do.	
138m	do.	lokuttaraṃ āhāraṃ bhāveti—'(when) he cultivates the supramundane nutriment'	do.	do.	do.	
138n	do.	lokuttaraṃ phassaṃ bhāveti—'(when) he cultivates the supramundane touch'	do.	do.	do.	
138o	do.	lokuttaraṃ vedanaṃ bhāveti—'(when) he cultivates the supramundane sensation'	do.	do.	do.	
138p	do.	lokuttaraṃ saññaṃ bhāveti—'(when) he cultivates the supramundane cognition'	do.	do.	do.	
138r	do.	lokuttaraṃ cetanaṃ bhāveti—'(when) he cultivates the supramundane volition'	do.	do.	do.	

138[8]	do.	lokuttaraṃ cittaṃ bhāveti—'(when) he cultivates the supramundane thought'	do.	*v*do.	do.	
142	jhānaṃ[(1)]	lokuttaraṃ jhānaṃ bhāveti	12 13 kāmarāgavyāpādānaṃ tanubhāvāya dutiyāya bhūmiyā pattiyā—'having reduced (the strength of) sensuality, passion and maliciousness, in order to attain to the second stage... 1	1 2	[1]	
143	do.	do.	12 14 kāmarāgavyāpādānaṃ anavasesappahānāya tatiyāya bhūmiyā pattiyā—'having avoided (all) sensuality, passion and maliciousness without residuum, in order to attain to the third stage... 1	1 2	[1]	
144	do.	do.	12 15 rūparāga arūparāga māna uddhacca avijjāya anavasesappahānāya catutthāya bhūmiyā pattiyā—'having avoidded (all) passion for form, (all) passion for the formless, (all) conceit, excitement and ignorance without residuum, in order to attain to the fourth stage... 1	1 2	[1]	

(*Cont.*)

No. of Case	Nomenclature of Thought	Sphere of Thought	Variants of Content No.	Trancic Variables No.	Objects of Thought No.	Mental Variables No.
145	cittaṃ	akusalaṃ— 'unwholesome'	0		1–6	1 9 diṭṭhigatasampayuttaṃ—'associated with views and opinions'
146	do.	do.	0		1–6	1 9 3
147	do.	do.	0		1–6	1 10 diṭṭhigatavipayuttaṃ—'dissociated from views and opinions'
153	do.	do.	0		1–6	11 domanassasahagataṃ—'accompanied by mental sorrow' 12 paṭighasaṃpayuttaṃ—'associated with (negative) reaction'
155	do.	do.	0		1–6	5 13 vicikicchāsaṃpayuttaṃ—'associated with perplexity'

156	do.	do.	0		1– 6	5 14 uddhaccasampayuttaṃ—'associated with excitement'
157	cakkhuviññāṇaṃ 'eye-consciousness'		15 kāmāvacarassa kusalassa kammassa kattā upacitattā vipākaṃ—'resulting from the ripening wholesome action wrought and stored up in the sensuous sphere' 0		1	5
158	sotaviññaṇaṃ ('ear-consciousness')		16 0		2	5
159	ghānaviññāṇaṃ ('smell-consciousness')		16 0		3	5
160	jivhāviññāṇaṃ ('taste-consciousness')		16 0		4	5
161	kāyaviññāṇaṃ ('body-consciousness')		16 0		5	5
162	manodhātu ('element of mind)		16 0		1– 5	5

(*Cont.*)

No. of Case	Nomenclature of Thought	Sphere of Thought	Variants of Content No.		Trancic Variables No.	Objects of Thought No.	Mental Variables No.
163	manoviññā-ṇadhātu ('element of mind-consciousness')		160			1–6	1
166	jhānaṃ[1]	rūpūpapattiyā maggaṃ bhāveti	171	rūpāvacarassa kusalassa kammassa katattā upacitattā vipākaṃ—'resulting from the ripening wholesome action wrought and stored up in the sphere of form'		[1]	
168	jhānaṃ[4]	arūpūpapattiyā maggaṃ bhāveti	1884	arūpāvacayassa kusalassa kammassa katattā upacitattā vipākaṃ—'resulting from the ripening wholesome action wrought and stored up in the sphere of formlessness'		[1] [19]	5
172	jhānaṃ[1]	lokuttaraṃ jhānaṃ bhāveti	1912 12[a]	lokuttarassa kusalassa jhānassa katattā bhāvitattā vipākaṃ—'resulting from the ripening wholesome trance wrought and experienced in the Supramundane sphere'	1 2	[1]	

222	cakkhuviññāṇam		20 akusalassa kammassa katattā upacitattā vipākaṃ—'resulting from the ripening unwholesome action wrought and stored...'		1	5
222[d]	kāyaviññāṇaṃ		20 0		5	15 dukkhasahagatam—'accompanied by suffering'
225	manodhātu		0 21 kiriyā neva kusalā nākusalā na ca kammavipākā—'(which is) an act (as such), neither wholesome nor unwholesome, and not resulting from the ripening action'		1– 5	5
226	manoviññāṇadhātu		0 21		1– 6	1
229	jhānaṃ(1)	rūpāvacaram... bhāveti—'he experiences in the sphere of form'	21 22 diṭṭhadhammasukhavihāraṃ—'happy abiding with seen dharmas' 1		[1]	
231	jhānaṃ(4)	arūpāvacaraṃ... bhāveti—'he experiences in the sphere of formlessness'	21 23 8 4		[19]	

Table VI. Mental States (MS) corresponding to each of 83 States of Consciousness (or dharmas—△△).[6]

No. of △	Name of △	No. of MS	Name of MS
Case No. 1A			
1	*phassa* (touch) [MS 1–4]	1	phassa—'touch'
		2	phusanā—'touching'
		3	samphusanā—'contact'
		4	samphusitattaṃ—'(being) contacted'.
2	*vedanā* (sensation) [MS 5–11]	5	manoviññāṇadhātu samphassajaṃ cetasikaṃ sātaṃ—'psychical ease born of contact with element of mind-consciousness'
		6	cetasikaṃ sukhaṃ—'psychical (ly) pleasant'
		7	cetosamphassajaṃ sātaṃ (vedayitaṃ)—'ease (experienced as) born of contact with the psychical'
		8	(cetosamphassajaṃ) sukhaṃ vedayitaṃ—'the pleasant experienced as (born of contact with the psychical)'
		9	cetosamphassajā sātā (vedanā)—'(sensation of) ease born of contact with the psychical'
		10	(cetosamphassajā) sukhā vedanā—'sensation of pleasant (born of contact with the psychical)'
		11	(vedanā)—'sensation'.[7]
3	*saññā* (cognition) [MS 12–14]	12	manoviññāṇadhātu samphassajā saññā—'cognition born of contact with element of mind-consciousness'
		13	saññānanā—'cognizing'
		14	saññānitattaṃ—'(being) cognized'

(*Cont.*)

No. of △	Name of △	No. of MS	Name of MS
4	*cetanā* (intention) [MS 15–17]	15	manoviññāṇadhātu samphassajā cetanā—'volition born of contact with element of mind-consciousness'
		16	sañcetanā—'intention'
		17	cetayitattaṃ—'(being) intended'
5	*citta* (thought) [MS 18–22, *19*, 23–27]	*18*	*citta*—'thought'
		19	*mano*—'mind'
		20	mānasa—'mental'
		21	hadaya—'heart'
		22	paṇḍara—'clear'(?!)
		19, 23	manāyatana—'base of mind'
		24	manindriya—'faculty of mind'
		25	viññāṇa—'consciousness'
		26	viññāṇakkhandha—'aggregate of consciousness'
		27	manoviññāṇādhātu—'element of mind-consciousness'
6	*vitakka* (reasoning) [MS 28–34]	28	takka—'ratiocination'
		29	*vitakka*—'reasoning'
		30	saṅkappa—'construing'
		31	appanā—'fixation'
		32	vyappanā—'focusing'
		33	cetaso abhiniropanā—'application of psyche'
		34	sammāsaṅkappa—'correct construing'.
7	*vicāra* (reflexion) [MS 35–40]	35	cāra—'procedure (of reflexion)'
		36	*vicāra*—'reflexion'
		37	anuvicāra—'application of reflexion'
		38	upavicāra—'approaching reflexion'
		39	cittassa anusandhanatā—'adjustment of thought'
		40	anupekkhanatā—'stabilization (of thought)'

(*Cont.*)

No. of △	Name of △	No. of MS	Name of MS
8	*pīti* (joy) [MS 41–49]	*41*	*pīti*—'joy'
		42	pamojja—'delightful'
		43	āmodanā—'delight'
		44	pamodanā—'delightfulness'
		45	hāsa—'mirth'
		46	pahāsa—'merriment'
		47	vitti—'felicity'
		48	odagya—'elation'
		49	attamanatā cittassa—'uprisedness of thought'.
9	*sukha* (pleasure) [as in △2]	*5–11*	
10	*cittassekaggatā* (one-directedness of thought) [MS 50–59)]	50	cittassa ṭhiti—'stasis of thought'
		51	(cittassa) saṇṭhiti—'constancy (of thought)
		52	(cittassa) avaṭṭhiti—'steadfastness (of thought)'
		53	avisāhāra—'unperturbedness of thought'
		54	avikkhepa—'unperplexity (of thought)'
		55	avisāhaṭamānasatā—'unperturbed mindedness'
		56	samatha—'quietude'
		57	samādhindriya—'faculty of concentration'
		58	samādhibala—'power of concentration'
		59	sammāsamādhi—'correct concentration'.
11	*saddhindriya* (faculty of faith) [MS 60–63, *60*, 64, 65]	*60*	*saddhā*—'faith'
		61	saddahanā—'having faith'
		62	okappanā—'confidence'
		63	abhippasāda—'assurance'
		60, 64	saddhindriya—'faculty of faith'
		65	saddhābala—'power of faith'.
12	*viriyindriya* (faculty of energy) [MS 66–82]	66	cetasiko viriyārambho—'physical inception of energy'
		67	nikkama—'exercise'
		68	parakkama—'exertion'

(*Cont.*)

No. of △	Name of △	No. of MS	Name of MS
12 (*cont.*)		69	uyyāma—'strive'
		70	vāyāma—'endeavour'
		71	ussāha—'zeal'
		72	ussoḷhi—'ardour'
		73	thāma—'stamina'
		74	dhiti—'firmness'
		75	asithilaparakkamatā—'(state of) unfaltering exertion'
		76	anikkhittacchandatā— '(state of) unabated desire'
		77	anikkhittadharatā—'(state of) unabated endurance'
		78	dhurasampaggāha—'strong grip of the burden'
		79	viriya—'energy'
		80	*viriyindriya*—'faculty of energy'
		81	viriyabala—'power of energy'
		82	sammāvāyāma—'correct endeavour'.
13	*satindriya* (faculty of recollection) [MS 83–85, 83, 86–89, *83*, 90–92]	*83*	*sati*—'recollection'
		84	anussati—'remembering'
		85	paṭissati—'recalling'
		83, 86	saraṇatā—'remembrance'
		87	dhāraṇatā—'mindfulness'
		88	apilāpanatā—'deep penetration (by memory)'
		89	asammusanatā—'unforgetfulness'
		83, *90*	satindriya—'faculty of recollection'
		91	satibala—'power of recollection'
		92	sammāsati—'correct recollection'.
14	*samādhindriya* (faculty of concentration) [As in △ 10)	*50–59*	
15	*paññindriya* (faculty of wisdom) [MS *93*–112, 93, 113–121, *97*, 122]	*93*	paññā—'wisdom'
		94	pajānanā—'understanding'
		95	vicaya—'search'

(*Cont.*)

No. of △	Name of △	No. of MS	Name of MS
15 (*Cont.*)		96	pavicaya—'research'
		97	dhammavicaya—'search of Dharma'
		98	sallakkhaṇā—'discernment'
		99	upalakkhaṇā—'discrimination'
		100	paccupalakkhaṇā—'differentiation'
		101	paṇḍicca—'erudition'
		102	kosalla—'proficiency'
		103	nepuñña—'expertise'
		104	vebhabyā—'pondering'
		105	cintā—'thinking'
		106	upaparikkhā—'analytical investigation'
		107	bhūrí—'breadth (of wisdom)'
		108	medhā—'sagacity'
		109	pariṇāyika—'(wisdom as) a guide'
		110	vipassanā—'intuition'
		111	sampajañña—'(being) conscious'
		112	patoda—'(wisdom as) a goad'
		93, 113	*paññindriya* —'faculty of wisdom'
		114	paññābala—'power of wisdom'
		115	paññāsattha—'sword of wisdom'
		116	paññāpāsāda—'palace of wisdom'
		117	paññāāloka—'lamp of wisdom'
		118	paññāābhāsa—'lustre of wisdom'
		119	paññāpajjota—'splendour of wisdom'
		120	paññāratana—'jewel of wisdom'
		121	amoha—'absence of delusion'
		97, 122	sammādiṭṭhi—'correct view'
16	*manindriya* (faculty of mind) [As in △ 5]	*18–27*	

(*Cont.*)

No. of △	Name of △	No. of MS	Name of MS
17	*somanassindriya* (faculty of mental gladness) [As in △△2, 9]	*5–11*	
18	*jīvitindriya* (faculty of living) [MS 123–131]	123	arūpinaṃ dhammānaṃ āyu—'duration of the formless dharmas'
		124	ṭhiti—'(their) stasis'
		125	yapanā—'(their) going on'
		126	yāpanā—'(their) keeping going on'
		127	iriyanā—'(their) progression'
		128	vattanā—'(their) continuance'
		129	pālanā—'(their) conservation'
		130	jīvita—'living'
		131	*jīvitindriya*—'faculty of life'
19	*sammādiṭṭhi* (correct view) [As in △15]	*93–122*	
20	*sammāsaṅkappa* (correct construing) [As in △6]	*28–34*	
21	*sammāvāyāma* (correct endeavour) [As in △12]	*66–82*	
22	*sammāsati* (correct recollection) [As in △13]	83–92	
23	*sammāsamādhi* (correct concentration) [As in △△10, 14]	*50–59*	
24	*saddhābala* (power of faith) [As in △11]	*60–65*	
25	*viriyabala* (faculty of energy) [As in △12, 21]	*66–82*	
26	*satibala* (power of recollection) [As in △△13, 22]	*83–92*	
27	*samādhibala* (power of concentration) [As in △△10, 14, 23]	*50–59*	

(*Cont.*)

No. of △	Name of △	No. of MS	Name of MS
28	*paññābala* (power of wisdom) [As in △△15, 19]	*93–122*	
29	*hirībala* (power of shame) [MS 132, 133]	132	hirīyati hirīyitabbena—'(when one) is ashamed of (what one) ought to be ashamed)
		133	hirīyati pāpakānaṃ akusalānaṃ dhammānaṃ samāpattiyā— '(when one is) ashamed of acquisition of sinful and un unwholesome dharmas'
30	*ottappabala* (power of remorse) [MS 134, 135]	134	ottappati ottappitabbena—'(when one) feels remorse of (what one) ought to be remorseful'
		135	ottappati pāpakānaṃ akusalānaṃ dhammānaṃ samāpattiyā —'(when one) feels remorse of acquisition of sinful and unwholesome dharmas'
31	*alobha* (disinterestedness) [MS 136–143]	*136*	*alobha*—'disinterestedness' alubbhanā—'(state of) not
		137	being greedy'
		138	alubbhitattaṃ—'(state of) not feeling greed'
		139	asārāga—'not infatuated'
		140	asārajjanā—'(state of) not being infatuated'
		141	asārajjitattaṃ—'(state of) not feeling infatuation'
		142	anabhijjhā—'not being covetous'
		143	alobho kusala mūlaṃ—'disinterestedness (as) a wholesome root'
32	*adosa* (non-hatred) [MS 144–149]	144	*adosa*—'non-hatred'
		145	adussanā—'non-hating'
		146	adussitattaṃ—'(state of) not feeling hatred'
		147	abyāpāda—'unmaliciousness'
		148	avyāpajja—'harmless'
		149	adoso kusala mūlaṃ—'non-hatred (as) a wholesome root'

(Cont.)

No. of △	Name of △	No. of MS	Name of MS
33	*amoha* (absence of delusion) [As in △△15, 19, 28]	*93–122*	
34	*anabhijjhā* (not being covetous) [As in △31]	*136–143*	
35	*abyāpāda* (unmaliciousness) [As in △32]	*144–149*	
36	*sammādiṭṭhi* (correct view) [As in △△15, 19, 28, 33]	*93–122*	
37	*hirī* (shame) [As in △29]	*132–133*	
38	*ottappa* (remorse) [As in △30]	*134–135*	
39	*kāyapassaddhi* (composedness of body) [MS 150–154]	150	vedanākkhandhassa saññākkhandhassa saṅkhārakkhandhassa passaddhi—'composedness of the aggregate of sensation, of the aggregate of cognition, and of the aggregate of synergies'
		151	paṭipassaddhi—'(their) composure'
		152	passambhanā—'(their) calming down'
		153	paṭipassambhanā—'(their) complete tranquillization'
		154	paṭipassambhatattaṃ—'completely tranquillized'
40	*cittapassaddhi* (composedness of thought) [MS 155–159]	155	viññaṇakkhandhassa passaddhi—'composedness of the aggregate of consciousness'
		156	paṭipassaddhi—'(its) composure'
		157	passambhanā—'(its) calming down'
		158	paṭipassambhanā—'(its) complete tranquillization'
		159	paṭipassambhatattaṃ—'completely tranquillized'.

(*Cont.*)

No. of △	Name of △	No. of MS	Name of MS
41	*kāyalahutā* (lightness of body) [MS 160–163]	160	vedanākkhandhassa saññākkhandhassa saṅkhārakkhandhassa labutā—'lightness of the aggregate of sensation, of the aggregate of cognition, and of the aggregate of synergies'
		161	lahupariṇāmatā—'(their capacity of) easy transformation'
		162	adandhanatā—'(their) non-sluggishness'
		163	avitthanatā—'(their) non-inertness'.
42	*cittalahutā* (lightness of thought) [MS 164—167]	164	viññāṇakkhandhassa lahutā—'lightness of the aggregate of consciousness'
		165	lahupariṇāmatā—'(its) capacity of easy transformation'
		166	adandhanatā—'(its) non non-sluggishness'
		167	avitthanatā—'(its) non-inertness'.
43	*kāyamudutā* (flexibility of body) [MS 168–171]	168	vedanākkhandhassa saññākkhandhassa saṅkhārakkhandhassa mudutā—'flexibility of the aggregate of sensation, of the aggregate of cognition, and of the aggregate of synergies'
		169	maddavatā—'(their) mildness'
		170	akakkhaḷatā—'(their) non-rigidity'
		171	akathinatā—'(their) non-stiffness'.
44	*cittamudutā* (flexibility of thought) [MS 172–175]	172	viññāṇakkhandhassa mudutā—'flexibility of the aggregate of consciousness'
		173	maddavatā—'(its) mildness'
		174	akakkhaḷatā—'(its) non-rigidity'
		175	akathinatā—'(its) non-stiffness'

(*Cont.*)

No. of △	Name of △	No. of MS	Name of MS
45	*kāyakammaññatā* (workability of body) [MS 176–178]	176	vedanākkhandhassa saññākkhandhassa saṅkhārakkhandhassa kammaññatā—'workability of the aggregate of sensation, of the aggregate of cognition, and of the aggregate of synergies'
		177	kammaññattaṃ—'(their) working ability'
		178	kammaññabhāva—'(their) being workable'
46	*cittakammaññatā* (workability of thought) [MS 179–181]	179	viññāṇakkhandhassa kammaññatā—'workability of the aggregate of consciousness'
		180	kammaññattaṃ—'(its) working ability'
		181	kammaññabhāva—'(its) being workable'
47	*kāyapāguññatā* (fitness of body) [MS 182–184]	182	vedanākkhandhassa saññākkhandhassa saṅkhārakkhandhassa paguṇatā–'good quality of the aggregate of sensation, of the aggregate of cognition, and of the aggregate of synergies'
		183	paguṇattaṃ—'(their) good quality'
		184	paguṇabhāva—'(their) being of good quality'.
48	*cittapāguññatā* (fitness of thought) [MS 185–187]	185	viññāṇakkhandhassa paguṇatā—'good quality of the aggregate of consciousness'
		186	paguṇattaṃ—'(its) good quality'
		187	paguṇabhāva—'(its) being of good quality'.
49	*kāyujukatā* (straightness of body) [MS 188–192]	188	vedanākkhandhassa saññākkhandhassa saṅkhārakkhandhassa ujukatā —'straightness of the aggregate of sensation, of the aggregate of cognition, and of the aggregate of synergies'

(*Cont.*)

No. of △	Name of △	No. of MS	Name of MS
49 (*Cont.*)		189	ujutā—'(their) rectitude'
		190	ajimhatā—'(their) undeflectedness'
		191	avaṅkatā—'(their) uncrookedness'
		192	akuṭilatā—'(their) untwistedness'
50	*cittujukatā* (straightness of thought) [MS 193–197]	193	viññāṇakkhandhassa ujukatā—'straightness of the aggregate of consciousness'
		194	ujutā—'(its) rectitude'
		195	ajiṃhatā—'(its) undeflectedness'
		196	avaṅkatā—'(its) uncrookedness'
		197	akuṭilatā—'(its) untwistedness'.
51	*sati* (recollection) (As in △△13, 22, 26]	*83–92*	
52	*sampajañña* (self-awareness) [As in △△15, 19, 28, 33, 36]	*93–122*	
53	*samatha* (quietude) [As in △△10, 14, 23, 27]	*50–59*	
54	*vipassanā* (intution) [As in △△15, 19, 28, 33, 36, 52]	*93–122*	
55	*paggāha* (grasp) (As in △△12, 21, 25]	*66–82*	
56	*avikkhepa* (unperturbedness) [As in △△10, 14, 23, 27, 53]	*50–59*	

(*Cont.*)

No. of △	Name of △	No. of MS	Name of MS
Case No. 5A			
2[a]	*vedanā*[8] [MS 198–200]	198	manoviññāṇadhātusamphassajaṃ cetasikaṃ neva sātaṃ nāsātaṃ—'neither psychical ease nor unease born of contact with element of mind-consciousness'
		199	cetosamphassajaṃ adukkhamasukhaṃ vedayitaṃ—'(what is) neither suffering nor pleasure experienced (as) born of contact with the psychical'
		200	cetosamphassajā adukkhamasukhā vedanā—'sensation of neither suffering nor pleasure born of contact with the psychical'.[9]
57	*upekkhā* (indifference) [As in △ 2[a]]	*198–200*	
58	*upekkhindriya* (of indifference) [As in △ △2[a], 57]	*198–200*	
Case No. 119A			
6[a]	*vitakka* [MS 28–34, 201, 202]	*28–34*	
		201	maggaṅga—'a component of the Way'
		202	maggapariyāpanna—'included in the Way'.
8[a]	*pīti* [MS 41–49, 203]	*41–49*	
		203	pītisambojjhaṅga—'joy (as) a component of Complete Awakening'.

(*Cont.*)

No. of △	Name of △	No. of MS	Name of MS
10[a]	*cittassekaggatā* [MS 50–59, 201–2, 204]	*50–59*	
		204	samādhisambojjhaṅga—'concentration (as) a component of Complete Awakening'
		201, 202	
12[a]	*viriyindriya* [MS 66–82, 201–2, 205]	*66–82*	
		205	viriyasambojjhaṅga—'energy (as) a compoment of Complete Awakening'
		201, 202	
13[a]	*satindriya* [MS 83–92, 201–2, 206]	*83–92*	
		206	satisambojjhaṅga—'recollection (as) a component of Complete Awakening'
		201, 202	
14[a]	*samādhindriya* [As in △ 10[a]]	*50–59*	
		201, 202	
		204	
15[a]	*paññindriya* [MS 83–122, 201–2, 207]	*93–122*	
		207	dhammavicayasambojjhaṅga—'a search of Dharma (as) a component of Complete Awakening'
59	*anaññātaññassāmītindirya* (the faculty [of those who] say: 'I shall know the unknown') [MS 93–122, 201–2, 207, 208]	208	dhammānaṃ anaññātānaṃ adiṭṭhānaṃ apattānaṃ aviditānaṃ asacchikatānaṃ sacchikiriyāya paññā—'the wisdom (that), seeing with (its) own eyes the unrecognized, unseen, unattained, unknown, and unfound dharmas, (says:) "I shall know the unknown" '.
		93–122	
		207	
		201, 202	

(*Cont.*)

No. of △	Name of △	No. of MS	Name of MS
19[a]	*sammādiṭṭhi* [As in △ 15[a]]	*93–122*	
		207	
		201, 202	
20[a]	*sammāsaṅkappa* [As in △ 6[a]]	*28–34*	
		201, 202	
60	*sammāvācā* (correct speech) [MS 201–2, 209–215]	209	catūhi vacíduccaritehi ārati virati paṭivirati veramaṇī—'leaving off, abstaining, totally abstaining and refraining from the four deviations of speech'
		210	akiriyā—'leaving (them) undone'
		211	akaraṇaṃ—'(leaving them) unaffected'
		212	anajjhāpatti—'not incurring guilt'
		213	velā anatikkamo—'not trespassing limit'
		214	setughāta—'destroying (their) cause'
		215	*sammāvācā—'correct speech'*
		201, 202	
61	*sammākammanta* (correct action) [MS 201–2, 216–222]	216	tīhi kāyaduccaritehi ārati virati paṭivirati veramaṇī—'leaving off, abstaining, totally abstaining and refraining from the three deviations of body'
		217	akiriyā—'leaving (them) undone'
		218	akaraṇaṃ—'(leaving them) unaffected'
		219	anajjhāpatti—'not incurring guilt'
		220	velā anatikkamo—'not trespassing limit'
		211	setughāta—'destroying (their) cause'
		222	*sammākammanta—'correct action'*
		201, 202	

(*Cont.*)

No. of △	Name of △	No. of MS	Name of MS
62	*sammā ājīva* (correct livelihood) [MS 201–2, 223–229]	223	micchā ājīvā ārati virati paṭivirati veramaṇī—'leaving off, abstaining, totally abstaining and refraining from the wrong livelihood'
		224	akiriyā—'leaving (it) undone'
		225	akaraṇaṃ—'(leaving it) unaffected'
		226	anajjhāpatti—'not incurring guilt'
		227	velā anatikkama—'not trespass ing limit'
		228	setughāta—'destroying (its) cause'
		229	*sammā ājīva—'correct livelihood'*
		201, 202	
21[a]	*sammāvāyāma*	66–82	
	[As in △ 12[a]]	205	
		201, 202	
22[a]	*sammāsati*	83–92	
	[As in △ 13[a]]	206	
		201, 202	
23[a]	*sammāsamādhi*	*50–59*	
	[As in △△ 10[a], 14[a]]	*201, 202*	
		204	
25[a]	*viriyabala*	*66–82*	
	[As in △△ 12[a], 21[a]]	*205*	
		201, 202	
26[a]	*satibala*	*83–92*	
	[As in △△ 13[a], 22[a]]	*206*	
		201, 202	
27[a]	*samādhibala*	*50–59*	
	[As in △△ 10[a], 14[a], 23[a]]	*201, 202*	
		204	
28[a]	*paññābala*	*93–122*	
	[As in △△ 15[a], 19[a]]	*207*	
		201, 202	
33[a]	*amoha*	*93–122*	
	[As in △△ 15[a], 19[a], 28[a]]	*207*	
		201, 202	
36[a]	*sammādiṭṭhi*	*93–122*	
	[As in △△ 15[a], 19[a], 28[a], 33[a]]	*207*	
		201, 202	

(*Cont.*)

No. of △	Name of △	No. of MS	Name of MS
39[a]	*kāyapassadhi* [MS 150–154, 230]	*150–154* 230	passadhisambojjhaṅga— 'composedness as a component of Complete Awakening'
40[a]	*cittapassadhi* [MS 155–159, 230]	*155–159* *230*	
51[a]	*sati* [As in △△13[a], 22[a], 26[a]]	*83–92* *206* *201, 202*	
52[a]	*sampajañña* [As in △△15[a], 19[a], 28[a], 33[a], 36[a]]	*93–122* *207* *201, 202*	
53[a]	*samatha* [As in △△10[a], 14[a], 23[a], 27[a]]	*50–59* *201, 202* *204*	
54[a]	*vipassanā* [As in 15[a], 19[a], 28[a], 33[a], 36[a], 52[a]]	*93–122* *207* *201, 202*	
55[a]	*paggāha* [As in △△12[a], 21[a], 25[a]]	*66–82* *205* *201, 202*	
56[a]	*avikkhepa* [As in △△10[a], 14[a], 23[a], 27[a], 53[a]]	*50–59* *204* *201, 202*	
Case No. 144A			
63	*aññindriya* (faculty of recognition) [As in △59]	*208* *93–122* *207* *201, 202*	

(*Cont.*)

No. of △	Name of △	No. of MS	Name of MS
Case No. 145B			
6[b]	*vitakka* [MS 28–33, 231]	*28–33*	
		231	micchāsaṅkappa—'wrong construing'
10[b]	*cittassekaggatā* [MS 50–58, 232]	*50–58*	
		232	micchāsamādhi—'wrong concentration'
12[b]	*viriyindriya* [MS 66–81, 233]	*66–81*	
		233	micchāvāyāma—'wrong endeavour'
14[b]	*samādhindriya* [As in △ 10[b]]	*50–58*	
		232	
64	*micchādiṭṭhi* (wrong view) [MS 234–249]	234	diṭṭhi—'view'
		235	diṭṭhigata—'current views and opinions'
		236	diṭṭhigahana—'thicket of views'
		237	diṭṭhikantāra—'wilderness of views'
		238	diṭṭhivisūkāyika—'distortion of views'
		239	diṭṭhivipphandita—'scuffle of views'
		240	diṭṭhisaññojana—'fetters of views'
		241	gāha—'grasping (of view)'
		242	paṭiggāha—'sticking strongly (to view)'
		243	abhinivesa—'inclination (towards view)'
		244	parāmāsa—'holding as paramount (one's view)'
		245	kummagga—'erroneous way'
		246	micchāpatha—'wrong path'
		247	micchatta—'wrongness'
		248	titthāyatana—'sectarian bias'
		249	vipariyāsaggāha—'grasping of inverted (views)'

(*Cont,*)

No. of △	Name of △	No. of MS	Name of MS
65	*micchāsaṅkappa* (wrong construing) ([As in △ 6^{b}]	*28–33* *231*	
66	*micchāvāyāma* (wrong endeavour) [As in △ 12^{b}]	*66–81* *233*	
67	*micchāsamādhi* (wrong concentration [As in △△ 10^{b}, 14^{b}]	*50–58* *232*	
25^{b}	*viriyabala* [As in △△ 12^{b}, 66]	*66–81* 233	
27^{b}	*samādhibala* [As in △△ 10^{b}, 14^{b}, 67]	*50–58* *232*	
68	*ahirikabala* (power of shamelessness) [MS 250, 251]	250	na hirīyati hirīyitabbena—‘(when one is) not ashamed of (what one) ought to be ashamed’
		251	na hirīyati pāpakānaṃ akusalānaṃ dhammānaṃ samāpattiyā—‘(when one is) not ashamed of acquisition of sinful and unwholesome dharmas’
69	*anottappabala* (power of unre-morsefulness) [MS 252, 253]	252	na ottappati ottappitabbena—‘(when one) does not feel remorse of (what one) ought to be remorseful’
		253	na ottappati pāpakānaṃ akusalānaṃ dhammānaṃ samāpattiyā—‘(when one) does not feel remorse of acquisition of sinful and unwholesome dharmas’
70	*lobha* (greed) [MS 254–261]	*254*	lobha—‘greed’
		255	lubbhanā—‘(state of) being greedy’
		256	lubbhitattaṃ—‘(state of) feeling greed’
		257	sārāga—‘infatuated’
		258	sārajjanā—‘(state of) being infatuated’

(*Cont.*)

No. of △	Name of △	No. of MS	Name of MS
70 (*Cont.*)		259	sārajitattaṃ—'(state of) feeling infatuation'
		260	abhijjhā—'covetousness'
		261	lobho akusalamūlaṃ—'greed (as) an unwholesome root'
71	*moha* (delusion) [MS 262–285]	262	aññāṇa—'nescience'
		263	adassana—'not-seeing'
		264	anabhisamaya—'un-comprehension'
		265	ananubodha—'not understanding'
		266	asambodha—'unawakened'
		267	appaṭivedha—'non-penetration'
		268	asagāhanā—'non-grasping'
		269	apariyogāhanā—'inability to compare'
		270	asamapekkhanā—'being unobservant'
		271	apaccavekkhanā—'non-consideration'
		272	apacakkhakamma—'inability to demonstrate'
		273	dummajjha—'stupidity'
		274	bālya—'childishness'
		275	asampajañña—'unawareness'
		276	*moha*—'delusion'
		277	pamoha—'utter delusion'
		278	sammoha—'complete delusion'
		279	avijjā—'ignorance'
		280	avijjogha—'flood of ignorance'
		281	avijjāyoga—'fetters of ignorance'
		282	avijjānusaya—'tendency towards ignorance'
		283	avijjāpariyuṭṭhāna—'obsession with ignorance'
		284	avijjālaṇga—'snares of ignorance'
		285	moho akusalamūlaṃ—'delusion (as) an unwholesome root'

(*Cont.*)

No. of △	Name of △	No. of MS	Name of MS
72	*abhijjhā* (covetousness) [As in △70]	*254–261*	
73	*micchādiṭṭhi* (wrong view) [As in △64]	*234–249*	
74	*ahirīka* (shamelessness) [As in △68]	*250, 251*	
75	*anottappa* (unremorsefulness) [As in △69]	*252–253*	
53b	*samatha* [As in △△10b, 14b, 67]	*50–58* *232*	
55b	*paggāha* [As in △△12bm 25b, 66]	*66–81* *233*	
56b	*avikkhepa* [As in △△10b, 14b, 53b, 67]	*50–58* *232*	
Case No. 153B			
2b	*vedanā* [MS 286–291]	286	manoviññāṇadhātusampassajaṃ cetasikaṃ asātaṃ—'psychical unease born of contact with element of mind-consciousness'
		287	cetasikaṃ dukkhaṃ—'psychically unpleasant'
		288	cetosamphassajamasātaṃ (vedayitaṃ)—'unease (experienced as) born of contact with the psychical'
		289	(cetosamphassajaṃ) dukkhaṃ vedayitaṃ—'the unpleasant experienced (as born of contact with the psychical)'
		290	cetosamphassajā asātā (vedanā)—'(sensation of) unease born of contact with the psychical'

(*Cont.*)

No. of △	Name of △	No. of MS	Name of MS
2^{b} (*Cont.*)		291	(cetosamphassajā) dukkhā vedanā—'sensation of unpleasant (born of contact with the psychical)'
76	*dukkha* (suffering) [As in △2^{b}]	*286–291*	
77	*domanassindriya* (faculty of mental sorrow) [As in △△2^{b}, 76]	*286–291*	
78	*dosa* (hatred) [MS 292–302]	*292*	dosa—'hatred'
		293	dussanā—'hating'
		294	dussitattaṃ—'(state of) feeling hatred'
		295	byāpatti—'maliciousness'
		296	byāpajjanā—'causing harm'
		297	byāpajjitatta—'harmfulness'
		298	virodha—'enmity'
		299	paṭivirodha—'hostility'
		300	caṇḍikka—'churlishness'
		301	asuropa—'abruptness'
		302	anattamanatā cittassa—'depression of thought'
79	*byāpāda* (maliciousness) [As in △78]	*292–302*	
Case No. 155B			
10^{c}	*cittassekaggatā* [MS 50]	50	
80	*vicikicchā* (perplexity) [MS 303–316]	303	kaṅkhā—'doubt'
		304	kaṅkhāyanā—'doubting'
		305	kaṇkhāyitattaṃ—'dubiety'
		306	vimati—'puzzlement'
		307	vicikicchā—'perplexity'
		308	dveḷhaka—'being in doubt (before two alternatives)'

(*Cont.*)

No. of △	Name of △	No. of MS	Name of MS
80 (*Cont.*)		309	dvedhāpatha—'standing at crossroads'
		310	saṃsaya—'succumbing (to hesitation)'
		311	anekaṃsaggāha—'uncertainty (indecision)'
		312	āsappanā—'evasion'
		313	parisappanā—'indecisiveness'
		314	apariyogāhanā—'lack of real grasping'
		315	thāmbhatattaṃ—'vacillation'
		316	cittassa manovilekha— mental perturbation of thought'
Case No. 156B			
81	*uddhacca* (excitement) [MS 317–320]	317	cittassa uddhacca—'excitement of thought'
		318	avūpasama—'agitation'
		319	cetaso vikkhepo—'psychical perplexity'
		320	bhantattaṃ cittassa—'turmoil of thought'
Case No. 157C			
2[c]	*vedanā* [MS 199, 200, 321]	321	cakkhuviññāṇadhātusamphassajaṃ cetasikaṃ neva sātaṃ nāsātaṃ—'neither psychical ease nor unease born of contact with element of eye-consciousness'
		199–200	
3[a]	*saññā* [MS 13, 14, 322]	322	cakkhuviññāṇadhātusamphassajā saññā—'cognition born of contact with element of eye-consciousness'
		13, 14	

(*Cont.*)

No. of △	Name of △	No. of MS	Name of MS
4^{a}	*cetanā* [MS 16, 17, 323]	323	cakkhuviññāṇadhātu samphassajā cetanā—'volition born of contact with element of eye-consciousness'
		16, 17	
5^{a}	*citta* [MS 18–26, 324]	*18–26*	
		324	cakkhuviññāṇadhātu—'element of eye-consciousness'
16^{a}	*manindriya* [As in 5^{a}]	*18–26*	
		324	
Case No. 158C			
2^{d}	*vedanā* [MS 199, 200, 325]	325	sotaviññāṇadhātusamphassajaṃ cetasikaṃ neva sātaṃ nāsātaṃ—'neither psychical ease nor unease born of contact with element of ear-consciousness'
		199, 200	
3^{b}	*saññā* [MS 13, 14, 326]	326	sotaviññāṇadhātusamphassajā saññā—'cognition born of contact with element of ear-consciousness'
		13, 14	
4^{b}	*cetanā* [MS 16, 17, 327]	327	sotaviññāṇadhātusamphassajā cetanā—'volition born of contact with element of ear-consciousness'
		16, 17	
5^{b}	*citta* [MS 18–26, 328]	*18–26*	
		328	sotaviññāṇadhātu—'element of ear-consciousness'
16^{b}	*manindriya* [As in 5^{b}]	*18–26*	
		328	

(*Cont.*)

No. of △	Name of △	No. of MS	Name of MS
Case No. 159C			
2[e]	*vedanā* [MS 199, 200, 329]	329	ghānaviññāṇadhātusamphassajaṃ cetasikaṃ neva sātaṃ nāsātaṃ—'neither psychical ease nor unease born of contact with element of smell-consciousness'
		199, 200	
3[c]	*saññā* [MS 13, 14, 330]	330	ghānaviññāṇadhātusamphassajā saññā—'cognition born of contact with element of smell-consciousness'
4[c]	*cetanā* [MS 16, 17, 331]	331	ghānaviññāṇadhātusamphassajā cetanā—'volition born of contact with element of smell-consciousness'
		16–17	
5[c]	*citta* [MS 18–26, 332]	*18–26*	
		332	ghānaviññāṇadhātu—'element of smell-consciousness'
16[c]	*manindriya* [As △ 5[c]]	*18–26*	
		332	
Case No. 160C			
2[f]	*vedanā* [MS 199, 200, 333]	333	jivhāviññāṇadhatusamphassajaṃ cetasikaṃ neva sātaṃ nāsātaṃ—'neither psychical ease nor unease born of contact with element of taste-consciousness'
		199, 200	
3[d]	*saññā* [MS 13, 14, 334]	334	jivhāviññāṇadhātusamphassajā saññā—'cognition born of contact with element of taste-consciousness'
		13, 14	

(*Cont.*)

No. of △	Name of △	No. of MS	Name of MS
4d	*cetanā* [MS 16, 17, 335]	335	jivhāviññāṇadhātusamphassajā cetanā—'volition born of contact with element of taste consciousness'
		16, 17	
5d	*citta* [MS 18–26, 336]	*18–26*	
		336	jivhāviññāṇadhātu—'element of taste-consciousness'
16d	*manindriya* [As in 5d]	*18–26*	
		336	
Case No. 161C			
2g	*vedanā* [MS 337–342]	337	kāyaviññāṇadhātusamphassajaṃ kāyikaṃ sātaṃ—'bodily ease born of contact with element of body-consciousness'
		338	kāyikaṃ sukhaṃ—'bodily pleasant'
		339	kāyasamphassajaṃ sātaṃ (vedayitaṃ)—'ease (experienced as) born of contact with body'
		340	(kāyasamphassajaṃ) sukhaṃ vedayitaṃ—'the pleasant experienced (as born of contact with body)'
		341	kāyasamphassajā sātā (vedanā) —'(sensation of) ease born of contact with body'
		342	(kāyasamphassajā) sukhā vedanā—'sensation of pleasant (born of contact with body)'
3e	*saññā* [MS 13, 14, 343]	343	kāyaviññāṇadhātusamphassajā saññā—'cognition born of contact with element of body-consciousness'
		13, 14	
4e	*cetanā* [MS 16, 17, 344]	344	kāyaviññāṇdhātusamphassajā cetanā—'volition born of contact with element of body-consciousness'
		16, 17	

(Cont.)

No. of △	Name of △	No. of MS	Name of MS
5^{e}	*citta* [MS 18–26, 345]	*18–26* 345	 kāyaviññāṇadhātu—'element of body-consciousness'
9^{a}	*sukha* [As in △ 2^{g}]	*337–342*	
16^{e}	*manindriya* [MS as in △ 5^{e}]	*18–26* *345*	
82	*sukhindriya* [As in △△ 2^{g}, 9^{a}]	*337–342*	
Case No. 162C			
2^{h}	*vedanā* [MS 199, 200, 346]	346 *199, 200*	manodhātusamphassajaṃ cetasikaṃ neva sātaṃ nāsātaṃ—'neither psychical ease nor unease born of contact with element of mind'
3^{f}	*saññā* [MS 13, 14, 347]	347 *13, 14*	manodhātusamphassajā saññā—'cognition born of contact with element of mind'
4^{f}	*cetanā* [MS 16, 17, 348]	348 *16, 17*	manodhātusamphassajā cetanā—'volition born of contact with element of mind'
5^{f}	*citta* [MS 18–26, 349]	*18–26* 349	 manodhātu—'element of mind'
6^{c}	*vitakka* [MS 28–33]	*28–33*	
16^{f}	*manindriya* [As in △ 5^{f}]	*18–26* *349*	

(*Cont.*)

No. of △	Name of △	No. of MS	Name of MS
Case No. 222C			
2^{i}	*vedanā* [MS 350–355]	350	kāyaviññāṇadhātusamphassajaṃ kāyikaṃ asātaṃ—'bodily unease born of contact with element of body-consciousness'
		351	kāyikaṃ dukkhaṃ—'bodily unpleasant'
		352	kāyasamphassajaṃ asātaṃ (vedayitaṃ)—'unease (experienced as) born of contact with body'
		353	(kāyasamphassajaṃ) dukkhaṃ (vedayitaṃ)—'the unpleasant experienced (as born of contact with body)'
		354	kāyasamphassajā asātā (vedanā)—'(sensation of) unease born of contact with body'
		355	(kāyasamphassajā) dukkhā vedanā—'sensation of unpleasant (born of contact with body)'
76^{a}	*dukkha* [As in △2^{i}]	*350–355*	
83	*dukkhindriya* (faculty of suffering) [As in △△2^{i}, 76^{a}]	*350–355*	

Table VII. Sets of Dharmas

D1 [△△1–56 (56)] No1^{A}

D2 [△△1–14, 16–18, 20–27, 29–32, 34, 35, 37–51, 53, 55, 56 (49)] No3^{A}

D3 [△△1, 2^{a}, 3–7, 10–16, 18–58 (55)] No5^{A}

D4 [△△1–7, 10–14, 16, 18, 20–27, 29–32, 34, 35, 37–51, 53, 55–58 (48)] No7^{A}

D5 [△△1–5, 8–19, 21–56 (53)] No10^{A}

D6 [△△1–5, 9–19, 21–56 (52)] No11^{A}

D7 [△△1–5, 10–16, 18, 19, 21–58 (52)] No12^{A}

D8 [△△1–5, 7–19, 21–56 (54)] No14^{A}

D9 [△△1–5, 6^{a}, 7, 8^{a}, 9, 10^{a}, 11, 12^{a}–15^{a} ,16–18, 19^{a}–23^{a}, 24, 25^{a}–28^{a}, 29–32, 33^{a}, 34, 35, 36^{a}, 37, 38, 39^{a}, 40^{a}, 41–50, 51^{a}–56^{a}, 59–62 (60)] No119^{A}

D10 [△△As in D9+△63 (61)] No144^{A}

D11 [△△1–5, 6^{b}, 7–9, 10^{b}, 12^{b}, 14, 16–18, 25^{b}, 27^{b}, 53^{b}, 55^{b}, 56^{b}, 64–75 (32)] No145^{B}

D12 [△△1–5, 6^{b}, 7–9, 10^{b}, 12^{b}, 14^{b}, 16–18, 25^{b}, 27^{b}, 53^{b}, 55^{b}, 56^{b}, 65–72, 74, 75 (30)] No147^{B}

D13 [△△1, 2^{a}, 3–5, 6^{b}, 7, 10^{b}, 12^{b}, 14^{b}, 16, 18, 25^{b}, 27^{b}, 53^{b}, 55^{b}, 56^{b}, 57, 58, 64–75 (31)] No149^{B}

D14 [△△1, 2^{b}, 3–5, 6^{b}, 7, 10^{b}, 12^{b}, 14^{b}, 16, 18, 25^{b}, 27^{b}, 53^{b}, 55^{b}, 56^{b}, 65–69, 71, 74–79 (29)] No153^{B}

D15 [△△1, 2^{a}, 3–5, 6^{b}, 7, 10^{c}, 12^{b}, 16, 18, 25^{b}, 55^{b}, 57, 58, 65, 66, 68, 69, 71, 74, 75, 80 (23)] No155^{B}

D16 [△△1, 2^{a}, 3–5, 6^{b}, 7, 10^{c}, 12^{b}, 14^{b}, 16, 18, 25^{b}, 27^{b}, 53^{b}, 55^{b}, 56^{b}, 57, 58, 65–69, 71, 74, 75, 81 (28)] No156^{B}

D17 [△△1, 2^{c}, 3^{a}, 4^{a}, 5^{a}, 10^{c}, 16^{a}, 18, 57, 58 (10)] No157^{C}

D18 [△△1, 2^{d}, 3^{b}, 4^{b}, 5^{b}, 10^{c}, 16^{b}, 18, 57, 58 (10)] No158^{C}

D19 [△△1, 2^{e}, 3^{c}, 4^{c}, 5,^{c} 10^{c}, 16^{c}, 18, 57, 58 (10)] No159^{C}

D20 [△△1, 2^{f}, 3^{d}, 4^{d}, 5^{d}, 10^{c}, 16^{d}, 18, 57, 58 (10)] No160^{C}

D21 [△△1, 2^{g}, 3^{e}, 4^{e}, 5^{e}, 9^{a}, 10^{c}, 16^{e}, 18, 82 (10)] No161^{C}

D22 [△△1, 2^{h}, 3^{f}, 4^{f}, 5^{f}, 6^{c}, 7, 10^{c}, 16^{f}, 18, 57, 58 (12)] No162^{C}

D23 [△△1–5, 6^{c}, 7–9, 10^{c}, 16–18 (13)] No163^{C}

D24 [(△1, 2^{a}, 3–5, 6^{c}, 7, 10^{c}, 16, 18, 57, 58 (12)] No164^{C}

D25 [△△1, 2^{i}, 3–5, 10^{c}, 16, 18, 76^{a}, 83 (10)] No222^{C}

D26 [△△1, 2^{i}, 3–7, 10^{c}, 16, 18, 57, 58 (12)] No224^{C}

Table VIII. Correspondences of cases of Rise of thought to the Text of Citta kaṇḍa of Dhs.

No of case	Section §, §§, §§§ etc.	p.	No of case	Section §, §§, §§§ etc.	p.	No of case	Section §, §§, §§§ etc.	p.	No of case	Section §, §§, §§§ etc.	p.	No of case	Section §, §§, §§§ etc.	p.
1.	1.1.1	18–27	48.	1.2.53	57	95.	1.2.100	68	142.	1.5.148	90–1	192.	3.1.38	127
2.	1.1.4	39	49.	1.2.54	57	96.	1.2.101	68	143.	1.5.149	91	193.	3.1.39	127–128
3.	1.1.5	39–40	50.	1.2.55	57	97.	1.2.102	68	144.	1.5.150	91	194.	3.1.40	128
4.	1.1.7	41	51.	1.2.56	57–8	98.	1.2.103	68	145.	2.1.1	92–7	195.	3.1.41	128–129
5.	1.1.8	41–2	52.	1.2.57	58	99.	1.2.104	68	146.	2.1.3	97	196.	3.1.42	129
6.	1.1.10	43	53.	1.2.58	58	100.	1.2.105	68	147.	2.1.4	98	197.	3.1.43	129
7.	1.1.11	43–4	54.	1 2.59	58	101.	1.2.106	68	148.	2.1.6	99	198.	3.1.44	129–130
8.	1.1.13	44–5	55.	1.2.60	58–9	102.	1.2.107	69	149.	2.1.7	99–100	199.	3.1.45	130
9.	1.2.14	45	56.	1.2.61	59	103.	1.2.108	69	150.	2.1.9	100	200.	3.1.46	130–131
10.	1.2.15	45–6	57.	1.2.62	59	104.	1.2.109	69	151.	2.1.10	100–101	201.	3.1.47	131
11.	1.2.16	46–7	58.	1.2.63	59	105.	1.2.110	69	152.	2.1.12	101	202.	3.1.48	131
12.	1.2.17	47	59.	1.2.64	59	106.	1.2.111	69	153.	2.2.13	102–103	203.	3.1.49	131
13.	1.2.18	47–8	60.	1.2.65	59–60	107.	1.3.112	70	154.	2.2.15	103	204.	3.1.50	132
14.	1.2.19	48	61.	1.2.66	60	108.	1.3.113	70	155.	2.3.16	104	205.	3.1.51	132
15.	1.2.20	48–9	62.	1.2.67	60	109.	1.3.114	70	156.	2.3.18	105	206.	3.1.52	132
16.	1.2.21	49–50	63.	1.2.68	60	110.	1.3.115	70	157.	3.1.1	107–108	207.	3.1.53	133
17.	1.2.22	50–1	64.	1.2.69	60–1	111.	1.4.116	70–1	158–161.	3.1.3	109–110	208.	3.1.54	133
18.	1.2.23	51	65.	1.2.70	61	112.	1.4.117	71	162.	3.1.5	111–112	209.	3.1.55	133–134
19.	1.2.24	51	66.	1.2.71	61	113.	1.4.118	71–2	163.	3.1.7	113–115	210.	3.1.56	134
20.	1.2.25	51	67.	1.2.72	61	114.	1.4.119	72	164.	3.1.9	115–117	211.	3.1.57	134
21.	1.2.26	51	68.	1.2.73	61–2	115.	1.4.120	72	165.	3.1.11	117–118	212.	3.1.58	134–135
22.	1.2.27	51–2	69.	1.2.74	62	116.	1.4.121	72–3	166.	3.1.12	118	213.	3.1.59	135
23.	1.2.28	52	70.	1.2.75	62	117.	1.4.122	73	167.	3.1.13	118	214.	3.1.60	135
24.	1.2.29	52	71.	1.2.76	62	118.	1.4.123	73	168.	3.1.14	119	215.	3.1.61	135–136
25.	1.2.30	52	72.	1.2.77	62	119.	1.5.124	74–84	169.	3.1.15	119	216.	3.1.62	136
26.	1.2.31	52	73.	1.2.78	63	120.	1.5.126	85	170.	3.1.16	119–120	217.	3.1.63	136
27.	1.2.32	52	74.	1.2.79	63	121.	1.5.127	85	171.	3.1.17	120	218.	3.1.64	136–137
28.	1.2.33	53	75.	1.2.80	63	122.	1.5.128	85	172.	3.1.18	120	219.	3.1.65	137
29.	1.2.34	53	76.	1.2.81	63	123.	1.5.129	85–6	173.	3.1.19	120–121	220.	3.1.66	138
30.	1.2.35	53	77.	1.2.82	64	124.	1.5.130	86	174.	3.1.20	121	221–222.	3.1.69	139
31.	1.2.36	53	78.	1.2.83	64	125.	1.5.131	86	175.	3.1.21	121	223.	3.1.71	140
32.	1.2.37	53	79.	1.2.84	64	126.	1.5.132	86	176.	3.1.22	121–122	224.	3.1.72	141

Table VIII (*Cont.*)

No of case	Section §, §§, §§§ etc.	p.	No of case	Section §, §§, §§§ etc.	p.	No of case	Section §, §§, §§§ etc.	p.	No of case	Section §, §§, §§§ etc.	p.	No of case	Section §, §§, §§§ etc.	p.
33.	1.2.38	53–4	80.	1.2.85	64	127.	1.5.133	86–7	177.	3.1.23	122	225.	3.2.73	141–142
34.	1.2.39	54	81.	1.2.86	64–5	128.	1.5.134	87	178.	3.1.24	122	226.	3.2.74	142–143
35.	1.2.40	54	82.	1.2.87	65	129.	1.5.135	87	179.	3.1.25	122–123	227.	3.2.76	144
36.	1.2.41	54	83.	1.2.88	65	130.	1.5.136	87	180.	3.1.26	123	228.	3.2.77	144–145
37.	1.2.42	54	84.	1.2.89	65	131.	1.5.137	87	181.	3.1.27	123	229.	3.2.78	145
38.	1.2.43	54	85.	1.2.90	65–6	132.	1.5.138	87–8	182.	3.1.28	123–124	230.	3.2.79	145
39.	1.2.44	54–5	86.	1.2.91	66	133.	1.5.139	88	183.	3.1.29	124	231.	3.2.80	145–146
40.	1.2.45	55	87.	1.2.92	66	134.	1.5.140	88	184.	3.1.30	124	232.	3.2.81	146
41.	1.2.46	55	88.	1.2.93	66	135.	1.5.141	88	185.	3.1.31	124–125	233.	3.2.82	146
42.	1.2.47	55	89.	1.2.94	66–7	136.	1.5.142	88	186.	3.1.32	125	234.	3.2.83	146
43.	1.2.48	55	90.	1.2.95	67	137.	1.5.143	88–9	187.	3.1.33	125–126			
44.	1.2.49	55–6	91.	1.2.96	67	138.	1.5.144	89	188.	3.1.34	126			
45.	1.2.50	56	92.	1.2.97	67	139.	1.5.145	89	189.	3.1.35	126			
46.	1.2.51	56–7	93.	1.2.98	67	140.	1.5.146	90	190.	3.1.36	126–127			
47.	1.2.52	57	94.	1.2.99	67	141.	1.5.147	90	191.	3.1.37	127			

5.1.0. It is in the contexts formed by content of thought, the contexts which otherwise could be termed 'the systems of content', where one can clearly observe (looking at Table V) how thought *operates*. And more importantly, one could see how, being *the subject* of different, mainly dhyanic operations, (i.e. those under variants of content in Table V) thought assumes different *names*. Each of these names denotes, in fact, a certain group of operations, substituting in each of these the term of 'thought' proper, i.e., *citta*. Speaking *semantically*, I am inclined to think of thought as present in dharmas in two essentially different ways: in the sense of its *connotations*, and in the sense of its *meanings*. So, speaking of *connotations* of thought, I may, for example, say that thought (*citta*) taken as a *dharma* (△5, *citta*) connotes all mental states in terms of which this *dharma* is interpreted (i.e., Ms.18–27 in the Table VI) together with these same mental states of $\triangle\triangle 16, 5^a, 16^a$, etc. Whereas, in dealing with *meanings* of thought, I have to establish the direct semantic relation of a *given term* by which thought is denoted in a given particular case, to a certain philosophical, psychological, or any other *content* revealed by means of the context where this term figures. [In the context of dharmas, 'a term' means 'a Pali term', so that in all *our* cases it will be *citta*, not 'thought', the meaning of which is to be revealed!] Therefore, when I say that '*citta* ("thought") is *viññāṇa* ("consciousness"),' the aspect of connotation is involved, while if I say that 'thought (citta) is a state of consciousness (dharma)'—this is, apparently a problem of meaning, which, as such, exceeds the confines of the *text* of *Dhs* and leads us to the Commentaries. I am, however, inclined to think that Buddhaghosa's *Atthasālinī* is of no real help in the understanding of *Dhammasaṅgani* or, more precisely speaking, it may help a lot to comprehend the concepts and notions of this book *syntagmatically* only. That is, the Commentary seems to have been meant to clarify and elucidate their meanings only in so far as they figured in certain, more or less stable and predictable, combinations and not having paid any attention to what could be conventionally named their 'positional semantics'. The last can be conceived of as the sum total of *all positions* of a given term (for example, *citta*), where each position is a *unique combination* of this term with other abhidhammic terms. Or, if we put it the other way around, *the meaning of each abhidhammic term consists* (or, *is the sum*) *of all its positional meanings and of all positional meanings of its connotations.*

5.1.1. The nomenclature of thought (see Table III) reflects in itself one *dimension of thought*, which could be conventionally called 'subjective'. This term I introduce only to underline the fact that, as far as we are concerned with *thought to which a content is ascribed* in the context of rise of thought, this thought could be deemed as what 'has arisen', i.e., as the subject of 'rise' understood in the sense of the most abstract and formal action of all thinkable actions. And such this 'subjectiveness' of thought is itself merely formal, for no more than merely formal is its predication by 'rise'. It is one of the ideas which I have repeatedly tried to *show* (not to *prove*, for it would be totally impossible to try to prove it!)—that *it is thought which thinks in dharmas, not a person.* [Though it is, as it were, a person (*puggala*) that is ascribed to thought (together with 'objects' and 'dharma-objects') by the great commentator, as we see it here in the beginning of Essay 4.] On this point I may go even as far as to assert that, if understood in the sense of 'subjective dimension', thought not only cannot be 'a person', but cannot, so to speak, *think of objects as persons*, for it thinks of objects as objects, and/or of dharmas as objects. [Unless, of course, it has begun thinking of objects as dharmas which, however, would lead us to an absolutely different *quality* of thought, that of 'wisdom' (*paññā*, △15.] The seven 'substitutes' of thought—T.3–9—are, in fact, the seven *modalities* of consciousness, in terms of which thought finds its *concretization*, which means that in these seven groups of cases we have no *one whole mentality* any more—it is given in the Abhidhammic observation as already analysed into seven modalities each of which substitutes thought on the one hand, and figures as or instead of, the whole mentality, on the other. So, for instance, the element of eye-consciousness *sees the visible forms as thought thinks of its objects* (i.e., of the objects which, by definition, belong to *all six* modalities).

The last idea, that thought (or mind, or consciousness) exists not only in its totality, but also in its concrete, 'sensory' as well as 'mental' modalities,[10] is, perhaps, one of the most interesting discoveries made in the Abhidhamma, anticipating some, not yet even 'current' ideas of modern psychology. The idea which becomes more complicated when one sees that the states of consciousness (dhammas) can be either wholesome (*kusala*) or unwholesome (*akusala*) only provided that mentality functions in its totality. Because, when those modalities of consciousness function analytically (we do not know yet whether such this functioning is synchronic or not), the dharmic composition decreases drastically, and the number of dharmas is reduced to 10–12 *indeterminate* dharmas (see Table VI, Nos. 157–222, and Table VII, DD. 17–26). This is probably what can be deemed 'pure' kinds of consciousness, pure not in the sense of any ethical, religious, or even yogic progress, but rather in the sense in which *matter or form* is regarded in the *Abhidhamma* as having nothing to do with either causes or fruits of any action and is, thereby, 'akarmic' (like Nirvana itself).

So, summing up what has been said about this subjective dimension of thought, we may state that thought, in assuming different terms from its nomenclature goes from, shall we say, 'quasi-natural' rises connected with uncontrolled motivations, through various stages of yogic (dhyanic) transformation (where motivations are controlled at first, and then eliminated), culminating in supramundane (*lokuttara*) trances, then, as it were, 'experiences' the regression of unwholesome states of consciousness and, finally, ends up in this digression to a total neutrality of separately functioning modalities of consciousness.

5.1.2. Quite another dimension of thought can be found in the large group of terms which denote dharmas (△△, 'states of consciousness') and dharmic connotations (MS, 'mental states'). It can be shown by the following example: To the thought (*citta*) that 'has arisen' in the context of 'rise' No. 1 (so called 'the first thought') a set of 56 dharmas (D.1) is related. The fifth state of consciousness in this set is also 'thought' (△5, *citta*). The latter, in turn, connotes ten mental states (MS.18–27) the first of which is 'thought' yet again (MS.18). Moreover, there is in this same set the *dharma* of 'faculty of mind' (△16 *manindriya*) the composition of which is the same as that of the *dharma* of thought, i.e., it contains exactly the same mental states (MS.18–27). So we have, so far, the four 'thoughts' termed by the same word (*citta*) and differing from each other only in their respective *positions* in Table VI: 'thought as arisen' (i.e., as 'subject of rise'), thought as △5, thought as MS.18 in △5, and thought as MS.18 in △16. [We can say, thus, that one and the same term, *citta*, has the four different *positional meanings*, for they are different indeed.]

Now, passing to the class of indeterminate dharmas (*dhammā abyākatā*), we see how in the reduced sets of dharmas (DD.17–26), the seven variants of the *dharma* of thought (△△5^a–5^f, and separately, △5) contain in their respective groups of mental states the terms T.3–9 of the nomenclature of thought, in the manner exactly the same as we have seen in the above-mentioned case of *citta:* 'element of eye-consciousness' (*cakkhuviññāṇadhātu*) figures as the subject of rise of thought (T.3), and as a particular mental state [△5^a (and 16^a); MS.324]; 'element of ear-consciousness' (*sotaviññāṇadhātu*, T.4) figures in △5^b and △16^b as MS.328; element of smell-consciousness' (*ghānaviññāṇadhātu*, T.5)—in △5^c (and △16^c) as MS.332, and so on.

We may conceive of this 'dharmic' dimension of thought as of what could be deemed of in a more *objective* way. This is so, not only in view of the fact that dharmas, at least in principle, are *the objects* [even apart from so-called 'dharma-objects' (*dhammārammaṇa*)] but, first of all, because in the context of rise of thought it is thought itself that assumes *the role* of subject *vis-à-vis* dharmas (see Table IX).

5.1.3. Apparently, the content of thought, as seen in Table V, shows that there could be found very few connotations of thought in the composition of its content. The word 'thought' (*citta*) we meet only twice, in the context of rise of thought, where thought is said to be 'superior' and 'dominated by thought' (*cittaṃ paṇītaṃ cittādhipateyyaṃ*, No. 111[b]; C.0; TV.13, 14). However, more important is that we can find in the content of jhanas some indirect indications that thought is present there implicitly as, perhaps, the primary material for subsequent dhyanic transformation. This, it seems to me, can be said of 'unwholesome dharmas' in the content of the first trance (No. 9; C.1). But can we apprehend all dhyanic transformation, or, more precisely speaking, all content of dhyanic thought as transformation of *thought itself?*

Not feeling myself able to answer this question, I would prefer to confine myself to two, so to speak, 'limiting remarks'. Firstly, one can state about each step of dhyanic progression (i.e., the first trance, the second, the third, etc., the first stage (*bhūmi*), the second, etc., and so on), that what each particular case of *dhyāna* has as its content is the *previous* thought (previous in the sense of yogic phasing, not the past in the sense of time external to *dhyāna*), so that each 'not yet transformed thought' is seen (or rather, thought of) as *residual*, not actual, whereas thought that 'has arisen' (as we have it in Nos. 1–8, for instance) is always *actual*. Therefore, the 'unwholesome states of consciousness' of the first *jhāna* might have meant the *specifically* unwholesome dhammas (marked as *akusala* in Table VI), and as such, might have been related to the previous and wholesome thought (*citta*) as *its* dharmas. [Or even, one may conjecture, these dharmas could have figured 'before and/or instead of' thought in their 'subjective' function (see Table IX.).]

My second remark is even more conjectural. There are, in the composition of the content of thought, some moments which point out the *threefold* structure of content, i.e., the implicit classification of content into 'the mental' (*manas* and its derivations), 'the psychical' (*cetas* and its derivations) and 'belonging to or possessing of, form' (*rūpa* and its derivations). This phenomenon of threefoldness—common place in the context of Abhidhamma as the whole, and particularly clearly seen in the lists of dharmas and mental states—could be traced in such elements of content as 'tranquillization of psyche' (No. 10; C.2), 'self-conscious' (No. 11; C.3), 'seeing the external forms' (No. 46; C.5), etc. But the main thing here is that thought itself (which also is present in dharmas in a threefold manner, as 'thought', 'mind', and 'consciousness') cannot retain its *stasis* in the context of a trance. That is why it can only be deduced as lying in the background of every dhyanic content, and externally unobservable.

5.2. What we have here summarily called 'sphere of thought' presents, in fact, the three very different things (see Table IV): the most general quality of thought, the most general quality of states of consciousness, and the most general quality of, shall we say, *sphere* (*avacara*) as such.[11] Needless to say, that in *Dhs.* and in the Abhidhamma in general, the *idea of sphere* was not yet crystallized into a quasi-ontological 'hierarchy of being' of the latest sections and schools of Theravada. In the context of dharmas, 'sphere' means, first of all, a sphere where, or within which, thought *operates*. Or, more precisely speaking, it implies something which, in itself, is no thought, having, at the same time, no concreteness of an empirical object. Or, it even can be said that sphere is a direction, orientation, or tendency of thought, implying, thereby, a certain place still to be attained (as in the case of the four jhanas) *by one whose thought* is, or has been, directed thereto, aimed at, or concentrated on. The concept of 'conscious karma' (*citkarma*) logically links this idea with that of karma so that, practically, one's bad (*akusala*) thought in the present is (in a way, of course!) what will be one's *state* (i.e., 'sphere', *avacara*, *dhātu*, *gati*) in the future. This, of course, is too primitive an explanation, for the whole context of dharmas shows us that this term itself must have been used primarily in some specific and technically determined yogic or dhyanic procedures. And here I will limit myself by simply stating that the very idea of *karma* or karmically caused conditions might have been conceived as one of the elements (or even objects') of 'dhyanic thinking' in early Buddhism.

As for wholesome, unwholesome, or indeterminate dharmas, the problem seems to be far more complex.[12] For it is the context of 'rise of thought' where we see the sets of dharmas separated from the content and, as it were, ousted from 'thought itself' into the very remote periphery of *the topos* of rise of thought. So, I surmise that 'the unwholesome dharmas', for example, mean in *Dhs.* something like 'the unwholesome conditions' with respect to a *thought* in question.

On the whole, the very idea of sphere in the Abhidhamma seems to be directly connected with what could be conventionally called 'the static model of the universe', or 'cosmology', as opposed to 'the universe as a dynamic system', or 'cosmogony'. The latter remained in Buddhism (as well as in other Indian philosophies where the conception of cycles always prevailed) rather undeveloped and was linked with the first by the idea of *thought* (unlike, for example, the Christian—or Judaeo-Christian—tradition, where the role of such link has been played by *man*). That is, perhaps, why the character of sphere is so fragile, changing and dynamic. It varies from a state or direction of thinking in a trance, through a mode of rebirth (*gati*), to a more or less stable (and as it were, 'naturally established') element of division of the universe (*dhātu*).

At the same time, however, this fourfold 'spheric' space-model of the universe might have served as a mere instance of yogic (dhyanic) technique, that is, as one of purely *formal* elements of the Abhidhammic framework of *dhyanic thinking on thought*.[13]

5.3.0. I deem that after looking at Table V, one may well have conceived a queer idea that what is seen as a *causal* interdependence between content, set of dharmas and mental variables, is in fact, a purely *topological scheme*, a certain spatial configuration—not a temporal sequence—determining *the type* of thought in a given case. That is, in 234 main cases of the rise of thought, enumerated in *Dhs.* we have 234 different configurations. Different in the sense that each of them differs from any other in, at least, one of the elements constituting the rise of thought. Moreover, I am even inclined to suppose that this 'topology of configurations' or 'sphere of differences'—instead of 'sequence of changes'—might have served in the time of the Old Masters of Abhidhamma as a very specific principle of establishing and recreating in recollection *the whole* picture of consciousness, as it is (can be, may be) configurated in the 'space' of rise of thought.

The principle of 'rise of thought' seems to me to be in itself radically different from a more formal (and mainly based on associations) principle expressed in the *mātikā* of *Dhs.* And, if I may surmise, it reflects in itself or is oriented to, an absolutely different kind of 'conscious memory', the memory which is not processual (i.e., 'cognized as a process'), which is not based on temporal associations, and the mechanism of which, supposedly, might have been of a quasi-visual (or 'eidetic') nature. This, in itself, is by no means unnatural, since a classical type of *oral* (repetitory) tradition of texts cannot be technically maintained only by means of verbal-auditive process, as in the case of a written tradition. It has to be reinforced and accompanied (say, 'doubled') by a kind of configurative reproduction, which can be, in its turn, regarded as a special state of consciousness.

[5.3.0.1. One may putatively suggest that this state of consciousness is *sati* ('recollection'), that is, △△13, 22, 26, 51 with their variants and corresponding mental states (see Table VI). Of enormous interest is the fact that *sati* is included only in the ten sets of dharmas (D1–10), i.e., in those consisting of wholesome dharmas only. So, it seems to be a wholesome dharma par excellence, and is, therefore, present only in the first 144 cases of rise of thought, being thus excluded both from karmically unwholesome dharmas and from those of karmically indeterminate kind (i.e., nearest to Nirvana). *Sati*, unlike *samādhi*, cannot be 'wrong' or 'mistaken' (*micchā* as opposed to *sammā*) and could, therefore, be seen as a 'quasi-natural' state, the state of *predisposition to the cultivation of recollection.* The term 'recollection' means neither the process of memorization or remembering, nor the sequence or order of the elements of the content of memory, but rather an ability to keep and maintain in one's mind simultaneously all elements of the spatial configuration of a given 'case'. The ability, for instance, momentarily to recollect *any thought* whatsoever together with its 'empty' content (empty because of its being reduced to contentless dharmas) and some additional thoughts of a general character, such, for instance, as that each thought is momentary, or that the continuity of thoughts of the past, present and future does not constitute an individual being.[14]]

5.3.0.2. Thus Table V can be regarded (if taken as a whole) as a space where all possible (not only actual, that is) types of thought are present synchronously (except those which do not belong to any type, of course). This, however, is not 'the space of psychology', for the psychological information included therein is not given to us in terms of mental phenomena taken in their formation or origin, evolution or development. There are these phenomena present, as if all their *processual* existence had been left far behind *before* they started coinciding with one another within the context of one or another rise of thought or, speaking metaphorically, before they entered *the space of types of thought* designed in Table V. One may even guess that what we indeed deal with in any European psychology whatsoever, is these very mental phenomena, but investigated from the point of view and in terms of, secondary processes of their *complex functioning.*

So, in trying to show the essential difference between the Buddhist theory of thought based on the principle of rise of thought and the theory of thought in European psychological tradition, I would emphasize that the latter commences its investigation of mental phenomena when they have already formed their sequential combinations with one another, assuming therewith the character and form of temporal causal processes. The Buddhist theory of thought starts with the second phase of investigation, that is, when we pass from the thought taken in its momentary (*khaṇika*) rise to *sequences* of rises of thought, and then we would have to leave this table, and pass to a far more complex picture. A picture where the microcosm of rise of thought would give place to the macrocosm of individual 'continuum (or stream) of thought' (*cittasantāna*) which, in its turn, will be waiting to be identified with a 'subject' (*puggala*) of thought. And then we will be able, taking this *puggala* as a new starting point, to return to our previous position—that of rise of thought with its subject, objects, dharmic objects, etc., and to re-start the play all over again. But unless we have performed this transition from the 'space of types of thought' to 'time sequences' of thoughts, no psychology could possibly be introduced—nor could it exist after we have left 'continuum of thought' and turned out attention to its 'subject'.

5.3.1. It can be clearly seen by now that, from the Abhidhammic point of view (understood as based on rise of thought and its topology), the sphere of psychology seems to be confined to the macrocosm of 'continuum of thought', and that is why all attempts to deduce the *processual* psychological knowledge from the pure phenomenology of the Abhidhamma have, so far, been proved to be so short-lived and futile.

It can also be said that, as far as the microcosm of rise of thought has no *inner time* of its own (in the sense that duration of *one* separate thought, though duration in itself, cannot allow any event to happen other than itself), the very idea of time here remains merely *formal.* And no less formal would then be the time of an occurrence or case (*samaya*) wherein a thought coincides with all other elements of rise of thought, shown in Table V. So, strictly, speaking, each separate case (and/or type) of thought constitutes its own *unique* spatial configuration within which no *temporal event* is possible. Given that there can be no psychology whatsoever without temporal interpretation of the inner causality in an objectively observed process, we may go even further and assert that the Buddhist *typology* of thought, being par excellence a *topological* typology, cannot be psychologically analysed. The *idea* of time may, therefore, appear only when we have not only sequences of rises of thought, but when there are thoughts of *more than one type* in such a sequence. That is to say, when we have observed what in the *Vijñānavāda* doctrine assumed the name of 'transformation' (*pariṇāma*) of consciousness, provided that time itself can be thought of only by this transformed consciousness and by nothing else.[15]

5.3.2. At the same time, it must be borne in mind that we cannot think of the whole scheme—(1) thought before (or outside) the rise of thought; (2) thought as the rise of thought, and (3) thought in the sequences of rises of thought

—as of a temporal model of thought too. This is so not only because, in the sense of this scheme, time would have different meanings (i.e., could be differently observed by an external observer), but also because in each of three phases of our scheme one would have *a different thought*. Or, to express it in terms of an external observer, a different *idea* of thought. So, in the first phase a thought can be thought of as dharmas only, while in the second phase it is *thought itself* with which dharmas do coincide in the configuration of a given case. And finally, in the third phase it is consciousness (*viññāṇa*) instead of thought. It is obvious that a *single* rise of thought cannot be observed: an observation is possible only when there are transformations in a thought (or in thoughts) observed.

Table IX shows the differences in three phases of the scheme discussed above.

Table IX. The Differences in Three Phases of Rise of Thought

Phase	Thought	Subject	Object	Time	Content
I.	**dharmas**	None	None	0	0
II.	**citta** (thought)	subject of thought **puggala**	**dharmas** and other objects	—	0—+
III.	**viññāṇa** (consciousness)	subject of continuum of thought **(purisa)**	**citta** and other objects and subjects	+	0

It is the second phase which is presented in Table V as the totality of all types of thought in all main cases of rise of thought. In observing the configurations of elements constituting these types (or rather, configurations of units constituting these 'rises') one may notice that some of the main features (if not all of them) are due first of all to the 'place' (*topos*) of a given type or group of types in Table V, and these features could hardly be understood from the description of the content of thought of a type in question.

5.3.3. The very formulation 'has arisen' (*uppannaṃ hoti*) constitutes the *minimum of content of thought*, and this is what we have in fact, when we deal with the first eight cases of rise of thought called in *Dhs*. 'The eight thoughts'. In these cases 'thought has arisen', having such objects as objects, the objects of senses, and dharmic objects, accompanied or not accompanied by and associated or dissociated from, five mental variables, and connected with a certain number of wholesome dharmas (varying from 56 to 49). The content of thought remains, however, the same in all eight cases—'has arisen'. And it is to be reckoned with a kind of *pure content*, that is, the content of thought which is neither complicated by a yogic process (as in further hundreds of cases), nor is drastically reduced, as when connected with indeterminate dharmas. This invariability of the minimum of content is pertaining to what can be called 'the normal thought', and remains as the unchangeable *basis* of all other contents when thought named as *citta*, *viññāṇa*, *manodhātu*, or *manoviññāṇadhātu*, is not substituted by a state of trance (*jhāna*). Although, even in the last case, when a trance is deliberately and consciously produced, induced, or attained (i.e., *upasampanna* instead of, so to speak, *uppanna*), the *form* of this basic content remains the same in all variants and combinations of variants of content of dhyanic thought. We may speak of this 'minimum of content' as of the 'zero content' of thought, and consider it as the 'contentless core' of each thought—the fact, as it were, of fixation of its becoming.

When we say 'content', and when, of course, the content in question is, so to speak, ampler than a 'zero content', that is, when we deal with one or another form of trance, then, what we mean by this very saying, is everything that is to be performed *within a thought*, here within a *jhāna* (and not only *by means of a jhāna*). Which in turn means—and to see it, is enough to look at Table V—that each of its units is a certain point of dhyanic transformation of what can be theoretically deemed to be psychically natural. [Note here, 'psychically', not 'psychologically', for, as a strictly descriptive discipline, psychology cannot be concerned with such evaluative categories as 'natural' or 'artificial'.] Psychically natural —which is, given primarily, before transformation, that is, merely on the strength of a rise of thought alone. And so we have—as is clearly shown by the first page of the table of content—the 'space' of psychical naturality, where the content is the zero-content, and where the eight rises of thought differ from each other not in content, but in mental variables and, to a lesser extent, in their dharmic composition.

5.3.4. Following the succession of types of thought in Table V from the case No. 9 downwards, we see how thought (*jhāna*—'trance', instead of *citta*—'thought') acquires its concrete content. And this is not only because of concrete and specific *yogic* objects of thought, such as dhyanic devices (*kasiṇa*), etc., but also because of concretization of thought itself in terms of its content. From this ensues that all characteristics of thought become its content (irrespective of whether this content is positive or negative). When, for instance, one is said to get rid of unwholesome dharmas (Table V, C.1), to suppress the reasoning and reflexion (C.2), to become dispassionate (C.3), or to avoid the pleasure and suffering (C.4)—all this constitutes, as it were, the inner content of thought which (in these very cases) is the 1st, or the 2nd, or the 3rd, or the 4th *jhāna* (trance). And when the dhyanic (trancic, so to speak) thought is said, for example, to be limited (No. 23, C.1, TV.5), 'limited' (*paritta*) here is not an abstract quality of thought (or, say, 'a name' as when we deal with dharmas), but an entirely concrete quality related to a certain step or stage in the yogic transformation of thought. [This in itself, is very significant particularly in view of the fact that 'a thought in general' (*citta*) cannot be either 'limited' or 'immeasurable' (*appamāṇa*, No. 25, TV.8) which qualities can be acquired in the context of a trance (*jhāna*) only.]

One may assert that each type of dhyanic thought possesses its own and unique system of content, within which one can discern a more or less definite twofold orientation of thought: the thought is *quasi-reflexive*, that is, directed to itself, but not to its subject (*puggala*) or to itself understood *as* its subject, and at the same time, this very thought is *quasi-objective*, that is, directed to objects internal and external.[16]

5.3.5. It is within these systems of content that one can observe such examples of, as it were, 'pure content' as exclamations and speech from the first or third person: 'Indifferent and recollectful, he abides in pleasure...' (No. 11, C.3), '[and saying] I know, I see...' (No. 46, C.5^b), '[saying] how beautiful!' (No. 92, C.7). This, it seems to me, shows that the *theory* of trance, as epitomized in *Dhs.* must have included certain cliches and patterns of expressions for specifically yogic content of a type of thought in question.

We may even consider the 'zero-content' of the first eight cases as opposed to the 'pure content' in the above-mentioned examples as to a sort of 'content within content'. The latter would thus be seen as the examples of, shall we say, *extreme contentfulness* in some of the cases of dhyanic thought. But there is another difficulty concerning the problem of content in *Dhs.* I think that, starting from the case of rise of thought No. 46 (C.5, 5^a, 5^b [1]), almost all contents become complex, i.e., are combinations of at least two different contents of thought (not to speak of objects of thought and trancic and mental variables). Looking at Table V, we see that from case No. 46 downward, these combinations grow more numerous, forming the huge 'combined contents' reminding one of gigantic molecules in biological chemistry. The principle of their formation, however, remains the same: no hierarchical order can be seen *within* those complex contents, and the very *fact* of rise of thought remains the nucleus, around which all contents in question are synchronously combined into one system of content, being, as it were, 'subsystems' thereof. The examples of so-called pure content might then be understood as a sort of *mark* by which the *objectivity* of dhyanic mental states included in the content of *jhāna* finds its formally subjective expression.[17]

5.3.6. As we have already asserted, almost all content of thought in *Dhs.* is trancic, i.e., either included in a *jhāna* or implied thereby. There can be practically no ordinary mental experience there. [Apart, of course, from 'thought has arisen' itself, which does not, in itself at least, contain any experience at all.][18] Moreover, this zero-content also could be seen as if it were not the initial, natural and pristine state of thought, but as the final result of reduction of some utterly complex yogic state (or states) of thought to the simplest thinkable element which can be given to thought only in a yogic analysis of the Abhidhamma. That is why we ought not to maintain the existence of any *natural psychology* at all. For the idea of *normal* mentality can be seen in the light of the Abhidhamma doctrine only as an *abstract derivation* or *reduction* from the states of 'yogic' mentality. Provided that such a result itself can be achieved in the process of a *jhāna* only.

This idea applies also to components of rise of thought other than its content. The 'vertical' hierarchy of the four spheres ('sensuous', 'belonging to form', 'formless', and 'supramundane') also may be regarded in the light of such kind of reduction. The sensuous sphere could be thought of as the place where thought does not attain any concrete stage, phase or level of *jhāna*. That is why this phase is sensuous, not the other way around. That is, we cannot state that there is no *jhāna* in this phase because there is sensuality (*kāma*) there, for sensuality itself appears not as an initial and 'natural' phase of mental development or evolution, but as an instance of dhyanic 'projection' of a state of thought without *jhāna*.

5.3.7. This may lead one to still another consideration of more general character: content of thought in *Dhs.* implies no *actual* yogic (or any other, for that matter) experience, but rather its *future* plan (projection). I use the term 'future' here not as a tense, but only in the sense of the *semantic reference* of an actual, past or future action, word or thought to the time when they *will have taken place* (in the context of the content of thought). So, when one says: 'I know (*jānāmi*)'—he knows it in the future, as well as he will master them (the forms) in the future (Table V, No.46, C.5^b). Moreover, when one's thought is said to be connected with the present dharma (*diṭṭhadhamma*—literally, 'the seen dharma' No.229, C.22), this *dharma* will be, as it were, 'presently' connected with one's thought in the future too. This phenomenon of projection reflects two very interesting trends in the early Buddhist yoga.

5.3.7.1. The first is that our notion of 'experience' can be, speaking terminologically, applied here with some reservation. The very meaning of *jhāna* implies that, whatever experience there might be, it had already been dispensed with *before*

Table X. Dhyanic Transformations of Mental States in the Content of the Four Trances

No. of Case	Negative Mental States	Positive Mental States	States of Dhyanic Transformation
0.		pre-dhyanic states	
9.	'sensuality', 'unwholesome dharmas' (C.1)	'reasoning', 'reflexion' (C.1^a, 1^b) 'joy and pleasure' (C.1^d)	'separation' (C.1^c)
10.	'reasoning', 'reflexion'	'joy', 'pleasure'' 'non-reasoning' 'non-reflexion' (2^a, 2^b)	'tranquillization and fixation of psyche' (C.2) 'concentration' (C.2^c)
11.	'joy and passion' (C.3)	'pleasure' (C.3)	'indifference', 'recollection', 'self-awareness' (C.3)
12.	'pleasure', 'suffering', mental gladness', 'mental sorrow' (C.4)	'without suffering and pleasure' (C.4)	'utter purity attained by recollection and indifference' (C.4^b)

one actually started his *anti-experience* of Buddhist yoga. I even dare suppose that a total *neutralization* of all previous experiences marks the point of departure of any yogic process. Then the whole content of dhyanic thought could have been imagined as three series of mental states—those *untransformed* and thereby to be got rid of, those, as it were, taking their place, and those which are specifically yogic or dhyanic in their character.

The right-hand column of Table X contains the terms of six dhyanic states by means of which the nine *ordinary* mental states (called 'negative') are eliminated from the content of dhyanic thought (called 'positive'). When seen *vertically*, this can be thought of as the process of *gradual* transformation of mentality where, however, the most significant moment of any experience is lacking: in the course of the dhyanic progression there can be no assimilation or accumulation of data of present or previous phases.[19] No new (dhyanic) state could appear in a *next jhāna* without disappearance of a *certain* mental state from the content of a given *jhāna*. So, we may say that the dhyanic transformation is directed, as it were, through the past to the future (with respect, of course, to dhyanic processes only), and then it can be said of the C.1 that it could have been eliminated from some 'pre-dhyanic' mentality by means of separation (C.1[c]) and, therewith, as it were, ousted into 'non-dhyanic' sphere (i.e., that of sensuous world) *before* the first *jhāna* started. This direction of dhyanic transformation of mentality as shown in the table is confined to *one given* sphere (see Table V). [Though in the case of the first *jhāna* it may be argued that the elimination of or separation (*viveka*) from, 'sensuality' and 'unwholesome dharmas' might have taken place in the 'non-yogic' space of the sensuous sphere.] This becomes evident when we have understood a merely dhyanic fact that *no progress within one sphere* (e.g., 'sensuous') could help one in the attainment of or the progress within, another sphere (e.g., 'sphere of form'). Therefore, if we conceive of experience as the consciously accumulated activity of the past, consciously actualized in the present, then such an experience would matter only within the sensuous sphere and, it can be said, within one's one life only. [For once experience becomes 'karmic' it ceases to be conscious, changing into an *objective* karmic factor, whereas once it becomes dhyanic (i.e., pertaining to the 'realm of form'), it begins being ousted into one's 'mental past'.] That is why, at least from the point of view of an external observer, the content of a yogic thought is present as a *conscious projection of what this thought is going to become through its separation from some elements of the 'previous' content.*

The term 'born of samadhi' (*samādhija*, C.2[c]) is particularly interesting, for it establishes a definite connection between these two most important terms in early Buddhist yoga—*jhāna* and *samādhi. Jhāna* figures here not in general, yet as a quite concrete *stage* of trance (the first, the second, etc.), and is deemed as attainable through, by means of, or, even *after*, some other yogic practices. This, of course, would not prevent *samādhi* from being practised *within* the first trance and taking therewith, the place of *viveka* ('separation', C.1[c]) which plays the same role as *samādhi*, though in the context of some pre-trancic (i.e., occurring *before* the first *jhāna)* yogic states. Therefore, there could be a reason to suppose that we probably have, as it were, two parallel series of yogic practices—*jhāna* and *sa-*

mādhi—and the latter can be seen as performed (or, performable) within the first, being a part of its content.

5.3.7.2. The second moment—far more important philosophically, though far less clear—is the conventional division of all dharmas into those of past, present and future. Such a classification implies their relation to thought and/or a person to whom the thought in question is ascribed. [And then one may even agree with some of the *Vaibhāṣika* purists in that they consider the present dharmas as more real, or even only real of these three.] If, however, thought is regarded as primary with respect to dharmas which, as we have seen in Table V, would find themselves as it were, in the periphery of content of thought—then the only 'more or less real' time is that wherein the content of thought is transformed, that is, the future. Given, of course, that, as has been mentioned above, we deal with *more than one* content of more than one thought, that these contents are differrent, and that we observe these differences as *transformations* of one thought into another, seen from an external point of view. For we know that thought's 'minimum-content' (not 'zero-content'!) is, shall we say, the minimum of dhyanic content, attributed to 'a subject' (*puggala*) whose (as it were 'previous') thought has already been transformed, as is seen from Table X, whereas states of dhyanic transformation (such as *viveka*, *samādhi*, *sati*, etc.) themselves always refer to a future actualization or realization. I may even dare to suggest that, what is deemed to be 'the dharmas of the present' is, in fact, a *reduced reflection* of future configurations of content of already transformed thought. [The zero-content—'(thought) has arisen'—may then be conceived as the 'maximum of reduction'.] This quasi-future thought, i.e., thought the content of which has been induced by a future dhyanic procedure, could be imagined as 'arisen' at this or that 'present' moment only because all cases (*samaya*) of rise of thought are listed in *Dhs.* and suchlike texts to be recollected as 'the past in present from the future'.

[5.3.7.3. The problem has been still more complicated by a typically European *compulsoriness of time* with respect to the 'discreteness' of dharmas. I think, that in the context of Abhidhamma the *topos* of *dharma* is a far more significant thing. One may say in a more than metaphorical way that dharmas belong to the *microcosmos* of thought i.e., to the 'rise of (a separate) thought' (*cittuppāda*) i.e., coincidence of a thought with its objects (including dharmas) and subjects (persons—*puggalas*). And this is said in the sense in which an individual 'continuum of thought' could be thought of as constituting the *macrocosm* of thought, and 'interpersonal' phenomenon of *citkarma* (i.e., karma of thought) as constituting its *cosmic* aspect.

The dharmas, however, have nothing to do with the dimension of time at all. For their own continuity is no more than a *method* of naturalization, which has been used in the latest Abhidhammic works to have the dharmas apprehended as the 'units of conscious being'. And the current Abhidhammic expression—'the dhammas of the present, past, and future'—in no way means that there is *time* where there are the dhammas. On the contrary, it is the dhammas that we represent *as time* in our own 'representational' consciousness or, speaking more exactly, 'time' figures as a *secondary* consciousness of, or with respect to, the dharmas. The same can be said, I suppose, about a current Mahayanic expression—'the Buddhas of the past, present, and future'. Moreover, the rendering itself of a *dharma* as 'a state of consciousness' allows for a possibility—if not a certainty—of interpreting *dharma* in an *achronic* way. And that is what W. James tried to do with his 'states of consciousness'.[20]]

5.4.1. The so-called 'trancic variables' are particularly interesting, because they constitute the only segment in the rise of thought which has, so to speak, no existence of its own, and figures only as the optional complement to some of the variants of the content of thought. In saying this I mean, on the one hand, that the characteristics of thought, which are used as trancic variables are not specific or essential to thought either taken in positive or in negative ways. So, when we see 'slow' or 'rapid' among them, we do not see them as inherent qualities which must be ascribed to dhyanic thought alternatively. On the contrary, the dhyanic thought can, with respect to these two variables, exist as either slow, or rapid, or as it were, without any reference to its being either. [This, by the way, means that we do not deal with any kind of binary opposition of quality in these variables, for 'slow' here is an independent quality of thought, not the absence of 'rapidity', and the absence of both these variables simply means that we deal with 'yet another case' of dhyanic thought.] On the other hand, none of those variables can figure without being connected with the *content* of a *jhāna*. That is, they cannot be met among other segments of rise of thought, as well as among states of consciousness (dharmas) or their connotations (i.e., mental states).

5.4.2. At the same time, however, one has to take into account that in two trancic variables (TV) out of sixteen we have the terms denoting two very important Buddhological categories: the process (or 'way', 'path', *paṭipāda*), and special knowledge (or 'super-knowledge', *abhiññā*). The first obviously refers to one's progression on the Path,[21] and deals with one's individual *intellectual* (rather than mental or psychical) capacity (such as cleverness, skilfulness, quickness of wit, etc.). The second refers to a far higher level of one's progress, probably involving also some karmic—i.e., not only dhyanic—factors, i.e., the level on which one finds oneself in possession of means to transform the *natural* properties, tendencies and propensities of one's psyche.

5.5. A lot has been said about objects of thought, more, perhaps, than about anything else in the inventory of the Buddhist yoga. So here I will limit myself to two brief observations concerning what seems to be the problem of *classification of objects* rather than objects themselves. And, indeed, it is enough to look at these objects in Table V to form a clear idea of their general classification and structure with respect to other segments of the rise of thought and, first of all, to its content.

The first observation is, that all objects of jhanas are divided into those presented to dhyanic thought as *devices* (*kasiṇa*) and those which are thought of and concentrated upon as *notions* (*saññā*—also 'cognition', 'apperception', 'perception', 'idea', and what not!) But why on earth, one may naively ask, two such *essentially* different objects as, say, 'a swollen corpse (No, 105; 0.9) and 'the basis of unbound consciousness' (No. 108; 0.20) must be seen as 'notions', whereas 'water' (No.45; 0.2) figures as 'a device'? My guess is that the *essence*, or *matter* of objects does not matter here at all. What we may have observed here is, probably, two different kinds of *thought*, or, more precisely, of *mental yoga*, with their respective sets of objects (denoted, consequently, by two different technical terms). One may even conjecture that 'devices' might have belonged to an older type of trance or meditation, and confined to the four *jhanas* only, while 'notions' could have appeared in some later description of, perhaps, more specifically *ascetic* yogic achievements.[22]

The second observation concerns quite another division of objects. In all cases connected with indeterminate dharmas, we observe a *reduction* in the number of objects (in Nos. 157–161 from six objects to one, in No. 162 from six to five, etc.), that could be regarded as one of the most common features to, practically, all kinds of yoga, though, speaking technically, those cases were not dhyanic (unless they have been combined with jhanas, as in Nos. 166–231). Moreover, taking into account that those cases are also related to the sets of dharmas with the number of dharmas drastically reduced (from 61 in No. 144 to 32 in No. 145 and to 10 in No. 157, see Table VII), we may surmise that the transition to Nirvana may be thought of as connected with a certain 'thinness', 'tenuousness' of consciousness (or even its 'compressed-ness'). This can find its expression either in diminution ('concentration') in objects, or reduction in dharmas, or in both.

5.6.1. As for *mental variables*, one may state with certainty that, at least if considered in the context of rise of thought, they link the content of a thought with a set of dharmas *corresponding* to this thought. That is, if taken, so to speak, in its most elementary type (No. 1; C.0; MV.1, 2), the thought corresponds to the set of dharmas (D.1) comprising all 56, shall we say, 'normal' states of consciousness. By saying 'normal' I mean, first of all, that they are 'wholesome' (*kusala*) and secondly, that they do not count variants among them, serving thereby, as a kind of an *exemplary* dharmic composure of the 'wholesome thought' (*cittaṃ kusalaṃ*). The two first mental variables—'mental gladness' and 'knowledge'—seem to make of the zero-content of the first thought (No. 1) a point of departure, opening the widest range of possibilities for further transformation.

However, unlike a *jhāna* in its connection with trancic variables, a thought cannot exist without mental variables. That is to say that, if, in the case of *jhāna* it may have one trancic variable or another, or not have any of them at all, in the case of thought a thought as such (i.e., when denoted by *citta*) must have at least two mental variables, although a *jhāna* can have one mental variable, as, for instance, the fourth *jhāna* has 'indifference' (MV 5) in No 104.

5.6.2. Now we could reformulate the last consideration by asserting that mental states called here 'mental variables', are related *unconditionally* to the *fact* of thought, and no more than optionally to its *content*. Let us be reminded now that, speaking strictly Abhidhammically, *the content of thought is what thought does to itself, or how it operates with itself.* Until this has happened thought can have its objects (as well as 'subjects' in the sense of 'quasi-personal' attribution), yet not its *own* content which is all in transformation and projection. Therefore, when one reads: '... thought has arisen accompanied by mental gladness and associated with knowledge...'—these two mental variables have to be understood as *what is happening with* thought and at the very moment of its *actualization*—that is, neither in retrospect nor, least of all, in projection!

So, the thought which, in this particular case (No. 1) is nothing but 'wholesome' (*kusala*), occurs *together with* 'mental gladness' and 'knowledge' which, as mental variables, connect this thought's 'zero-content' with the corresponding set of dharmas (D.1) where mental gladness figures as △17 (*somanassindriya*—'faculty of mental gladness'), whereas 'knowledge' (*ñāṇa*) does not figure either among the dharmas of any set, or among their connoted mental states. This can, indirectly at least, speak in favour of a suggestion that in mental variables we have a kind of mental states relatively independent from the thought's dharmic composition and, if looked at from the point of view of an external observer who is observing them *together with thought*, determining the dharmic composition of a thought in question. [And this is lucidly shown by the position of mental variables in the context of rise of thought in the first eight 'thoughts' of *Dhs.*]

5.6.3. And, finally, looking at Table V, we see yet one more feature of mental variables, that seems to be of a considerable metaphysical significance. I dare define this feature in the following way: When a mental state in question (e.g., 'mental gladness') is *absent* (as in No. 5) this, in itself, does not imply the presence of its opposite. That is, in this particular case it can be stated that it is opposed not to 'mental sorrow' [*domanassa*, N.153; MV.11; △77 (*domanassindriya*)], but to 'indifference' (*upekkhā*, MV.5 and △△57, 58). This, in turn, suggests that the last is opposed to both 'mental gladness' and 'mental sorrow' not taken together (for there is no such a context in *Dhs.*), but regarded in their concrete respective contexts only. So, there can be no binary opposition there. At the same time, such mental variables as 'association with knowledge' and 'dissociation from knowledge' (MV. 2, 4) must be seen not as negative with respect to *one another*, but as totally independent mental states of the wholesome thought which necessarily *connotes the knowledge* (either in negative or in positive ways). This can be seen as yet another example of the Buddhist philosophical attitude to see negative notions as independent, not as denying the respective positive ones.

5.7.0. In speaking about dharmas here, I will confine myself strictly and rigidly to the merely *formal* aspect of their presence within the context of rise of thought only, which means that neither the problem of their *general meaning*, nor the problem concerning their *analytical meanings* [i.e., their figuring as aggregates (*khandha*), elements (*dhātu* etc.] are not going to be touched upon in this section (see below, in Essay 6).

According to the scheme outlined in the second essay, the dharmic line is regarded as one of the three ways by which or through which the Buddhist theory of thought and or consciousness can find its *approximate* or*pression.* But again, this expression would necessarily remain formal unless we have endowed it either with a psychological meaning, or with an ontological status. What we indeed can and must do here, is to ask the simplest question: What are the dharmas in connection with and with respect to the thought within the context of 'rise of thought'?

In answering this question, I will make four remarks.

5.7.1. By paraphrasing what has been said in 5.1, we can say that a *dharma* is a state of consciousness, not only generally related to a given (i.e., arising in one of 234 cases) thought as *one* of the dharmas of a given set of dharmas, but also connoted by this thought in a more specific way, i.e., bearing one of its *positional meanings*. So, it is through a positional meaning that a *dharma* or a mental state can be, in an *inverse* order, identified as this thought or thought in general. What, however, we must constantly bear in mind is that this identification is absolute only in an *individual* case of 'rise', not for a group of cases or all cases taken together.

5.7.2. When we look at 'thought' as a *dharma* (No. 1; D.1; △5, *citta*) we see that it connotes ten terms of mental states (MS.18–27) and contains eleven positional meanings (for MS.19—*manas*—figures there twice, the first time in the natural order of numbers, and the second between MS.22 and 23). This also means that, apart from the most general sense in which all dharmas 'are the thought' (or mind), there is the 'cluster' of meanings with each of them, and with all of them taken together, thought may become identified. Thus all thinkable dharmas can be thought of, at a given moment of rise of a given thought, of course, as *this* thought taken in all *its* states. The problem, however, is, in fact, far more complicated, and requires yet one more angle of consideration.

5.7.3. It is, perhaps in the context of rise of thought only, that all dharmas are presented from the point of view of 'thought arisen', and in no other way, for the very formula 'when such-and-such thought has arisen,... then there are such-and-such dharmas' tells nothing at all about the way of their (i.e., dharmas') origination, coming into existence or 'flowing into' one's individual stream of thought. Because, now we deal neither with 'one' nor 'a stream', but with a *separate thought* to which no aspect of mind (*manas*) can be ascribed. And in this connection I cannot help conjecturing about one thing already touched upon in the third essay. It is not at all strange that the first two lines of the Dhammapada have not been commented upon in the tradition of so-called Great Commentation. For *mind* it was, not *thought* (*citta*), of which, from which, and because of which the dharmas were spoken of as *made*, *originated*, etc. And this was their (dharmas') *manner of being* (or, at least, becoming), not the way in which they were *thought of*. And that is, probably (nobody can be sure!) why the 'dharmic question' was then, as it were, 'dismissed' as taken for granted, and did not appear any more in the Dhammapada.

5.7.4. One may, however, take one step further and go on speculating on the possibility of seeking, if not finding out, in this very direction, the main difference between the natural dogmatic vision in the Suttas, and the dhyanic *theory* in *Dhs*. Therefore, in the latter the set of dharmas (D) does not change when the thought changes, or, speaking more technically, when we pass from one *case* to another (see 5.0.3. and Table VII). On the contrary, when we have a certain thought arisen, it *connotes* (or, shall we say, 'is thought of as') a certain set of dharmas and *through* them, the respective complexes of mental states (MS). So, in the sense of such a theoretical approach, one cannot even assert that a *dharma* is a discrete state of consciousness, for this particular consciousness (thought) is already given to us as a discrete and momentary *case*. So, bearing in mind what has been called 'the dharmic line' in Buddhist theory of thought (in the beginning of the second essay), on the one hand, and what we have so far said about positional meanings of thought, on the other, we may venture and come to the conclusion that *all positional meaning of thought in Dhs. constitute, side by side with, and apart from, the unity of thought, its variety and even plurality*. And then we can say that one thing is thought as such, i.e., taken in its individual rise only, quite another is thought as △5, yet another as △16, yet another as MS.18, and so on. And all this, of course, not to speak of *non-dharmic* differences of thought itself as, for example, is the difference between thought in the case No. 1 and thought in the case No. 2, etc.

5.7.4.0. The classification of dharmas presents an aspect of the theory of dharmas (*dharmavāda*) very different in its character and scope from the aspect of content (i.e., not content of dharmas, of course, but 'content' understood as a point of view, from which one can consider them).

No classification of dharmas can help us in our attempts to understand their nature, for all dharmic classifications are *relational*, while the idea of the nature of dharmas (*dharmatā*) implies, in principle at least, an *inner* point of view. Thus, the classification of 56 wholesome dharmas into eleven groups, to which we will return a little later, the classification of all dharmas into 'variants' and 'invariants', and even the very division of dharmas into 56 kinds of dharmas can be seen as made from the point of view of thought or, more precisely, of 'rise of thought'.

Then a very interesting question may arise: Can there be any other approach to dharmas? That is, an approach which would be based on a point of view even more *universal* than that of thought.

5.7.4.1. One may assume, for example, that the division of dharmas into *saṃskṛta* and *asaṃskṛta* could be seen as one of such classifications, for its basis is Nirvana which is, speaking technically, neither thought nor dharmas. It can be said then that all 56 dharmas of *Dhs.* would be put under the first rubric, for according to this classification they are in combinations and, thereby, belong to the sphere of empirical consciousness in one way or another. Whereas Nirvana does not figure as a *dharma* in *Dhs.* at all. So, the following dharmas will be present, according to this classification: (1) △△1–56 (or, practically 1–83, see Table VI); (2)—none.[23]

This same classification could be seen as the *classification of everything* into (1) what is 'aggregate' (*khandha, skandha*), and (2) what is 'element' (*dhātu*);[24] provided, however, that *dhātu* itself is regarded as a category more fundamental and universal than *dharma*.[25]

5.7.4.2. Another classification is based on 'form' (*rūpa*) and is, to a degree, analogous to the first classification. So, from a merely *technical* point of view, all our 56 (or 83) dharmas are 'formless' (*arūpino dhammā*). This means (among other things) that forms are not considered as *states of consciousness* proper (for 'conscious' or 'mental' they are not) first, and that they are not karmic (i.e., cannot be either wholesome or unwholesome with respect to karmic *effects*) Secondly, that is why they are *indeterminate* (together with those of states of consciousness which are marked by C in Table VI, and *asaṅkhata dhammas* not included in the dhammic list of *Dhs.*).

At the same time—and this is of overwhelming philosophical relevance and interest—these very 'forms' can be regarded as that 'substrative material' (but not 'matter') of which mental, psychical and karmic *mechanisms* are built. Or, one may say that 'form' is a *symbolic term* (not a concept!), which symbolizes those *non-conscious* energies which are interpreted by consciousness in a *purely objective* way, but, meta-philosophically speaking, cannot be found *outside* the conscious interpretation. We may, therefore, state that 'hatred' (*dosa*, △78 in Table VI) is a state of consciousness, i.e., a dharma understood in the sense of consciousness and thereby, a formless one—whereas the mechanism responsible for a *phenomenal* manifestation of 'hatred' (a reflectory mechanism, for instance) will be understood as 'form'. And the same could be stated about karma: hatred is one of unwholesome (*akusala*) dharmas, i.e., a 'formless' state of consciousness producing the bad karmic effects, while the *mechanism* of production of these effects, i.e., *karma* itself, can be related to 'form'.[26]

5.7.4.3. The classification of dharmas into 'wholesome', 'unwholesome' and 'indeterminate' is particularly important to us for two main reasons. First, its field is much broader than that of dharmas taken in the sense of states of consciousness, and covers practically *all* dharmas taken in the rather Sarvastivadin sense of 'everything thinkable'. Secondly, the very principle on which this classification is based is, in itself, far broader than *karma*. This means that 'indeterminate' are the 'things' which are not only indeterminate in respect of their karmic effect, but also *indeterminable* par excellence with respect to any other thinkable qualification or definition.

So, all 'formal' dharmas, all *rūpa*—are indeterminate for the reason that they are not conscious. Therefore, the 'basis of bodily sensibility' (or of 'touch'), being *rūpa* (in the sense of previous classification into 'form' and 'formless'), is karmically indeterminate, because all form is indeterminate. But 'element of the incomposite' (i.e., *asaṅkhata-dhātu*) is not a *rūpa* and, at the same time, has nothing to do with *karma* by definition. Its indeterminability lies elsewhere, and cannot be grouped, for it is ungraspable and unthinkable (*acintya*)—that is, not because it is unconscious or akarmic. The very introduction of indeterminability in the Abhidhammic philosophy might have had an especial meaning—indeterminability might have been meant as *an indication of the limits of the Abhidhammic philosophical discourse itself.* [We can, therefore, explain why the dharma of 'correct views' (*sammādiṭṭhi*, △△19, 36) is wholesome, and why the dharma of 'wrong' views (*micchādiṭṭhi*,

△64) is 'unwholesome', but we cannot explain why *asaṅkhata-dhātu* is indeterminate, because it is not meant to be explained.]

Now, returning to our list of dharmas I will show how this triple classification works.[27]

A. *Wholesome dharmas:* △△1–63.
Variants: △△2^{a}, 6^{a}, 8^{a}, 10^{a}, 12^{a}–15^{a}, 19^{a}–23^{a}, 25^{a}–28^{a}, 33^{a}, 36^{a}, 39^{a}, 40^{a}, 51^{a}–56^{a}.

B. *Unwholesome dharmas:* △△1–5, 7–9, 16–18, 57, 58, 64–75, 80, 81.
Variants: △△2^{a}; 2^{b}, 6^{b}, 10^{b}–12^{b}, 25^{b}, 27^{b}, 53^{b}, 55^{b}, 56^{b};
△10^{c}.

C. *Indeterminate dharmas:* △△1, 3–9, 16, 18, 57, 58, 82, 83.
Variants: △△2^{a}–5^{a}, 9^{a}, 16^{a}, 76^{a};
△△3^{b}–5^{b}, 16^{b};
△△2^{c}–6^{c}, 10^{c}, 16^{c};
△△2^{d}–5^{d}, 16^{d};
△△2^{e}–5^{e}, 16^{e};
△△2^{f}–5^{f}, 16^{f};
△2^{g};
△2^{h};
△2^{i}.

If we substract from this enumeration all variants, and single out only those dharmas which belong specifically to one of these groups only, we will get the following result:

A △△13–15, 19–24, 26, 28–52, 54, 59–63 [=41△△].
B △△64–75, 80, 81 [=24△△].
C △△82, 83 [=2△△].

Now, by subtracting all dharmas after △56 of the list of wholesome dharmas, we will have four groups of dharmas: *A*–36 *specifically* wholesome dharmas (△△13–15, 19–24, 26, 28–52, 54); *B*–8 dharmas figuring as wholesome and unwholesome (△△11, 12, 17, 25, 27, 53, 55, 56); *C*–12 dharmas figuring as wholesome, unwholesome, and indeterminate (△△1–10, 16, 18).

The composition of these three groups of dharmas (i.e., *A*, *B* and *C*) shows that the very fact of their being 'wholesome', 'unwholesome', or 'indeterminate' is absolutely *external* in respect of dharmas themselves. The degree of their (i.e., dharmas') 'karmic speciality' is very low, if any, which is clearly seen from the fact that, strictly speaking, only wholesome dharmas (A) can be regarded as specific (A'). And from this might follow that what we deal with in this classification is, in fact, the set of *wholesome* dharmas (D1, seen here in Table VII), some of which can also figure (when the *case* is present) as unwholesome, and some as indeterminate.

5.7.4.4. As has been stated in the beginning of this essay, the dharmas are different either because of difference in their *composition* [i.e., in mental states (M.S.) in the sense in which they are interpreted in *Dhs.*], or because of difference in their *position* (i.e., in their △number), or because of both of them. Table VI shows with utmost clarity the following types of dharmas regarding these differences:

α. *Homonymous* dharmas, i.e., dharmas denoted by the same term, e.g., dharma of 'correct views' (*sammādiṭṭhi*), which figures twice in the list of wholesome dharmas (△△19, 36). Under this rubric one must place, of course, all variants of dharmas, which are homonymous par excellence in relation to their respective *invariants*. So △2^{a} is a homonym of △2 (*vedanā*), though possessing of a different set of mental states (△2–MS.5–11, △2^{a}–MS.198–200), while both two dharmas of 'correct views' possess one and the same set of mental states (MS.93–122).

β. *Synonymous* dharmas, i.e., dharmas denoted by different terms but having the same set of mental states. Such are, for example, △△5, 16 (i.e., 'thought' and 'faculty of mind', MS.18–27). [One can observe very easily that no variant can be a 'synonym' of its invariant!]

γ. *Isotopic* dharmas, i.e., dharmas occupying *the same* place in the traditional arrangement of the 56 wholesome dharmas in eleven groups (marked I–XI in Table XIII). Besides all variants, isotopic par excellence in relation to their invariants, △△57–83 are also isotopic in the sense that each of them is placed instead of and within the same group as, *one* of these 56 dharmas (which, of course, are *heterotopic* with respect to one another, by definition).

Table XI. (α) The list of homonymous dharmas

△2 —△△2^{a}—2^{i}.	△15— △15^{a}.	△33— △33^{a}.
△3—△△3^{a}—3^{f}.	△16—△△16^{a}—16^{f}.	△36— s.△19.
△4—△△4^{a}—4^{f}.	△19—△△36, 19^{a}, 36^{a}.	△39— △39^{a}.
△5—△△5^{a}—5^{f}.	△20— △20^{a}.	△40— △40^{a}.
△6—△△6^{a}—6^{c}.	△21— △21^{a}.	△51— △51^{a}.
△8— △8^{a}.	△22— △22^{a}.	△52— △52^{a}.
△9— △9^{a}	△23— △23^{a}.	△53—△△53^{a}, 53^{b}.
△10—△△10^{a}—10^{c}	△25—△△25^{a}, 25^{b}.	△54— △54^{a}.
△12—△△12^{a}, 12^{b}.	△26— △26^{a}.	△55—△△55^{a}, 55^{b}
△13— △13^{a}.	△27—△△27^{a}, 27^{b}.	△56—△△56^{a}, 56^{b}
△14—△△14^{a}, 14^{b}.	△28— △28^{a}.	△76— △76^{a}.

5.7.4.5. What Tables XI–XIII demonstrate is that all 56 wholesome dharmas form a certain 'topological space', where each *dharma* is a *topos* (or, more precisely speaking, the name of each of the 56 dharmas is the term *denoting* a 'topos') characterized by two main properties: *x*—the property to be *empty* of any concrete dharma (including its variants and isotopes), i.e., the property to remain a 'zero topos' awaiting, as it were, to be filled with *its* dharmas in one other case of 'rise of thought'; and *y*—the property to have variants and isotopes.

Table XII. (β) The list of synonymous dharmas

A.
△2—△△9, 17.
△5— △16.
△6— △20.
△10—△△14, 23, 27, 53, 56.
△11— △24.
△12—△△21, 25, 55.
△13—△△22, 26, 51.
△15—△△19, 28, 33, 36, 52, 54.
△29— △37.
△30— △38.
△31— △34.
△32— △35.
△57—△△58, 2^{a}.
△59— △63.
△6^{a}— △20^{a}.
△10^{a}—△△14^{a}, 23^{a}, 27^{a}, 53^{a}, 56^{a}.
△12^{a}—△△12^{a}, 25^{a}, 55^{a}.
△13^{a}—△△22^{a}, 26^{a}, 51^{a}.
△15^{a}—△△19^{a}, 28^{a}, 33^{a}, 36^{a}, 52^{a}, 54^{a}
△15^{a}—△△19^{a}, 28^{a}, 33^{a}, 36^{a}, 52^{a}, 54^{a}.

B.
△64— △73.
△65— △6^{b}.
△66—△△12^{b}, 25^{b}.
△67—△△10^{b}, 14^{b}, 27^{b}, 53^{b}, 56^{b}.
△68— △74.
△69— △75.
△70— △72.
△76—△△77, 2^{b}.
△78— △79.

C.
△5^{a}— △16^{a}.
△5^{b}— △16^{b}.
△5^{c}— △16^{c}.
△5^{d}— △16^{d}.
△82—△△2^{g}, 9^{a}.
△5^{e}— △16^{e}.
△5^{f}— △16^{f}.
△83—△△2^{i}, 76^{a}.

Table XIII. (γ) The list of isotopic dharmas

I.
△2—△△2^{a}—2^{i}
△3—△△3^{a}—3^{f}
△4—△△4^{a}—4^{f}
△5—△△5^{a}—5^{f}

II.
△6—△△6^{a}—6^{c}
△8—△8^{a}
△9—△△9^{a}, 57, 76
△10—△△10^{a}—10^{c}

III.
△12—△△12^{a}, 12^{b}
△13—△13^{a}
△14—△△14^{a}, 14^{b}
△15—△15^{a}
△16—△△16^{a}—16^{f}
△17—△△58, 77
△59—△63
△82—△83

IV.
△19—△△19^{a}, 64
△20—△△20^{a}, 65
△21—△△21^{a}, 66
△22—△22^{a}
△23—△△23^{a}, 67

V.
△25—△△25^{a}, 25^{b}
△26—△26^{a}
△27—△△27^{a}, 27^{b}
△28—△28^{a}

VI.
△31——△△70, 78, 80, 81
△33—△△33^{a}, 71
△34—△△72, 79
△36—△△36^{a}, 73

VII.
△38—△74
△38—△75

VIII.
△39—△39^{a}
△40—△40^{a}

IX.
△51—△51^{a}
△52—△52^{a}

X.
△53—△△53^{a}, 53^{b}
△54—△54^{a}

XI.
△55—△△55^{a}, 55^{b}
△56—△△56^{a}, 56^{b}

If looked at from this 'topological' angle, all 56 dharmas would be seen as 56 *places* in their relation to their respective *concrete* dharmas.

Table XIV

△	X	Y	△	X	Y	△	X	Y
1^{I}	—	—	20	+	+	40	+	+
2	—	+	21	+	+	41	+	—
3	—	+	22	+	+	42	+	—
4	—	+	23	+	+	43	+	—
5	—	+				44	+	—
			24^{V}	+	—	45	+	—
6^{II}	+	+	25	+	+	46	+	—
7	+	—	26	+	+	47	+	—
8	+	+	27	+	+	48	+	—
9	+	+	28	+	+	49	+	—
10	—	+	29	+	—	50	+	—
			30	+	—			
11^{III}	+	—				51^{IX}	+	+
12	+	+	31^{VI}	+	+	52	+	+
13	+	+	32	+	—			
14	+	+	33	+	+	53^{X}	+	+
15	+	+	34	+	+	54	+	+
16	—	+	35	+	—			
17	+	+	36	+	+	55^{XI}	+	+
18	—	—				56	+	+
			37^{VII}	+	+			
19^{IV}	+	+	38	+	+			
			39^{VIII}	+	+			

From Table XIV it can clearly be seen that there are only eight dharmas (△△1–5, 10, 16, 18) whose *topos* cannot remain empty—there can be no case (*samaya*) without all of them being present. So, we may regard them as *fundamental* with respect to any rise of thought enumerated in *Dhs.* The two of them, however,—'touch' and 'faculty of living' (△△1, 18)—could be regarded as the most fundamental 'points' or even 'focuses' in the whole 'dharmic space' of rise of thought. And this is not only because they are irreplaceable and unsubstitutable but, probably, also because of an extraordinary and specific function of theirs: 'touch' and 'faculty of living' could be fathomed as two *loci* through which one rise of thought is connected with or continues into, another, forming, thereby, a kind of *axis* to a continuum of thought (*cittasantāna*).

It is in the cases of indeterminate dharmas (Nos. 157–234) that this topological character of dharmas becomes particularly obvious. And, indeed, the list of 56 dharmas seems to be a kind of 'periodical system' of chemical elements, where the possibility is always implied, that however many or few of them there might be there, each element, when and if it appears would invariably be positioned in its own place. So, it can be supposed that all but the above-mentioned eight dharmas are the *places* of dharmas, first of all, and only secondly, dharmas. And one can only guess what happens to these places when they are not filled with *actual* dharmas.

One may conjecture whether or not these eight dharmas could be conceived as 'the most natural ones'. It is, however, obvious enough that all 56 dharmas are, as it were, 'the point of departure' for all possible changes and modifications, while these eight seem to be the most *ethically* (i.e. karmically, in this context only) neutral.

NOTES TO ESSAY 5

1 One cannot, however, even call the rise of thought an event, for no event can have ever taken place without it or apart from it. That is, the very notion of an event implies that 'thought has already arisen', and that an event itself is, therefore, no more than one of the thinkable elements in this occurrence or coincidence. Thus, the rise of thought, as such (i.e., regarded with respect to thought only), is not an event, whereas any of its synchronous components (the meditation on a swollen corpse, for example) could be thought of as an event.

2 *Dhs.* does not mention 'a subject' or 'a person' (*puggala*) who figures in *As.* as an important element in each occurrence (*samaya*) of the rise of thought (see above 4.1).

3 *Dhs.* p. 111–113. There are 234 main particular cases of rise of thought in this text. In saying 'main' I mean that some of them contain a number of 'sub-cases' (when treated in the table below they are marked by letter). As to their 'particularity' I want to emphasize that each case, though corresponding to a *type* of thought, seems to be *extreme* in its concreteness. That is, as a case, it cannot be more concrete.

4 S. 10–11 in this table do not belong, speaking strictly terminologically, to the segment of 'sphere' of rise of thought or, one may say, the idea of sphere is not relevant in the cases Nos. 221–228.

5 The asterisks mark the five-fold system of trance. The first trance is one and the same for both systems. The content of the 2nd trance in the four-fold system is 'split' between 2nd and 3rd trances of the five-fold system. The 4th trance in the five-fold system is as the 3rd in the four-fold, and the 5th trance in the five-fold system is as the 4th in the four-fold.

6 This table comprises the 56 dharmas of the 'wholesome' class and their variants. It does not include in itself such 'analytical' categories as 'aggregates' (*khandha*), 'elements' (*dhātu*), etc., that is, it does include them only when they figure as *mental states* connoted by one or another of dharmas. So, for example, we see the aggregate of consciousness figuring as one among ten mental states of 'thought' (*citta*, △5; MS. 26). All first 56 dharmas of this list are ascribed to the case No. 1 (so called 'the first thought', *paṭhamaṃ cittaṃ*, *Dhs.*, pp. 18—39). Further on the dharmas of each other (new) case will be separated by a horizontal line. The classes of dharmas are marked by capital letters (A—wholesome; B—unwholesome; C—indeterminate), e.g. No. 1 A: i.e. the case in which the dharmas are wholesome. Not being a Pali scholar, I have been constantly consulting various translations of *Dhs.*, and first of all, *Dhs. tr.*, and *Dhs. fr.*

7 It is my mistake to single out *vedanā* here as a *separate* mental state (MS.11). I have let it remain here to avoid some further *formal* complications of rather textual nature. See below on this table, △2^a.

8 All variants of dharmas (marked by letters) and all additional dharmas (i.e., 57–83) are placed within this table after the 56 dharmas of the first 'wholesome thought'. The traditional division of the 56 dharmas into eleven groups is marked here by roman numbers. See in *Dhs.* Introduction, pp. xxx–xxxviii.

9 See here Note 7.

10 I mark these two terms with single quotes because until now in the modern Western psychology, the term 'sensory' has implied a more analytical meaning, while 'mental' has assumed a far too speculative meaning. However, in the Abhidhamma (as in any other Indian teaching dealing with consciousness) consciousness is seen as the *source* of any sensory activity (i.e., by any means not the other way around!), which contains in itself all general as well as analytical functions of all potential as well as actual sensory mechanisms.

11 Perhaps, the term 'plane' would be more appropriate than 'sphere', particularly when we deal with *avacara* as a specifically dhyanic technical term. See Vimuttimagga (p. 43).

12 So, as we have already seen in Table III, both thought and dharmas are termed 'wholesome' (Nos. 1-8, 111-112) in all dhyanic states, and sphere is wholesome by implication, whereas in cases Nos. 221–228 sphere as such is not relevant (see Note 4 above).

13 Needless to say that 'thinking' (as a process par excellence) cannot be reduced to 'thought', and belongs to an absolutely different level of our problem. See below 6.16 and Note 66 to Essay 6.

14 That is why, I think, it is almost impossible to treat *sati* in the sense of a merely instrumental function by means of which mind is refined or purified (or, say, is purifying itself). And this is the main way in which *sati* is understood in the suttas and commentaries. See in Rune E. A. Johansson (1979, pp. 170–1, 174).

15 The term, when rendered as 'transformation' (i.e., not as 'maturation' or 'development') can have either *neutral* or *negative* meaning in the *Yogācāra* doctrine (I. Yamada, 1977, pp. 161–4).

16 So, in the first case I use 'quasi' because the very notion of reflexive procedure implies necessarily a certain relatedness to a real subject of thinking, while here there is neither the process of thought, nor a 'person' related to as its subject. In the second case, it is because the Abhidhammic idea of object is very different from what the modern psychology calls an object in the sense of 'objective methodology' (and this is particularly so in the psychology of visual and auditory perception). For in the Abhidhamma the majority of objects are *dhyanically construed*, and include also the notion or cognition (*saññā*) of object, used *as an object* in trance and meditation. See, for example, the dhyanic objects which are the corpses in different stages of disintegration and putrification (Table V, Nos. 105–106^{h}; 0.9–18).

17 The 'subjective' in the Abhidhamma means one's relation to oneself (*ajjhatta*) and cannot be directly, and in an absolute sense, opposed to 'the objective'. So, from the Abhidhammic viewpoint, one cannot even say that one's words are more objective than one's feelings not yet expressed (which would have been qualified by L. Wittgenstein as a complete nonsense). It is *the relatedness to oneself only*, which makes one thing more subjective than another in the Abhidhamma, by no means their (i.e., these things') observability from the point of view of an external onlooker.

18 That is, one may, however, state that, while passing from one to another of the eight thoughts (Nos. 1–8), one may accumulate the experience of 'mental gladness', 'knowledge', 'synergic activity', and 'indifference' as well as the experience of not experiencing them (see Table V, MV. 1–5).

19 One of the factors accountable for this 'anti-experience' could be seen in the elimination of the *normal* (or 'progressive') individual memory or the so-called 'actual' memory giving way to a kind of super-memory (*sati*). This might vaguely correspond to the duality of 'actual' and 'depth-memory' in the classical Indian yoga [where all memory figures as a modification (*pariṇāma*)—here it is not transformation!] See G. Feurstein (1980, pp. 60, 69, 70, 73).

20 It is very interesting to note the general *inner* (i.e., often not disclosed) tendency of European and American psychologists and psychological philosophers to reduce time to a certain type of consciousness (memory, attention, etc.). E. Cassirer (1957, pp. 176–7) wrote: '... multiplicity of temporal determinations occurs within the *indivisible moment of time* [as *kṣaṇa* in the Abhidharma, A. P.]... the total content of consciousness given in the simple noun is distributed over present, past and future. This form of phenomenal differentiation constitutes the true problem'. This almost Buddhist formulation entails that time is inherent in the 'nature' of consciousness (the *minimal* act of which is, theoretically, timeless), and that to say 'a state of consciousness' is, practically, the same as to say 'the moment of time'. W. James (1910, pp. 250–2) also tended to intuit time as the 'consciousness of simultaneousness' in states of consciousness. The main problem, however, has remained the same: we have to make distinction between *time as an objective external condition, and time as a type of consciousness.* We may infer about time in the first sense from the principle of interdependent co-origination (*pratītya-samutpāda*), but it would not give us any idea about 'time of thinking' (or, say, dharmic time). And it seems to me, that this distinction cannot be performed in the context, of a positivistic scientific approach where 'time' and 'continuity' are seen as equivalents. See, Lilian Silburn (1955, pp. 1, 3, 191, 192–3).

21 Usually it is translated as 'practice', see, for instance in Upatissa (pp. 43, 44).

22 This could be historically (or, rather, 'mythologically') accounted for by the fact that the Ascetic Gautama left his teachers Arada Kalama and Udraka Ramaputra who had been teaching the concentration on 'nothingness' and 'neither notion nor non-notion', respectively [see Table V, Nos. 109, 110; 0 0. (21), (22)] and then, as he said it in his tale to Aggivessana,

he, as it were, 'returned' to the first *jhāna* [No. 9; C. 1; 0. (1)] placed in his early childhood. See, Andrew Bareau (1963, pp. 14–27, 47–8, 52; 1974, pp. 107–8, 410).

23 In applying this apparently sarvastivadin principle of division to apparently theravadin list of dharmas, I assume that this principle was realized in the *Vibhaṅga* of the *Abhidhamma-piṭaka* in the notion of *asaṅkhata-dhātu* ('element of the incomposite' rather than 'incomposite element'). The most that could be said about this element is that it is 'absent in the five aggregates (*khandha*)' or, what is more, cannot *be* aggregated. See A. Bareau (1951, pp. 23–6), Th. Stcherbatsky (1923, pp. 6–10. 75–6).

24 That is to say, that *asaṅkhata-dhātu* is also a *dharma*, but in a far more general sense: not as 'a state of consciousness', but indeed as 'a thing': 'What are the unobstructive and un-apposite (*appaṭigha anidassana*) dharmas? (They are) the aggregate of sensation, the aggregate of cognition...and also...the element of the incomposite...' *Dhs*., pp. 147, 239.

25 Also see in 4.3.6 and Notes 50–52 to Essay 4.

26 I cannot help seeing a direct analogy between the Abhidhammic category of *rūpa* (as opposed to *arūpino dhammā*) and the Jaina category of *adharma* (as opposed to *dharma*). Or, what is more, a certain analogy could also be noticed between Jainist *jīva* and Abhidhammic *arūpa*, particularly in view of the fact that in Jainism 'time' and 'space' are *ajīva* (non-soul), while according to the Abhidhammic classification, they are definitely *rūpa*.

27 My very remote meta-philosophical conjecture is that the category of 'indeterminate' can be referred to or connected with idea of 'pure objectivity' or 'pure object'. The latter can be construed in several ways, of which one is to reduce consciousness or 'the conscious' to its 'bearer' or 'carrier' as something *non-conscious* par excellence. This may well mean that *dharma* and *dhātu*, taken *as such*, are as non-conscious as *rūpa* and, even, as Nirvana. It is Nirvana of which one can think as 'non-conscious', though only in the sense in which thought (*citta*) *is* conscious, and in no other way.

It would be very instructive, in the context of our considerations concerning the indeterminate, to remember E. von Hartmann, the first European proponent of the idea of the unconscious. He ascribes to the unconscious two main negative properties: (1) It does not suffer (*erkrankt nicht*); (2) It does not discontinue. These two characteristics of the unconscious could be very easily juxtaposed with two main Buddhist characteristics of the conscious, namely: (1^1) It does suffer; (2^1) It discontinues (i.e., it is *discrete*). See, E. Von Hartmann (1870, p. p. 327–334). We may only suggest that these Hartmannean characteristics could be applied to *rūpa* and Nirvana alike and, therefore, could be regarded as the characteristics covering all which is indeterminate, with the exception of 'indeterminate states of consciousness' proper.

6. A PRELIMINARY DISCOURSE ON DHARMAS

6.0.1–2. It is, it seems to me, in Buddhism, that the first serious attempt was made to look at thought and consciousness (*citta*) as an *object*. That is, to depersonalize and desubjectify the thought to such an extent as to be able to see it as entirely devoid of any specifically psychological functions or properties. At the same time, the Buddhist Masters of old tried to combine this idea of 'thought as an object' with quite another idea of 'all objects as objects of thought' (i.e., not existing without the context of thought or apart from it), as a result of which all 'objects of thought' were endowed with functions and properties of a more or less psychological character.

6.0.3–4. It is only after having considered this methodological dualism of 'thought as object' versus 'object of thought' that we would be able to start thinking of introducing the notion of *dharma*. The notion that, if treated purely and merely in an 'Abhidhammic' way, would be seen as *complementary* to that of thought in both above-mentioned senses. Because *dharma* itself, taken in its connection with thought, would inevitably assume its duality: (a) on the one hand we have dharmas as 'specific objects of thought' (i.e., the objects which figure in the Abhidhamma among and side by side with, other objects of thought put under the rubric '0.6', see above, 5.0.4 and 5.7), (b) while on the other hand, dharmas are present as embracing all varieties of thought, actual as well as potential, those with their objects as well as those taken in a more subjective and psychological way.[1] Given of course, that in the latter case the very term 'thought' is used in its most general sense, i.e., as covering both 'consciousness' (*viññāṇa*) and 'mind' or 'mentality' (*manas*).

6.0.5. The term 'a state of consciousness' may then be used to render a *dharma* understood either as *one state of consciousness of unspecified kind*, or as *one kind of states of consciousness*, or as *a specific category of* objects of thought named 'dharma-objects' [*dhammārammaṇa*]. I have preferred 'state of consciousness' as the English equivalent of *dharma*, not because it is the best, but because it is less definite than any other.

[6.0.6.1. Now it is becoming clearer and clearer that the core of the problem of 'rendering' of *dharma*, if not the key to its solution, lies in the sphere of distinctions between language and meta-language, i.e., between inner functioning and the external theoretical description of these two terms. And unless an Indologist or even a Buddhologist becomes aware of these distinctions all his or her attempts to 'translate' *dharma* into a language, shall we say, external or culturally so far alien to the Buddhist culture, would remain futile in spite of philological discernments of one and philosophical insights of the other. And 'rendering' has been chosen here instead of 'translation' in order to stress a less technically obligatory and more self-conscious character of my observations.[4] In saying this I mean, first of all, that rendering here figures as a certain *kind of interpretation* which implies a phenomenological analysis of what we are doing ourselves when we are interpreting one term in the sense of another, one text in the sense of another, or one culture in the sense of another, for that thing.]

[6.0.6.2. The basic and most elementary form of distinction between meta-language and language with respect to *dharma* can be seen in a certain ambiguity of definitions and characterizations of the term in the works of those among modern scholars who tried to deal with it in a systematic way. That is, to regard *dharma* as belonging to the *theoretical system* of Buddhist philosophy, i.e., the Abhidhamma of the Pali Canon and late Theradavin Commentaries, or the Adhidharma of the Sarvastivadins and its derivations. It was nobody else other than E. Burnouf who in all naivity wrote: 'The psychological and metaphysical terms used in the Buddhist philosophy are enumerated in a certain order. Each of these terms constitutes a *Dharma*, that is a Law, a condition, or a thesis; for nothing is so extended as the meaning of this word...'[5] But of course, E. Burnouf could not have conceived that his very definition (or characterization) of *Dharma* as 'the Law extended', was reflecting the role of *dharma* as a meta-concept in the Buddhist philosophy (to the extent the last was then known), that is, as a concept which denoted *the forms and principles of organization* of the texts, remaining as it were, neutral to their content. Though he might have (probably) vaguely surmised that in European philosophical tradition (and particularly in Cartesianism) something like 'Law', or 'Order', or 'Method', or even 'Form', had been, indeed, used as means of theoretical description of thinkable content in a philosophy. The very fact of translation of *dharma* as 'Law' indirectly showed that in the case of E. Burnouf (as in those of some of his predecessors and successors) the *phenomenal* character of any philosophical theory was not yet understood [in the sense that method was still opposed to phenomenology, or (in some other cases) to ontology, or even to 'theory as such' etc.][6]

6.0.6.3. The numerous cases, however, when *dharma* has been used to denote the entirety of Buddhism as religion or the wholeness of Buddha's Message, induced some European scholars, and rightly so, to translate this term as 'the Religion', or 'the Teaching', or 'the Law of the Buddha', acquiring therewith the meaning more or less synonymous with that of 'Buddhism'. In which case, it has found itself to be, quite naturally, differentiated from 'a dharma' of the Abhidharma (or 'a dhamma' of the Abhidamma) as the general or universal principle (or Truth) from a particular or more concrete case or manifestation of the same principle.

And this, probably, already contained in, or carried with itself, the possibility of a specifically *religious* approach to *dharma*, not infrequently in the disguise of an *ontology opposed to ethics* (as we see it in the works of de la Vallée Poussin and Mrs. Rhys Davids), or to the theory of cognition (as in Th. Stcherbatsky, O. Rosenberg, M. Liebenthal and E. Obermiller).[7] Moreover, I am even inclined to think that such a radically new translation of *dharma* as 'a state of consciousness' reflected in itself not so much the psychological trends in English Buddhology in the second half of the nineteenth century, as the 'religious moralism' of English moral philosophy at that time. For it is not any earlier than in the eighties that the very notion of the 'state of consciousness' (and totally irrespective of any dharma) started acquiring its psychological meaning.

6.0.6.4. Thus, Burnouf's definition of *dharma* remained yet another Cartesian intuition which was soon almost forgotten, as we see it now, for example, in the works of the most prominent Buddhologist of Burnouf's lineage, André Bareau, who translates *dharma* now as 'dharma', now as 'thing'.[8] And by the time 'state of consciousness' became a standard equivalent of *dharma*, the question of meta-language arose again, and in a quite different atmosphere (or shall we say 'field') of philosophical apperception. For gradually, it became obvious that the seemingly insurmountable difficulty of the rendering of *dharma* could not be accounted for in terms of a remote epoch or an alien culture. Even a superficial knowledge of Buddhaghosa's and Dhammapala's commentaries would show that to a contemporary of theirs, or perhaps even to a contemporary of the first perpetuator of the Oral Tradition, the meaning of *dharma* (and probably, samskaras too, to some extent) was known to them as one of the most important notions and terms of their own *culture*. In Buddhism, however, it was not only extracted from its previous (and contemporary) cultural and religious context, but (as partly in Jainism) totally *neutralized* and *denaturalized*, having been turned into a kind of term of purely theoretical description of anything to be described and, at the same time, into a term denoting the chief object of description.[9] Moreover, one may argue that this very neutralization and denaturalization became in early Buddhism singled out as a specific and separate process of non-reflexive thinking, i.e., as *one of the dharmas*. [*Dharma* as a 'theory-making instrument' does not seem impossible within the framework of the Abhidhamma, but (and this is an extremely difficult thing to conceive of) it was itself also an *object* of the Buddhist yoga (here—*sati* or *jhāna*).]

6.0.6.5. In any event, what we have here on the side of English translators in the case of *dharma* as 'state of consciousness', is a clear synthesis of 'ethos' and 'ethics'[10] so typical of any European world-outlook of the second half of the nineteenth century, and it was between the purely descriptive and the explanatory translations like 'state of consciousness' and purely nominal ones (when 'dharma' is rendered as *dharma*), that D.T. Suzuki appeared with his translation of 'samskaras' as 'confections',[11] boldly following the way of 'calque' or 'semantic construction' of the Tibetan translations of the Sanskrit Buddhist terminology. And of course, if asked about the exact *meaning*, he would have replied, that in both 'samskaras' and 'confections' the terminological meaning would (and should) remain undisclosed, but that one would (and should) be able to understand at least such a simple thing as the analogous *semantic structure* of both words together with the fact, that their not yet known terminological meaning had already severed *all* associations with their respective ordinary meanings (such as 'a type of ritual' in the first case, and a 'type of sweets' and/or women's dress, in the second). Moreover, we may conjecture that it is this very *negation* of the *other* meaning (or meanings) that constituted a part of the content in the *terminological* meaning of samskaras, which implies that the very task of rendering this or similar terms into English or any other language, would necessarily include the finding and establishing of a calque-equivalent. This also, or even first of all, would necessitate a much more complex process—that of *reinterpretation* by the renderer of the notions and categories of his own culture, i.e., making them neutral, 'non-usable' with respect to this culture so that they would be able to convey the fullness of *other* meanings. ['Other' in the sense of being broader than that of 'other culture', for within this context, the meanings of *dharma* and samskaras had been cultural, but stopped being so, exceeding the limits of any cultural understanding, which must have involved the same process of reinterpretation.] But had not Burnouf already suggested that *dharma* was no more than an *expression* of a certain universal *content?* The content that, probably, could not have been *thought* outside or beyond this *form* of expression. In fact, Burnouf did not go as far as that, not only because he was not aware of the *cultural* limits of his language, but also because he had no theory from the point of view of which any language could have been treated in its cultural relativity. [For I think that the very *phenomenon of translation* is an 'expression' of such relativity.[12]][13]

I think that the second stage was marked by the appearance of *Problems of Buddhist Philosophy* by Otto Rosenberg[14] who synthesized the whole previous experience of understanding the dharmas in terms of European philosophy and, at the same time, made an extremely courageous attempt to assimilate in his description of the theory of dharmas some elements of inner Buddhist approach to the problem. Strictly following Vasubandhu and the commentaries on the *Abhidharmakośa*, he was induced to consider *dharma* not as an element or concept belonging to the whole of the Abhidharmic theory, but as *a system in itself.* That is, his intuition was that all connotations of *dharma* formed, or constituted a certain 'space of meanings', so that whenever a thought or idea happened to find itself in the dharmic space, it immediately assumed a 'dharmic' meaning (losing, thereby, its own).

6.0.6.6. In saying this I, to some extent at any rate, modernize the Rosenbergean conception of *dharma*, and cannot help doing so, because he was, probably, the first Buddhologist who made the first step towards an understanding of 'dharma' *culturally untinted*, and it is very tempting to jump to the next stage. One thing, however, remains to be clarified: he conceived of this dharma system as *a system of content.* Which, from the Aristotelian or Cartesian point of view, would be seen as mere nonsense, for no form could be implied, because even as a 'concept' or 'notion', *dharma* remains in Rosenbergean interpretation *a unit of content* or, shall we say, a fact which cannot find its interpretation in the context of any binary opposition and, first of all, that of 'content/form'. Therefore, *dharma* cannot be rendered in any way other than 'dharma', for any other equivalent inavoidably finds itself, so to speak, *already being* in the 'system of dharma' as a purely *contentful connotation* of the last. Or, more precisely speaking, *all that has been included into the Abhidharma is dharma by definition.* What follows is that this theory (*dharmavāda*) cannot be defined in terms of epistemology as opposed to metaphysics, or ontology as opposed to ethics, because all these terms would be seen only as those of *secondary interpretation* of the meanings which might be generated within the system of dharma-contents.

6.0.6.7. Thus, samskaras too are treated by Rosenberg as bearing certain dharmic content (and not having a content of their own), which is very significant in view of the fact that *dharmas cannot have any content other than their own.* Given, of course, that the content of *dharma* cannot be defined by any means external to *dharma*, which means that such a content is undefinable outside the dharma-system itself, or even that, from an *external* point of view, dharmas may be thought of as contentless, but ... by no means as 'forms' or 'formal', for the opposition 'content/form' is not a part of the dharma-system. Then, following Rosenberg, we may say that samskaras are concretizations of dharmas' content, and render this into 'dharma-processes', which would reflect on it our purely cultural attitude to describe all phenomena in terms of 'entity/process' opposition.

6.0.6.8. Rosenberg's interpretation of *dharma* may invite yet another understanding of this term, i.e., as 'the theory', for there is *one* theory of dharmas as well as of anything else in the sense of dharmas. One can accept this rendering in the sense analogous to that in which the term 'quantum-theory' is used. That is—there is one quantum-theory, for the term implies one definite concept of theoretical physics as its content. [We may even go further and say that *dharma* can be understood as 'theory together with its object', but it would be another instance of a sheer *cultural synthesis.* For in the context of our theoretical thinking it would mean two different things covered by one concept, whereas in *dharmavāda* itself it means one and the same thing (*dharma*) which could be secondarily interpreted in two different ways.]

6.0.6.9. Th. Stcherbatsky's works on *dharma* established a completely different and far more descriptive approach to the problem. Dharmas and samskaras complement one another in the context of the meaning given to 'existence' (*bhava*) of things and facts.

Th. Stcherbatsky writes: 'When the principle "everything exists" (*sarvam asti*) is set forth, it has the meaning that nothing but the twelve bases (*āyatana*) exists... An object which cannot be viewed as a *separate* object of cognition (*viṣaya*) or a separate faculty of cognition (*indriya*) is unreal, as e.g., the soul, or the personality. Being a congeries of separate elements it is declared to be a name, and not a reality, not a *dharma*'.[15] It is, however, self-evident that we cannot turn this Buddhistic explanation of existence into a definition of *dharma*. For, if reinterpreted in the sense of ordinary European philosophical thinking, this explanation would leave us with an inevitable confusion of two predicates—'real' and 'existent'. The existence of dharmas cannot be either proven or disproven, because, not belonging to *empirical objects*, the dharmas are seen as what makes these objects existent, figuring as the *non-empirical basis* of these objects, and possessing a certain degree of reality, but only *with respect to* and *in relation with*, these objects. At the same time, the very term 'existence' implies another and more difficult idea: for 'everything exists' only to the extent in which dharmas are thought as existent (and their existence is no more than a generalizing metaphor). Everything does exist as a certain objectivity, the very existence of which is due not only to the 'basic' existence of dharmas, but also to the 'forces of co-existence' which make all things *exist as composite*, for to exist as a composite thing and to exist—are synonymous in Buddhism. So 'existence' is itself 'composed' of (a) being dharmic, and (b) being composite, and it is in this sense, first of all, that *dharmas* are opposed to samskaras (see 2.1–2).[16]

If, then, we try to conceive of all dharmas as *separate* and of all things as *complex* or composite, we will clearly see that each individual object has its existence which is dharmic, and its individuality which is samskaric and which bears the individual name (*nāma*) as the sign of its complex-ness and unreality in the sense of dharma. Therefore, when we read here about *separateness* of objects we must understand it as the *secondary* separateness, i.e., derived from that of dharmas which are *discrete* par excellence, though their discreteness is a totally abstract quality, while in the case of objects it is concrete and cognizable. [We may even say that discreteness in objects is a dharmic quality (together with the discrete character of cognition itself), while their being composite is a samskaric quality.] At the same time, we have to bear in mind that the separateness of all *subjects* (i.e., continuums of consciousness, i.e., all sentient beings) cannot be established analytically or as an inference from separateness of all objects; possibly though, it may constitute a special class of objects. It would be interesting to represent dharma as a cluster of abstract qualities which serve as differentiating indices:

saṃskāras

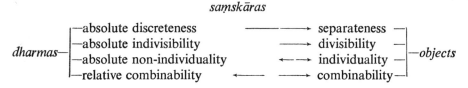

dharmas—	—absolute discreteness	——→	separateness —	—*objects*
	—absolute indivisibility	——→	divisibility —	
	—absolute non-individuality	←—→	individuality —	
	—relative combinability	←— —→	combinability—	

This scheme shows that it is dharmas which cause the objects to be dharmic, but it is samskaras which cause the very *existence* of objects. That is, in the absence of objects (including individuals) there can be no samskaras, while dharmas remain as they are, i.e., as *pure objects* (given that their last quality is induced *from* samskaras). That is, samskaras do not have their own existence, while dharmas do have it, though only with respect to and in comparison with, objects. [Which would be seen not only from the Cartesian, but even Husserlean point of view, as a complete nonsense.][17]

6.0.6.10. However, dharmas cannot be viewed in terms of 'philosophical method' (not to speak of 'means of knowledge' or 'instrument of cognition', *pramāṇa*). Or, let us say it differently; the principle 'all (that is there) is *dharma*' does not imply any possibility of a *methodological* postulation, which, of course, would have been absolutely impossible in the context of any 'serious' European philosophy of the last two centuries. Because, as the central principle, *dharma* is loose enough to allow for too many contradictory postulates to exist simultaneously. And that is why the term 'methodology' can be applied to the Buddhist philosophy in general in a strictly objective (i.e., in the sense of an external observation) way only.

The very notion of 'method of cognition' appears, technically speaking, only provided that a certain (however simply and elementary it might be) *analysis of cognition* has already taken place. Whereas in the context of Abhidharma proper, it is an *analysis of consciousness*, not of cognition or knowledge, that was being performed and developed since the third century B.C. up to, at least, the third century A.D. The Buddhist epistemology came into being as something quite definitely derivative from and secondary to, the Buddhist theory of consciousness, on the one hand, and as a more or less simultaneous reflex of and reaction to, the epistemological developments in the contemporary non-Buddhist teachings (darshanas) of the middle of the first millenium A.D. But even then an epistemological position of a Buddhist Master like Dharmakirti or Dignaga remained an external one and mainly externally (polemically) oriented. The theory of dharmas, *dharmavāda*, never became a *darśana*, and *dharma* itself never became a 'category of pure (or any, for that matter) reasoning'. That is why all parallels with Kant have, so far, remained futile and fruitless. And *dharma* is a *category* only in an *inner* sense, that is, as the universal object *within* the Abhidharma, but not as a category in terms of which an external observer could describe *his* method of observation (together with his culture, among other things), for it does not belong to *reason* as it has been understood in the European philosophical tradition since Kant. We can render 'reason' as a 'dharma' (that is, one of the dharmas, such, for instance, as △6, of the *Dhs.*, *vitakka*), but we cannot *translate* 'dharma' as 'a category'. For if taken as 'a category' in the context of the classical European philosophy, 'reason' stands as an abstraction acquired in the process and as a result of, *the analysis of reflexive thinking*. Whereas in the *dharmavāda*, dharma figures as the only predicate in, practically, all the initial postulations of this theory.

6.0.6.11. The post-Stcherbatskean development of the dharma-problem can be classified into three variants. In the first, very much influenced by Stcherbatsky, *dharma* figures in an utterly ambiguous way sharing, as it were, the properties of *a notion* and *a thing* at one and the same time: it is still rendered as 'a category', but assumes the marks of an entity.[18] This means more than a methodological confusion, it reflects on itself an obvious impossibility to express the *content* of one system in terms of another *meta-system*. For Stcherbatsky himself was almost aware that, if used in the Kantian sense, such a term as 'a nominal category' never did imply any *thing-ness*. In the second we have a kind of return to a relative 'thingness' of dharmas understood as an undefinable phenomenon, and described as 'ultimate, durationless, incomparable entities which flash into existence...'[19] [The term 'phenomenon' here is used not in the phenomenological way, but in a broader context of its cultural uses.] The third variant is present in a happy marriage of a very rigid Ceylonese Theravadin Buddhism with a kind of modern psychology. [The latter is usually given in a little 'pre-modern', very generalized and, I am afraid more cultural than strictly scientific manner.] With *dharma* rendered now as 'mental image', now as 'mental process',[20] we constantly have to bear in mind that this 'scientific mentalism' is no more than a consequence of an arbitrary application of the objective psycho-physiological methodology to the 'psychological metaphysics' of dharmavada.

There is yet another conception of *dharma*, which stays apart from these three variants. It counts among its adherents the late Edward Conze who tried from the early fifties to work out a stressedly ontological understanding of dharma. *Dharma* is only one of the three fundamental staples of this approach—the other two are *svabhāva* ('own-nature' or 'own being')[21] and *pratītyasamutpāda* ('interdependent co-origination'). *Dharma* is conceived there not in the sense of a phenomenal existence subject to the universal law of causes and effects,[22] but as the *pristine spiritual entity* which is, 'as such', outside any series of causality and stays, as it were, 'before', or in another dimension than that of ignorance (*avidyā*), i.e., the first link of *pratītyasamutpāda.*[23] So, what could be thought of (*cintya*) as *dharma*, could be thought of as 'state' (or 'modality') of consciousness, whereas what could not be thought of (*acintya*) is *dharma* in its ineffability (*anupalambha*). It seems to me that this conception, where dharmas are a kind of equivalent to 'ontological entities', reflects such an important (and so far neglected by scholarly observers) element of European culture of the twenties to forties of our century as the revival of gnostic tendencies ('Perennial Philosophy'), which took part of the Theosophy and Anthroposophy of the previous period. [In general, I think that the conscious experience of rendering *dharma* shows an obviously obscuring role of the 'cultural synthesis' in modern Buddhology. And if we cannot avoid this kind of obscuration, we ought, at least, to be aware of it in order to be able to control our capacity to make mistakes.]

6.1.0. Trying to understand *dharma* from the meta-philosophical point of view, that is, taking it out of the context of Buddhist interpretation, and positing it as *an outer object* of our own investigation, we would see very soon that its 'object-ness' itself is no more than that of a mode of *thinking on thought*. But what would happen, if we stop thinking on thought? Then it would be said of thought, that *it exists in the absence of a thinking subject*, *that is*, so *to speak*, *being a pure object* (or, shall we say, the purest object), and then the very notion of *dharma* would not enter the 'scene of consciousness', for a *dharma* is an object only when there are other objects (*ārammana*) and subjects (*puggala*) on the scene. Which means, in its turn, that though all *my* thinking about any thought, consciousness or mind would be dharmic (i.e. interpreted and interpretable in terms of states of consciousness), it would not eliminate the possibility of thought as an absolute object (i.e., not interpretable in terms of states of consciousness). Given, of course, that in the early Abhidhamma this possibility was only *de facto* introduced by postulation of the 'rise of thought' (*cittuppāda*) and did not acquire its theoretical foundation before the appearance of the Yogacara Treatises. And was this not a very strange point of departure to the whole movement of thought, which eventually resulted in what could be named 'the metapsychology' of the Abhidhamma? Because the idea itself of psychology simply cannot exist in the absence of, shall we say, a mentality investigating another mentality. However, the Kantian distinction between the phenomenal and the noumenal is not applicable here, for the Abhidhamma could have, in principle at least, accepted the idea of mentality that could 'mentate', but could not think, while in Yogacara it was rather the other way around.[24]

6.1.1. This point seems to me to be of extreme importance and enigmaticality. Because the very elimination of 'subject' or 'self' of thinking suggests that, on the one hand there can be a 'mere mentation' (or 'having the states of consciousness', i.e., dharmas) without thinking, while on the other hand, there can be 'thinking without mentation'. Therefore, even if we admit that in our 'modern' approach to the problem the term 'mentality' (or 'mind') is no more than the name by which we denote the way of thinking on our own thinking (which of course, would have been totally unacceptable to both Kant and Husserl), then we have to admit that in both these cases there will be no psychology whatever. For in the first we will have a typical case of *meta-psychology*, where the mind is interpreted as 'states of consciousness only' (*dhamma matta*), while in the second there can be no psychology at all, for 'thought' (or 'consciousness') would thus figure without any psychological predicates, i.e., as 'thought only' (*citta matta*) wherefrom all mentation is dismissed.

6.1.2. I have used the term (meta-psychology) here only to emphasize all contrariness and direct opposition of the Abhidhammic approach to mind to that of each and every sort of *reductionist* psychology. *The subject of investigation* (one must not confuse it with, for example, object of *thinking*) in meta-psychology is the conditions and/or states of our own thinking *about* mind, while in a reductionist psychology it is the substrata of mental processes. And it is in this sense that the term 'Abhidhamma' itself may be rendered as 'meta-psychology', though in a merely conventional way. But if it is so, we would have to take all consequences, and I am entirely aware that to say that 'an egg can mentate' is a metaphor not less senseless than to say 'a combination of atoms can think'.[25] However, even in saying that an egg or a plant can have a mentality, we impose on their 'conduct' the conditions and states (i.e., dhammas in an Abhidammic sense of the term) of our own thinking which, in the final analysis reveal themselves as *not ours*, or at least, *not only ours*. That is, so to speak, they reveal themselves as *objective correlates* between *mental thinking* of an observer (or investigator) and *mentality without thinking* of the observed. Or, we may say, between *subjective thinking* and *objective mentality*. Then the above mentioned 'thinking without mentation' may have been seen as an 'absolutely objective thought'.

6.1.3. To seek for an explanation or understanding of what *dharma* is in terms of 'content', seems to me to be an utterly futile affair, first of all because *dharma has never been meant to be explained or understood as the subject of any philosophical proposition.* Or, putting it in a different way, one may say that *dharma has been always understood as something in the sense of which some or all other things were to be interpreted*—that is, it was meant to serve a sort of *universal predicate*. There is not a single *context* in either Abhidhamma or in the Suttas, in which *dharma* could be defined. Each context, however, where it happens to figure, may have suggested about its various uses and connotations revealed in its contextual connections with other terms and notions, and first of all, of course, with the triad of 'thought-consciousness-mind-or-mentality' (*citta*, *vijñāna*, *manas*). And it is only in juxtaposition with these three, or all of them together, that *dharma* assumes its *relative meaning* of '*a state of*' consciousness, but not acquiring any of their content. So to say 'a *dharma* is a state of consciousness' is a tautology rather than a definition. That is why, by the way, nothing like that was ever said in the Buddhist texts. It would be not only entirely wrong as an adjustment to our own cultural habit of conceptualization. We simply cannot say that 'a *dharma* is... (a predicate follows)', because a *dharma*, in fact, 'is' no thing, yet a term *denoting* (not being) a certain relation or type of relation *to* thought, consciousness or mind. That is, *dharma* is not a concept in the accepted terminological sense of the latter, but a purely *relational notion*. Given, of course, that we look at it as an *object of thinking*, not that of meditation, that is.

6.1.4. The mere fact of *naming* a *dharma* by its name (may I remind here that 'state of consciousness' is not a name!) cannot help fixing in this *dharma* of some 'inherent' psychological properties, for they are given in the name itself.[26] So, for example, let us look at 'lightness of thought' (*cittalahutā*, △42 of *Dhs.*, see Table VI). This, however tempting, must not be understood in the sense that one object ('thought') is endowed with a certain property ('lightness') also objectively existing either as one among other properties of thought,[27] or as a property independent from thought. On the contrary, let us try to think that 'thought' here is devoid of any inherent qualities, and that 'lightness of thought' (not 'lightness' alone) is a certain modification postulated prior to or side-by-side with, 'thought'. Then the very *relation* of ascribing the latter to the former is named as a 'dharma of lightness of thought' [in the sense of in 6.0.5]. And that is why the *description* (not a definition) of this *dharma* is made in such a nominal (one may even say—lexicographical) way: 'Lightness of thought is, in this case, the lightness of aggregate of consciousness (*viññāṇakkhandha*), its elasticity and quickness..., its...' These three terms ('lightness', 'elasticity', 'quickness') denote the *definite* properties presented as if they were actually to be found in thought or consciousness. While in fact, they are no more than the *moments of interpretation of 'thought' as a state of thought*, whereas these moments themselves remain, as such, uninterpretable or interpretable in all possible ways, which amounts to the same thing.

6.2.0. Let me try another and rather risky explanation of my own understanding of *dharma* as a state of consciousness. When I think of mind in a *general* psychological way, that is, as covering all describable mental functions and capacities, I am still bound to admit in my awareness of the fact of my thinking about mind, that my thinking about mind cannot be, here and now at least, included in what I am thinking of as 'mind' (not *my* mind, but mind as an *object* of *my* thinking). And likewise, when I am aware of my thinking on mind, I have to admit that if there is such an object of awareness as my thinking, then this awareness is to be excluded from what is labelled as 'my thinking'. And in both cases we have a certain *framework of interpretation*—in the first 'I think...', in the second

'I am aware...'—which itself cannot be interpreted in the sense of its object (in the first case 'mind', in the second 'thinking'), and which does not allow for any interpretation other than purely nominal. If we conceive of *dharma* in the sense of 'framework of interpretation of consciousness', we would be able to produce a series of formal propositions, such as 'dharma is an object of visual meditation' (*bhāvanā*), or 'dharma is a word', or 'dharma is a central notion of Buddhist philosophy'. None of these, however, has anything to do with the *content* of interpretation. What, for instance, the first of these propositions is establishing, is no more than the *fact* of thinking about *dharma*, wherefrom cannot be inferred that 'a dharma is an object'.[28] This is to be understood in the sense that *no psychology can be deduced from meta-psychology*.[29] [In saying this I mean that the first proposition does not even touch on the nature or character of the object in question, but deals entirely with the conditions wherein *dharma* is operated with, and the very term 'object' belongs to these conditions, not to *dharma*, that is.]

6.2.1. The thing, however, is that as far as the Abhiddhamma goes, it is consciousness that acquires its *states*, not the *subject* of consciousness or person whose presence at the 'rise of thought' (see 4.1) is merely nominal.[30] From the point of view of consciousness, it can be said that, *when consciousness is conscious of one's mind, thought or consciousness directed to their objects*,[31] *then it is 'being conscious of' that may be named 'a state of consciousness' or a dharma.* This, however, must not be seen as a definition of *dharma*, but rather as an *indication* to where, when, and in connection with what a *dharma* might be sought.[32] This formulation I am going to comment on in a more or less strictly Abhidhammic way, and following the sequence of words.

(1) 'When' denotes a *coincidence* of (4), (5) and (6), which, however, does not take place in time. On the contrary, there is no time without, outside, or apart from these coincidences (*samaya*) which, in fact, constitute what we call the time.[33]

(2) 'Consciousness' is conceived here as an entirely non-psychological category, i.e., not related, as such, to (4) and (5) [or, more exactly, to (5) or (4)], though it is related to them *when* [in the sense of (1)] it is conscious of (5) in the sense of (3).

(3) 'Is conscious' denotes such a state of (2), when (2) is related to (5) [and/or to (4) through (5), and/or to (6) through (5), etc.] It is this *relation* that implies the opposition of 'consciousness' in the sense of (2) to 'consciousness' in the sense of (5).[34] For it is (5) that may become an object of psychology, and (2) that cannot, while (3) remains as the real formulation for a meta-psychological approach. The *states* of consciousness, or say, the moments of 'being conscious of' [the moments in the sense of (1)] retain their psychological 'names' in the absence of any psychological content of their own.[35]

(4) 'One' here is a person (*puggala*), not a 'sentient being' (*satta*). Because, to the latter the thought had already been ascribed (though in a merely 'formal' way, see Essay 2), while to the first it would be ascribed only *when* [in the sense of (1)] there would be the *case* (samaya). But even in this case 'one' stays, as it were, apart from any psychology unless it is *one's mind*, in which case it is 'mind', not 'one', which would assume some psychological characteristics.

(5a) 'Thought'. (5b) 'Consciousness'. (5c) 'Mind'. In this case, i.e., in the sense of this formulation, they can be seen as interchangeable with respect to (4), though with respect to (2) the situation will be far more complex. In this case, however, they are taken in a purely objective way, as the 'pure objects' of (2), that is.

(6) 'Objects' here could be conceived as either 'thought', 'consciousness' and 'mind', or all *other* objects.

6.2.2. One of the main obstacles to our understanding of *dharma* is, of course, our inability to grasp the meaning of the term 'object', when used both in and with respect to, the Buddhist philosophy. Setting aside some details on which I was concentrating in Essay 5, I would like now to stress the four chief distinctive traits of the Buddhist *conception of object.*

(1) An object is *always* conceived as 'object of thought', i.e., by any means not opposed to thought and not considered as, say, 'more objective' than thought.

(2) Therefore, even when it is not a 'dharma-object', it is to be considered dharmically all the same. That is, perhaps, why *dharma* is sometimes translated as 'object'. [Given, of course, that one cannot state that "a dharma is an object', though one could maintain *ad hoc* that 'this dharma is an object of...' etc.] And that is, by the way, why Nirvana could be thought of as *an object among other dharma-objects*—that is, so to speak, that Nirvana is not an especial object, yet an especial *dharma* (i.e. *asaṃskṛta dharma*).[36]

(3) One ought to be aware of a clear methodological difference between our own and Buddhist approaches to the idea of 'a different object'. For, given all varieties and variations, we would call an object 'different' because of its *objective* difference (or differences) from other objects. While from the Buddhist point of view, it would be seen as different, in principle at least, when present in *another situation of thought*, and/or *another state of consciousness* (i.e. *dharma*). That is, we may say, that to an Abhidharmist, any object of another thought (or even another moment of thought) would be another object, for this mere reason. [This would be true, at least, with respect to *saṃskṛta* dharmas.] Which in turn, might mean that the very notion of 'objectivity', if tentatively applied to Buddhism, would cover the thought directed to another object or, shall we say, both thought and its object, as if they were *one* other object.

(4) One may see in the Abhidharmic *concept of object* that it contains the most fundamental and, at the same time, the most elementary *type of relation* within thought (or any modification or modality of the latter), which could be called 'the pure objectness' or an *extreme case of object.* This is when any sort of relation between 'object' and 'thought' in an 'object of thought' becomes reduced to the pure nominality, i.e., not implying any other (be it logical, ontological, semantic, etc.) relation. In such a case the following three trends might be observed:

α. When the *name* of an object includes the negative prefix 'a' (as in *asaṃskṛta dharma*), it would not mean that the object itself consists of another object and its negation.[37]

β. When the *name* of an object is a compound one (as, for instance, *samudayanirodha*—'cessation of production') this object cannot be thought of as containing any relation between its two (or more) parts other than purely nominal, and this is particularly important with respect to *causal* relation.[38]

γ. When the *name* of an object consists of 'object' and of something of which this is an object, then this something cannot be thought of as caused by or 'materially' (*vastutaḥ*) related to, object'.[39]

6.2.3. So in the final analysis it can be said of all objects that they are dharmas in the sense in which it can be said of all dharmas (i.e., both *saṃskṛta* and *asaṃskṛta*) that they are *asaṃskṛta* dharmas (whereby the differentiations made in 6.0.5 become superfluous).[40] And the paraphrase of this would be to say that, a *dharma*, if understood as 'a state of consciousness' is the same thing as an object understood as in 6.2.2 (4).

If, however, we return to a strictly metaphilosophical position in the question of 'object-dharma' relation, we will see that neither 'object', nor *dharma* can be understood, even approximately, as 'a phenomenon'. Which is due not only to their being *a priori* hypostasized but, first of all, to the very fact that *the type of general relation fixed in the notion of dharma is, as it were, 'methodologically' reflected in the type of general relation fixed in the notion of object* (*ālambana, ārammaṇa*). That is, so to speak, in both we have the thought etc., related to whatsoever it might be, but in *dharma* this relation is established as prior to any actual thinking (or, say, to any observable *fact* of thinking), while in the object thought is seen as dealing already with all 'objects', including all dharmas.[41] Therefore, 'methodologically' here does not imply an epistemology, because we simply choose to look at dharmas from the point of view of objects, whereas it is quite possible to do it the other way around. That is, when the relation itself ('thought-object' relation) would be seen as realized within one or another dharma *objectively*, i.e., irrespective of whether or not one cognizes it, and if one cognizes it, irrespective of *how* he does it.

6.3. The last consideration raises one other question of utmost difficulty: does 'dharma', as a *notion*, belong to a *theory*, or being a purely *relational* notion, it is no more than a term of merely *meta-theoretical* description of the universal relation of thought (and/or consciousness) to its objects and states? The answer cannot be a simple and clear one. Because, if we still conceive of thought as a thing (i.e., not an object only), then, as it was already said above (6.1.1), *dharma* would be understood *meta-psychologically*, i.e., as one of conditions of *thinking*,[42] but by any means not of knowledge. [For knowledge (*ñāṇa*) in the Abhidhamma may or may not become *conjoint* (*sampayutta*) with thought (*citta*),[43] being thereby, an additional factor and not figuring as a separate *dharma*.][44] On the other hand, if taken in its absolute objectivity, i.e., as 'the highest object' of philosophical (and soteriological) 'theory', *dharma* would lose its relational character and assume its quasi-ontological status depriving thereby the thought of its 'thingness'.[45] And finally, we may again return to a purely relational interpretation of *dharma* as a 'pure' state of consciousness in the sense of which the consciousness (or thought) interprets itself, and it is then only that we may understand dharma as a term of meta-theory of consciousness which would become again void of any thinkable 'thingness'. In the last case this 'thingness' would be relegated to thought, as we see it later, in the Vajrayana Buddhism.

6.4. Is it not quite evident that no theory of knowledge is possible without a special reflexion on the cognizing person as an *independent entity*?[46] Or, if we put it in a little different way, no epistemology is possible until the process of reflexion on the *subject* of knowledge (whereby the subject finds its place not only outside knowledge, but also outside this very reflexive process) is completed. But it has not been completed in Buddhism, let alone the Abhidhamma where all reflective procedures find their place *within* the rubrics of several dhammas.

6.5. On the whole, I am inclined to think that, for the sake of our understanding of Buddhist *philosophy* as a system (which, of course, does not mean that it is a system in *itself*), or, shall we say, to produce our *own* meta-philosophical understanding of it in a systematic way, it would be interesting to imagine it as having, as it were, three entries: thought (and/or consciousness), *dharma* (state of consciousness) and object. This, of course, must not be understood in the sense that such was primarily the genuine scheme of the Buddhist philosophy itself, for what I am suggesting now is no more than a scheme of *our* understanding of the 'object' named 'The Buddhist Philosophy'. Each of these notions might be used with respect to each other, or as a meta-concept, or even as a thing (given that in the last case both negative and positive interpretations are possible). So that by means of this 'triad' the whole region of the theory of dharmas could become described, or at least made describable.

This becomes particularly interesting if we try to apply this triadic scheme of approach to main categories of Buddhist philosophy itself. Nirvana, for example, though unthinkable (*acintya*), is an object, and though not a thought (*na citta*), is a *dharma*.[47] *Karma* (also understood in a more general way, i.e., as 'an action'), albeit being neither a *dharma* nor an object, can be reduced or made phenomenologically reducible to consciousness or thought.[48] While *rūpa*, the form, can be regarded as an object and a *dharma*, yet never as consciousness, etc.[49]

So within the framework of the Abhidharma proper we are left with 'object' as the most *universal* category (the broadest entry, shall we say, provided of course, that we look at the Abhidharma from an entirely external position). For from an *internal* point of view, 'object' would be seen as the category shifting from *dharma* to thought and the other way around or, if present in the situation of 'the rise of thought', as opposed to thought and *objectively* different from 'a person' (*puggala* of the Abhidhamma).[50]

6.6. There is another thing of extreme methodological importance for our understanding of 'object' in and with respect to, the Abhidharma: we have to make clear distinction between an object given in investigation ('subject of investigation') and an object of thought (or of 'thinking'). Because, *a thought, when present in the Dhammasaṅgaṇi, is seen as a single, non-composite, and absolutely separate object*. But it is an object of investigation here, in the sense that our own investigating cognition (*saṃjñā*)[51] has not been reflected upon as 'another thought', or, shall we say, *objectified* as 'a thought'. In this case, as it was said elsewhere, this thought is cognized as having its own objects, dharmas, etc. At the same time, these very objects (and dharmas) can be seen, as it were, 'internally', that is, from the point of view of thought itself, and as its own objects, or let us put it stronger, seen as existing ('arising') only in connection with this thought and as solely its objects. This is where we would deal with them as 'objects of thought', which indirectly means that *dharmas cannot be objects of direct investigation.*[52] That is, they can be investigated only as *states of consciousness which have already become objectively connected with thought, and only provided that whenever we start this investigation, they are already there.*

And then would it not be obvious that an 'investigator' could not investigate his own dharmas, for they are *anattā?* Because they cannot be anybody's objects, but only those of 'a thought' which throughout the Abhidharma is given *objectively*, and whose 'rise' (*utpāda*) includes 'a person' (*pudgala*) as one of its co-factors, and it is this 'objectivity' of thought which would even forbid an investigator to identify himself with this 'person' in any way other than metaphorical.

6.7. The term 'objective' (in its adjectival meaning) is used here as a term of a meta-philosophical approach and, therefore, only partly coincides with the meaning of the word 'object' in the Abhidharma. And that is why it is to be stressed that its use here is confined to *methodology* of our investigation. So, in this sense only, we can say, for example, that when there is an object of thought, it means that *our* object of investigation here and now is not this thought, but this object (which, as it was said above, would not prevent this thought from being an object at another time or in another place).[53] And this, once limited by these 'spacio-temporal' conditions, could be formulated in such an operational way: *object is all that at this given moment of investigation is not thought or consciousness.* This dichotomy, however, is not absolute, because there is always an external observer or investigator, whose attention shifts from 'thought as an object' to 'an object of thought', and whose presence can be neither accounted for nor reduced to, the objectivity of dharmas.

6.8. All situations observed (and observable) by an observer have the 'rise of thought' as their extremal and, at the same time, most elementary case. And it is at this very moment of observation of 'rise of thought' with its person, objects and dharmas, that the observer himself cannot be thought of as an object [unless, of course, he starts observing or investigating 'his own' thought, in which investigation he would then figure as a person (*puggala*) with respect to objects, etc.]. But nor could he be taken for a subject (in the sense of the opposition 'object/subject'), for his observation is totally devoid of any traits of *reflexion.* That is, it is not related to himself as to *its* subject, so that the inferences like the Cartesian formulation do not apply here at all, and he would not be able to say, I think, therefore I exist'—for in his observation his very thinking is not related to *him* as an observer.[54] We may then sum all this up in saying that an observer of thought with its objects can neither observe himself as 'a subject', nor can he be observed by others as 'an object'. The classical dichotomy of 'object-subject' is here transformed into a much more complex 'construction', where the 'complete objectification' can be achieved only provided that there is no subject any more. That is, such a construction where its constituents—'thought-objects-dharmas'—would be conceived as simultaneously present and *excluding* each other in the thought of an observer.

6.9. It would be an utter mistake to say that the Buddhist Masters of old conceived the world as being or consisting of dharmas. Nor did they think that their cognition was brought about in or by means of dharmas. There was neither a mere dharmic ontology, or a mere dharmic epistemology there. And in the framework of our meta-philosophical approach, it can be contended that, speaking terminologically, dharmas do not carry any *information* about the world or the psychology of men, because dharmas are not *specific*. On the contrary, they are as unspecific as one could imagine. And this is so because of their (with the exception, of course, of *asaṃskṛta dharmas*) *relatedness* to thought and/or consciousness, which is, in itself absolutely non-specific in the sense that is covers what in our philosophical terminology is regarded as conscious as well as non-conscious, subjective as well as objective, material as well as non-material, etc.[55] For to say that, for example, 'emotion is thought' is, Buddhistically speaking, possible only because emotion is a *dharma* (in a broader sense, of course), and each *dharma* is, in a certain sense, thought. That is to say, an emotion (or perhaps, in an exacter manner, this emotion in question) is a dharmic object and, on the strength of its being 'dharmic', is as 'conscious' as thought or consciousness itself.

6.10. I am in full awareness that the last point would present to an investigator some insurmountable difficulties, particularly because in the further and latest developments of the Buddhist theory of consciousness the universal self-consciousness of thought was asserted with such a force that, practically, the distinction between a thought having itself for an object, and a thought having for an object something else, has completely disappeared. The most essential point here is, that if (and when) such a difference existed—and it did exist indeed throughout the whole Abhidhamma—then each and every thought which is not self-conscious would inevitably be regarded on the same level as an emotion, a sensation, an effect, an instinct, or any other mental, psychical or bio-psychical phenomenon, however primitive and elementary such a phenomenon might be. However, it is to be reminded here that the main and crucial difference between the Abhidhamma and, practically, any European epistemology is that in the latter the very prefix 'self' in its connection with 'consciousness' means 'a subject' or 'a person' *thinking*, while in the former it means *the direction of thought towards itself.* But even understood in the former way, the self-consciousness cannot be applied to dharmas, and it is in this sense that we think of Nirvana as of a *dharma*, not a 'thought'. We may even take risk to say that dharmas are not the thought in the sense that they do not think on themselves, however nonsensical it might sound. But it is the thought of an observer that may think of *itself* (not himself) in terms of dharmas, that is, in terms of its relatedness to all *thinkable* objects (including those *thinking*).

So, for example, the thought (*citta*) is a *dharma* (or, a kind of dharmas, listed as △5 in the Abhidhammic list of dharmas) *to* (but not 'of') an observer of thought, provided that he observes the thought *generally*. ['Generally' means here that the thought is observed neither as an object of thought of the observer himself, nor as that of 'a person' (*puggala*), but as one of abstractly conceived 'dharmic objects'.] In the case of such an observation, an observer not only cannot have 'this thought' attributed to him, but cannot even bring about an 'ideal' substitution, saying, 'If I were a person to whom this thought might be attributed...'—for there cannot be such a 'person' here at all. And a *dharma* named 'thought' would be thought of outside any thinkable *reflexion* and, thereby, as a totally impersonal one (by any means not the other way around). 'Thought' as 'a state of consciousness', cannot be thinkable in the context of a reflexion, and that is why it can be attributed to 'someone' only by means of some other things or agencies (which, themselves, are not states of consciousness) such as, for instance, *karma*. And this, Buddhistically speaking, may be exemplified by the fact that ultimate Nirvana is nobody's—and the same can be said of all dharmas taken *as such*.

6.11. It is in the late and modern Abhidhamma, however, where the dhammas now and again assume a merely *naturalistic* explanation and become the measurable fundamental entities whereupon the whole phenomenal world is resting. In spite of many reservations and clarifications made by modern Buddhist Theravadin scholars to the effect that what we deal with in dhammas is a mere psychology, they could not prevent dhammas from becoming a sort of 'psychological ontology'. And this, I guess, is, at least partly, due to the influence of some European epistemological tendencies. One point, however, remains very difficult to explain, and I will try to interpret it by means of a metaphysical comparison of the terms ontology and *svabhāva* ('own nature').

6.11.1. The notion of 'ontology' within almost all *theoretical contexts* of European culture—and irrespective of all differences between these contexts—implies a certain abstract, non-specific *quality* with which things and events may or may not be endowed, yet which remains universal and universally applicable in both positive and negative ways. 'Realism/nominalism', 'rationalism/empiricism', 'monism/dualism', 'materialism/idealism'—in all these oppositionally marked contexts 'the being' retains this quality invariably, the unique predicate ascribed now to one thing, now to its opposite. The only thing here that is left to logical analysis is to investigate the degree of universality and/or reality of what we deal with in each particular case of the predication of 'being', ranking from 'pure ontology' of God's being as one of His perfections to 'being' as secondary to thinking in the Cartesian formula. A *dharma*, in the context of Abhidharma at least, cannot be non-specifically predicated by 'being'. So that to say, in a little artificial manner, that 'the dharmas *are*...', or even to interpret them in a 'quasiontological' way, saying that '(there are) dharmas only' (*dharmamātra*)—would inavoidably place us in an utterly *trivial* position. And this is so, because dharmas *cannot be*, *but are what and as they are* (i.e., in the sense of *yathābhūtatā*). We can, of course, state that the time of 'existence' of a 'dharma of thought' is $1/10^{21}$ second, which indeed, in this *theoretical* context would not mean any 'being' lasting for $1/10^{21}$ second.[56] Moreover, this would not even mean that this dharma's 'being as it is' includes this duration for, in the sense of 'as it is', it is totally irrelevant. So we are allowed to say that even *when* they 'are', dharmas cannot be predicated with 'being' for in this case it is 'when' [i.e., not in the sense of duration, but in that of 'happening'] that matters, not 'are'.

6.11.2. If taken with respect to dharmas only, *svabhāva* would be seen as *their own* being, in the sense in which they do not differ from one another, though if understood all of them as sharing of this one being, their 'dharma-ness' (*dharmatā* or *tathatā* of all dharmas), they would differ very strongly from all that is not a *dharma*. So, that in the last sense their 'being' would be seen not as their *being*, but as their being what *they are* in distinction, for example, from *karma*, or *duḥkha* ('suffering'), or any other *thinkable* thing which is not one of the dharmas.

6.11.3. Therefore, in the sense of 'being' in general, dharmas *are not*, while in the sense of their *own* being they can not be classified even into *saṃskṛta* and *asaṃskṛta*, being, in fact, *the same*. Their classification is very conventional and relative, that is, they may be classified in one way or another, but always with intimation that in classifying them one always thinks or meditates on them as related to something which, at this given moment at least, is not a *dharma;* or, returning to our previous problem of object, which is not a 'dharmic object'.

6.12. One of the simplest and at the same time, the most enigmatic things[57] in the whole Abhidhamma is that the *dhammas are considered as already existent when the thought is stated as arisen.*

Given that one thing is to think of *thought* as related to dharmas, and quite another is to think of dharmas[58] in their relation to thought (the former is discussed in Essay 4 on 'The Rise of Thought'), and concentrating on the latter, I can say that a *thought arisen* is, in the Abhidhamma, *the only primarily given fact.* The fact in the absence of which there is nothing to observe, conceive of, or meditate on. The fact wherein the universe of objects and subjects[59] is contained, or wherefrom it can be derived for an *external* observer, be it an observer of the thought in general, his own thought or any thought whatsoever. That is, without the rise of thought there is no field of observation at all in Abhidhamma, and without external observation there can be no Abhidhamma as the systematic exposition (or fixation) of the theory of dhammas.

So, speaking of rise of thought as a fact,[60] we may say: 'There is a thought there', or 'there is no thought there', or 'this is one thought or another', or as is said in *Dhammasaṅgani*, 'the first thought, the second thought, the third thought, etc.' The dhammas, however, *are there, as various discrete forms in which each thought assumes its interpretation of continuity and process.* This is a limited and relational definition of dhammas. Relational, because they are regarded here not *as such*, but in their relation to *thought only*, that is, to a situation when and where a thought is already detected in its factuality. This needs to be explained in a more detailed way.

6.12.1. Firstly, no dhammas can be a fact *per se*, for *one dhamma* cannot merely be thought of as existent, because no thought can be interpreted in the sense of one *dhamma*, but solely in the sense of the combination of an infinite number of dhammas of one or several kinds (much more often several than one).

6.12.2. Secondly, the thought is given in observation as a *separate* fact or, let us say, in separate facts the succession of which is *externally* established (whether empirically or ideally) by an observer acting, speaking and thinking *separately* from what is observed. While the continuity of dhammas is postulated as *the precondition* of any thought, be it that of observer or of those observed. One *may* think of various and different continuities of dhammas as separate, but only *after* the fact itself of thought is already observed, though one may know, none the less, that this or that continuity of dhammas had been existing before an observation began and will exist after it has finished, so that the very problem of 'otherness' would be totally irrelevant in the context of such a consideration. Unlike William James' idea that one's psychical and mental life is *manifested* in states of consciousness, the Masters of Abhidhamma maintained that what, in fact, we see as one's psychical and mental life is the manifestation of unmanifested dharmas. That is to say, *any thinkable activity of thought is thought to be 'dharmic'* and, therefore, is to be interpreted in terms of discreteness (discontinuity) of states of consciousness as well as in terms of continuity of states of consciousness, if we chose to interpret the *process* of thought, not its act of rising only. The basic thing here is, however, that any epistemological criteria remain inapplicable to dharmas, because these criteria are valid only *within* the system of interpretable objects, and entirely non-valid with respect to the things constituting the basis of interpretation, for the latter belong to quite another system.[61]

6.12.3. Thirdly—and this point I consider highly important—the factuality of thought, when this thought is interpreted in the sense of dhammas, cannot be understood as or in terms of, psychological empiricism. To the contrary, throughout the Abhidhamma the thought (*citta*), even when used not in its dhammic sense (i.e., when it does not figure as one of the kinds of dhammas), implies a much higher degree of abstractedness than any *empirical* idea of thought.

6.13. It is worth mentioning, at last, that the *predicates* of dharmas do not make dharmas *contentful*, even if they imply a certain definite content themselves. So from the expression 'the dharmas of the present, past and future' one can not infer anything at all about the possibility of different interpretations of these three 'kinds' of states of consciousness, in terms of content. The same is when we try to interpret the first line of Dhammapada 'Mind-made are the dharmas, etc.', or a proposition that 'all dharmas are signless (*alakkhaṇa*)'. Because, if we take the last example, we will have to admit that the very *meaning* of 'signlessness' exists only with respect to dharmas and in no other way. [Unlike, shall we say, the meaning of 'mortal' in the proposition: 'all men are mortal'.] This is to say that practically all sentences where 'dharmas' figure as the subject of the logical construction, are mere tautologies. Which means that the meaning of a predicate related to 'dharmas' cannot be reduced to any 'content' other than dharmas themselves.

Thus to assert that 'everything that exists is dharma', would mean that everything *thinkable* in terms of content could be thought of only in the context of certain states of consciousness, i.e., dharmas, but not the other way around. And that is exactly what W. James bore in mind in stating that one and the same thing may be 'I' in one state of consciousness, and something else in another. [From which we may easily 'deduce' that there is no such a state of consciousness as 'I' on the one hand, and that in terms of content 'I' (as well as 'non-I') can exist (i.e., 'be thought of as existing') only when related to one or another *dharma*, on the other hand. But neither 'I' nor 'non-I' become a *specific content* to any dharma.]

The use of the word 'content' is no more than an element of the meta-philosophical approach, because all contents of *thought*, speaking Buddhistically, belong to the level quite different from that to which thought itself does belong. The 'level of content', if taken apart from thought, would be inevitably ousted in the realm of 'as it were psychology' in our investigation.

6.14.0. The time, if seen from the point of view of the Abhidharma, does not stand out as a phenomenon, nor is this surprising, because, not being one of the states of consciousness (dharmas), it also cannot be reduced either to one of them, or to any of their combinations. And in this case, we have to return back to *thought* in the sense of which time may have figured as something, as it were, positively *thinkable*, though not necessarily as one of the *objects* of thinking. In saying this I do not exclude the possibility or, even, necessity of other points of approach to the problem of time in Buddhism. Moreover, I am going to suggest a very tentative scheme of such a 'Buddhistic' investigation in the following way.

6.14.1.

(1) Firstly, we must investigate the *conditions of thinking* about time which means that there can be supposed several various cases, situations, or contents in which and about which time is to be predicated as *content* of thinking.

(2) Secondly, we must observe the cases, when thinking itself, i.e., in its various acts and instances, may be interpreted as different (i.e., one or the other, not one and the same) with respect to time.[62]

(3) Thirdly, we pass to a situation, when thinking, taken in one of its modalities, would be objectively conceived *as* time. That is to say, that there is, in thinking, a certain *psychological subjectivity* which is objectified (or naturalized) as time. (Time as an epiphenomenon of thinking.)

(4) Fourthly, we return to the states of consciousness (dharmas), and consider them in their connections with thinking containing time as its content.

(5) Fifthly, we then would explore the states of consciousness with respect to their own time, or timelessness.

(6) Sixthly, we may then conclude, by making a meta-philosophical stipulation about the *abstract* possibility to construe a *structure of consciousness* (not a state of consciousness—this distinction here is overwhelmingly important) that can have included time as its own *objective* content. This stipulation could be hardly

considered as Buddhistic—let alone 'Buddhist'—though we still can refer to the Yogacarin metaphysics, where time is regarded as one of the 'contents' of non-individual *ālāyavijñāna* ('stored consciousness').[63]

6.14.2. Speaking of conditions of thinking when time figures as object and content of thinking, we find ourselves in a position that is, itself, at once subjective and objective. Subjective, because when thinking of time, our thinking concentrates necessarily on some reflexive procedures related to duration of one's own or somebody else's thinking, or any *act* of thinking which is prior to, coinciding with or following any act of non-thinking. In the latter case time would be conceived of as that of *sequence* or *seriality* of thinking. However, a very strong intimation remains there that no sequence or seriality in time of acts of non-thinking alone can be conceived of or stipulated. [So, for instance, a sequence of Texts (*sūtrānta*) or of their expositions (*dharmaparyāya*) is *temporal* only on the strength of their stressedly *conscious* character.][64] The very idea of all Buddhas of past, present and future, if understood as a merely Buddhological idea, might be seen as *one of such conditions* of thinking of time. That is, while thinking of all Buddhas, one *brings in* the idea of time—not the other way around. That is to say, that the time here cannot be *an independent object* of thinking, because it depends on its conditions.[65]

6.15. *A hidden postulate about thinking*

In one of his unpublished metaphysical essays M. Mamardashvili says: 'Isn't it astonishing that such a thing as thinking simply *cannot be*, though we know that it *is* there, as like as not?' And it is in Buddhism that we find no instrument whatever to deal with thinking, though a *yogic* concept of thinking is constantly present there.[66]

From the point of view of an empiricist, this impossibility is too evident to be questioned, for no thinking can be discovered *by our reflection on our thinking*. In the case of the Abhidhammic approach the situation with thinking would be far more complicated. For in the Abhidhamma this reflection is always, as it were, already objectified as one or another mental state and therefore thinking itself cannot be found *in* (that is, not *by* as in the previous approach) our, or somebody else's, reflection on thinking. The theory of dhammas could hardly be considered as a method of analysis or a method of interpretation of reflexive procedures only. And the thing is, that reflection on thinking, though present within at least six dhammas out of 56, still continues to figure as a 'non-dharmic' and, thereby, entirely *subjective* state of mind. While thinking itself cannot be fixed in the dharmic analysis of any reflexive procedures, for its presence within these procedures is purely *objective* and not subject to any reflection. This, I conjecture, might have been observed by some of the Abhidhammic Masters as early as the time of the composition of the earliest 'dhammic lists'. We may even assert that, though it has been grasped, classified and denoted by such quasi-synonymous terms as 'thought' (*citta*), 'mind' (*manas*), 'consciousness' (*viññāṇa*) and in the late Mahayana, 'sentient-ness' or 'thought-ness' (Tib. *sems-ñid*), thinking itself remained unidentified and even unidentifiable with any of the Abhidhammic or Abhidharmic categories or concepts. Moreover, when we say 'objective', this implies that a certain thing has been changed from a 'subjective' into an 'objective' thing, which can be achieved through a dharmic analysis or through the process of *dhyāna*, or by some other means. Yet when we say that there cannot be thinking, we assume that this thinking, irrespective of whether it could or could not be there, cannot be thought of otherwise than as *primarily* objective, or that its objectivity is primary. The dharmas then would be seen as thinking's secondary objectifications, and reflexive procedures as its subjective interpretations.

Quite another difficulty in our understanding of thinking as impossible is due to the fact that, speaking generally, thinking itself *is not natural.* More than that—it is utterly unnatural, provided of course, that the opposition 'natural/unnatural' belongs to our own culture and has nothing to do with the cultural background of early historical Buddhism. [Where what we would have called 'natural', figured, indeed, as 'conditioned'. Thus for example, fear (*bhaya*) was described by the Buddha as arising in even highly experienced ascetics on the strength of their being subjected to certain conditions (utter solitude, jungles, ghosts and spirits in forests and wilderness etc.), but not because of their own 'human' nature, etc.] That is, Budhistically speaking, thinking does not come as rain, for even if we do not know the causes of the latter, they are supposed to exist. Thinking as such (i.e., apart from its direction, character, etc.) simply *happens*, and the only, though remote enough, analogy to this 'happening of thinking' can be seen in the process of *dhyāna* understood in its most general way. *Dhyāna* cannot, of course, provide one with a key to the understanding of the problem of thinking but can indirectly indicate some possibilities of such an understanding. In saying this, first of all I mean the existence of *specifically dhyanic texts*, which not only contained (or were themselves) the objects of or terminological fixations for *dhyāna* (and in particular, *sati*, yogic 'recollection'), but also served as a sort of *framework for thinking*. That is to say, that thinking, when and if actualized, did actualize within and in terms of these dhyanic texts, which by no means suggests that they can be regarded as 'texts of thinking'. Because a 'text of thinking' implies that a certain thinking (or thinking of a certain type) has already taken place either as preceding a text, or as coinciding (or *being one*) with its coming into being. It seems to me, however, that in the case of the Buddhist *dhyāna*, these texts, whether oral or written, have existed as 'contentless' units of merely potential and latent thinking which might or might not have found its actualization therein. So, taking the *Dhammasaṅgaṇi* as an example, we would dare to assert that it would not be possible, even to a highly experienced yogin, to reconstruct the text of this book from *mātikā*, though it may be possible, *knowing* the book, to actualize the whole text (in one's recollection) as a text of thinking, following the *mātikā*. In other words, we may say that in the European philosophical tradition a text, however lapidary or condensed it might be, still can be seen as a 'text of thinking', i.e. a text can be identified with a text of thinking hypothetically at least and, as such, might be continued or discontinued, reproduced or destroyed. While in the Abhidhammic tradition, no text of thinking could be created or annihilated, for it exists in its potentiality which, in itself, is not textual.

Thus, speaking meta-philosophically, we may conjecture that in European culture (broadly understood) each text can be imagined as an *actual* cultural reflection on thinking which itself does not exist outside this reflection, which comes into being and perishes with this reflection and, thereby, cannot be imagined at all without the text of its (i.e., thinking's) *cultural* actualization. In the Buddhist tradition the very idea of culture is totally synonymous with tradition itself and, therefore, physically the text remains virtually irrelevant to the potential existence of thinking. Any actual text is given to us as *thinkable* (audible, readable, writable, meditatable etc.) content. Yet it is this *thinkability*, that is, not a text or its content, through which thinking itself is revealed as *impossible*—not only in its impossibility to be thought of, but in its impossibility *to be*. Because, there is nothing *between* an object in the content, and a text whereby this content (or more exactly, we ourselves) might find its expression. So, the classical duality of 'level of content/level of expression' is totally inapplicable to the problem of thinking.

Speaking metaphilosophically, we may well remark that any phenomenology is no more than an investigation of ways or methods (or say, laws or rules) by means of which a thought could be interpreted in its *cultural fixations* (named 'notions', or 'concepts', or 'ideas'). Ascribing to the remark made above a more 'general' (and more Kantian) character, we can even assert that *each phenomenon is a thought already interpreted* in the sense of content, and then all such notions as 'text', 'content', 'form', 'sign' etc., would be seen as terms of interpretation of thinking, not of thinking itself. Moreover, from a Buddhistic point of view, these notions could even be seen in the sense of opposition or contrariness to thinking, given the reflexive and thereby subjective character of all abstract interpretations of thinking on the whole. [I am even inclined to regard such yogic formulations as, for instance *cittavṛtti* ('fluctuation of thought') in the sense of opposition of thinking as such to all possible interpretations of thinking as anything else.] The remarkable idea of the formalists—yogacarins, that each thought or consciousness is 'self-illuminating' (*svaprakāśa*) bore an entirely objective meaning. That is, it never had anything to do with a 'subject', be it 'me', 'thou', or 'we'. Because it was thought itself that was thought of as aware of itself, not 'I' or 'thou'. And that is why Jinendrabuddhi in his commentary denotes this state of *subjective* awareness of an idea by the word 'buddhi' which is used as a term of secondary interpretation of thinking.[67] One of the most essential philosophical moments in the Abhidhamma, an absolutely discrete character of the states of consciousness (dhammas), finds its complete analogy in the absolute separateness of all thoughts from each other in space and time. A given thought (*citta*) thus arises within an occurrence or happening (*samaya*) where and when it is connected with dhammas, objects (*ārammaṇa*), subjects (*puggala*), and *karma*. But even described in such a quasi-realistic way, a given thought never *becomes* (*bhavati*) what it *is* (*hoti*), however brilliant Mrs. Rys Davids' considerations on the subject might have been. It actually cannot *be* even as a single act or instance of thinking. So, it can only *happen* or *occur*, or flow 'from nowhere' into a 'stream of thought', given that the last figures as no more than still one more interpretive concept whereby a subjectively attributed continuity of discrete states and things is formally established. Thinking could be theoretically conceived of as being either in the interval between its being in 'nowhere' and into the stream, or as being in the interval between one thought and the other, but this seems to be a speculation never attempted by any of the Abhidhammic masters. But then quite another problem arises: how can we pass from where there is no thinking to where there is thinking? To Descartes as well as to Wittgenstein such a transition would not be possible. For any indication to the points or moments 'without thinking' would be void for either of them, though for quite different reasons. To the former this is *ontologically* impossible (i.e. irrespective of his methodology) on the strength of the parallelism of two 'beings', conscious and natural: they could not cross—and this is conceived *objectively*. To Wittgenstein thinking itself is, unlike that in Buddhism, an entirely natural, or more exactly, naturalized concept. That is, my thinking is as natural as my speech (and my language is as natural as my speech too). However, when he comes to where he cannot spot the thinking, he cannot help introducing some other means to show why he cannot do that.

Wittgenstein writes about men looking like automats: 'As if they were acting not on their own will ...' (1978, p. 99). But of course, this will, is it not undetectable? That is, it can be *traced*. [Literally: its traces could be observed, or rather, the traces or symptoms of its *absence*, not of its presence. And then he says: 'they behave like automata ...'] But it could never be realized in its *actuality*, save the cases when the actuality of its absence is demonstrated. And of course, Wittgenstein could not help seeing it as a *personal* will, the being of which is uncertain, while that of his own is evidently certain and, thereby, 'describable'. So, the will is a thing which might or might not be, though it cannot be realized as *one* in, say, all men. All the more that to Wittgenstein the *other will* must have been *marked* by its absence rather than by its presence, while his own was *felt* (behind and beyond his philosophical investigation i.e., indescribable or 'ineffable') to have been present because of his ... *thinking*.[68] That is to say, it could have been realized in the *fact* of his thinking, which otherwise would have never reached the 'surface' of his text and remained forever as something utterly latent and potential in the depths of his mind. Something about which he would have to keep silent.

However, in order to acknowledge the presence of 'other will' or at least admit its possibility, an observer has to allow for its being *thought of* by another person. [No will can be deduced from mere observation of self-observation.] Returning to an old Buddhist argument, we may say that though 'desire to act' can be deduced from the fact of an outer (outwardly observable) movement, and the same with thought, speech etc., it will be no more than a *formal* desire conceived of as an inner component of an outer action. Some deeper factor still lies undisclosed, awaiting for its being explored and analysed in the late Abhidharma where 'a thought arisen' and its concomitants are to be considered as a *coincidence* brought about by this very factor of *vāsanā* (*bags*) understood as an *objective will.* To Wittgenstein it is always subjective, i.e., his own. That is why he discards 'thinking' when he speaks of people looking as if they were the automata, i.e., deprived of their subjectivity, while constantly speaking of himself in terms of subjectivity only. And the contrary position is succinctly shown, for example, in the *Bodhicāryāvatāra* (see 4.2) where the 'automata' are described as devoid of consciousness, not of will, that is, for, as a phenomenon, the thinking cannot *become* by itself, but can *happen* i.e., be brought into a stream by means of *vāsanā*. Because, as it was shown above, the stream is nothing but an *objectification* of thought or consciousness in its quasi-temporal aspect, while thinking requires, necessarily, the work of a constantly acting factor.

My very vague conjecture is that in some of the texts of the Pali Canon (not only in the Abhidhamma) the main concern is about *singularity of thinking*, not about its typology. That is, about those 'points of fixation' of thinking where it cannot correlate with *the general* typologically, does not ascend historically to any prototype, and must not be reduced to any initial principle logically. The considering thinking in such fixations can be seen as one of the *metaphilosophical* preoccupations. I am ready even to go as far as to conjecture that so widely known and wildly misinterpreted a phenomenon as *samādhi* (and, particularly, *satori* in Zen Buddhism) can be seen as that absolute stopping of thinking, wherein everybody who happens to enter there, *does not think* in his own unique way. The way which would differ from any other way of non-thinking much more than any one way of thinking may differ from any other.

However, this singularity has absolutely nothing to do with *a person* not thinking (or thinking): It is his thinking, not himself, that is singular. [M. Mamardashvili would have said that 'his non-thinking *does not occur* in one and the same structure of consciousness with his "I" (not to speak of the fact that there is no such a structure of consciousness as "I" in Buddhism at all).'] From this follow all so-called 'paradoxes of *samādhi*', which, in fact, are neither paradoxes, nor metaphors, but *terms of consciousness*, which cannot be related to or correlated with, a person understood as *the subject* of *samādhi* in question. So, the notorious Zen expression 'the Buddha—a lump of shit'—is nothing but *the occurrence of two terms of consciousness within an interval of non-thinking*. Although these terms are *pronounced in thinking*. That is, when pronounced in thinking, they present a certain type of *discursiveness*, though carrying in (or with) themselves the traces of non-thinking; which traces are usually qualified (and very stupidly so) as paradoxes or metaphors.

These 'fixations' of singularity cannot be conceived of or worked through in a philosophy, for unthinkable are they as objects of any *contentful* thinking. Only in the context of a phenomenological or meta-philosophical investigation one could ponder over them. I might also note in this connection, that 'non-thinking' of *samādhi* is not a natural (i.e., psychological, etc.) phenomenon, that is, it is *absent* in the nature of individual thinking. One may, approximately of course, think of non-thinking as belonging to the *objectivity* of consciousness. That is, it can be *thinkable* as one of the states of consciousness (i.e., as a *dharma*), or as one of the structures of consciousness, where individual thinking is deemed as possessing the potency of becoming *non-natural*.

6.16. *Some additional remarks on 'otherness'*

To understand—or even to start understanding—the concept of 'other thought' in a perspective broader than that provided not only by the Buddhist but also by a Buddhistic approach, one would have to get rid of entirely all possible epistemological solutions, however tempting they might be.

In the following remarks I will try approximating to such an understanding by tackling the whole problem of 'other thought' from the point of view of 'otherness', i.e., not from that of 'thought'.

(1) Speaking logically, there is, on the part of a speaker, a very strong *implication of choice* in the notion of otherness; that is, to say 'other' does not mean 'any other', though there are no rules according to which such a choice is to be determined. [Which, of course, does not mean that it is not determined.]

(2) 'Other' does not necessarily imply here 'not this one' or, least of all, 'the same as this' (as in the expression '... in this case as in many others...'), although it certainly implies 'other than mine' which, seemingly only, narrows the class of 'others' and, thereby, the sphere of choice.

(3) An 'other' does not necessarily mean a 'different object', for it may well be the same object, *yet seen as* the other. The main difference between European and Indian methods of one's self-observation is that in the former I see myself from the point of view of another person, while in the latter I see myself as another person. That is, in the first case, I externalize my observation of myself, while in the second I externalize myself as an *object* of observation, transforming myself into an *other* object. This is, in fact, the beginning of *objectification.*

So, the 'otherness' here might be subdivided into two cases: (a) the classical case of 'other' in the Suttas, where one thing is recommended to be seen as another (and, thereby, not as itself), or where one is recommended to see another thing *instead of* the first one, provided that the first one is thought of as less real, or not real at all. As, for instance, when it is asserted that there is no 'I', but there are the five skandhas, or that there is no 'I', but there are samskaras (instead), etc.;[69] (b) the no less classical case where a thing is commended to be seen as *other*, i.e., not mine (or thine) but, as it were, alien (which very often coincides with the notion of the Third Person).

(4) So, in the light of this remark, 'other thought' is to be reduced to some *essential* otherness. The otherness by means of which my own thought can be changed into an *absolute* object (i.e., 'object of all objects', etc.). I may even assert that the only real (i.e., essential) otherness is that of thought. That is, there is not any other thing as other as thought.

(5) Wherefrom Buddhologically it follows that, what is objectified by the Buddha as other thought, could be achieved by *me* in the objectification of my own thought which becomes, therewith, as it were, the other. But, of course, I cannot achieve this objectification with a thought other than mine.

(6) Therefore, phenomenologically speaking, other thought is reduced to what I have called an 'essential otherness' and an 'object'. And then my thought is reduced to other thought in order of objectification. Perhaps the Buddhist masters of old knew about an independent position of 'otherness' as to what the very

idea of 'object' was to be reduced, not the other way around. To us an object seems to be obviously a kind of primary category, whereas to them it remained a sort of complex concept needed to have been reduced to its basic determinants among which otherness was to be considered the first. 'Other stream' then, would be seen not as any other thing, but as 'the most other' thing in the universe or, say, as the only *really* other thing. I see that saying this, I find myself in direct contradiction to the idea that it is *my* stream, not other, than could be cognized directly. But let us not forget that this idea belongs to the epistemological aspect of our problem, not to metaphysical or Buddhological, that is.[70]

Moreover, I am inclined to think that what is implied in the idea of direct knowledge of 'my stream' is entirely different from what the idea of 'absolute object' implies. For there is no distinction between a direct and indirect knowledge in the objectification, because this distinction also belongs to epistemology par excellence.[71]

NOTES TO ESSAY 6

1 The terms 'subjective' and 'psychological' are used partly synonymously here, in the sense that they both imply the existence (or even, the postulation of existence) of individual psychical mechanisms to be investigated. But by no means in the sense that psychology is considered as more subjective than any other way of investigation of psychical mechanism.

2 As, for instance, when one would identify any fact observed or experienced by an individual (headache or outburst of anger, for example), saying: 'This is a state of consciousness'. Provided that this would not necessarily fall under the rubric of one or other *kind* of states of consciousness in Abhidhammic or any other classification of states of consciousness.

3 Thus this second meaning would embrace the cases where a fact is identified with a state of consciousness falling certainly under the rubric of one or another kind of dharmas of the Abhidhamma, as well as the cases, when we deal not with particular dharmas but with *kinds of dharmas* in general. An example of the first: 'My thinking now is (corresponding to) a dharma of thought (*citta, dhamma* △5 of the first Abhidhammic list of dhammas)'. An example of the latter: 'The dhamma of thought and the dhammas of reasoning and reflection (*vicāra,* △7: *vitakka,* △6) are answerable for the process of investigation'.

4 We may guess that 'rendering' would require just another kind of mental discipline.

5 E. Burnouf (1876, p. 391).

6 One may conjecture to what extent Burnouf might have been influenced on this point by the works of Brian Hodgson, the real Father Founder of British Buddhology. The extreme felicity of Hodgson's approach to Buddhism is amazing. He saw Buddhism as, first of all, a religion and, moreover, as *one* (though motley and variegated as it was) religious system. And besides, he happened to be one of the very few Buddhologists who happily evaded an inner intellectual confrontation between Buddhism and his own culturally acquired Christianity, theism, or atheism; 'Matter endowed with intrinsic intelligence' he called dharma! B. H. Hodgson (1874, pp. 40,72). See also T. E. Colebrooke (1873, pp. 420–1).

7 L. de la Vallée Poussin establishes in his rendering a stressedly metaphysical meaning of dharmas, calling them 'unstable and substanceless elements' (1909, p. 54). Whereas Kern, in a more Kantian way, prefers to use the term phenomenon (dharmas are 'all mental and physical phenomena'). See S. Kern (1896, p. 51). The use of this term by Mrs. Rhys Davids is very different: 'The ultimate data [of Theravada Buddhism] were phenomenal, and yet they were very real'. See C. Rhys Davids (1914, p. 65); the formulation of a kind unheard of in a Kantian school.

8 *Dhs. tr.* (pp. 42–3 et *passim*).

9 It evidently invites parallels and comparisons of a more speculative character. So, for example, speaking of *sanātana dharma* of Hinduism, we may state that it includes its own description. At the same time, we usually do not take note of such an evident fact of our own culture (*conceptually* understood, not empirically), that it is also impossible without or outside its own description.

10 This or suchlike classification may be particularly useful in the study of Hindu rituals, where the term 'ethos' was first introduced by A. F. Stenzler (1865, pp. 149–63 and especially pp. 154–5).

11 D. T. Suzuki (1974, p. 26).

12 I would go so far as to suggest that the core of primary Buddhist instruction might have consisted of the series of such like interpretations, the *results* of which in the *form of terms* had had to be memorized and thereafter used to describe one's mental experience as 'no one's' (i.e., in an entirely desubjectivized sense), which in turn means that these experiences were described as already transformed from those of one's into those of nobody's, and such terms as 'dharma' and samskaras meant only to *confirm* this transformation. I think that in the context of such an instruction, the very concept of 'common (or ordinary) use' of language as opposed to 'theoretical' is getting superfluous and futile. Let us look in this connection at such a passage from L. Wittgenstein (1978, p. 184): 'People who on awaking

tell us certain incidents (that they have been in such-and-such places etc.). Then we teach them the expression "I dreamt", which precedes the narrative. Afterwards I sometimes ask them, "Did you dream anything last night?" and am answered yes or no ... That is the language game. (I have assumed here that I do not dream myself...)'. This place, which Stcherbatsky would have qualified as 'very sanskritic' or 'very Buddhist', is in itself a brilliant example of 'half-conscious' character of Wittgensteinian 'analysis of language' ('half-conscious' means 'not phenomenlogical enough' here). For the central term here, 'to dream', cannot be classified as belonging to either 'common speech' or 'language of theory'. It is, as a matter of fact, a term of description of man's untransformed mental experience in terms of 'language only'. That is why Wittgenstein classifies this term as an 'expression'. Dharmakirti would have called it 'a way (or manner) of speaking' (*vacana mātra*), stressing thereby, that it is simply *instead of saying one thing* (here what is *in* the narrative) *we say the other* (what precedes it). So, it is 'the expression' that figures as a meta-term here, not 'the dream' or 'to dream'. But this meta-term does not form the *theory* of mental experiences in this passage, for it has been introduced only to show that what in common language is 'such-and-such incidents', in meta-language of linguistical analysis is 'dream'. So, speaking Buddhistically, Wittgenstein is 'a Buddha the other way around', for he teaches the dreamers *their own* language (i.e., not his, for he does not dream), establishing, confirming them in their own *dharma*. Because, his own language has remained uninvestigated *as such*, that is, he had no *dharma* of his own, so to speak, to teach them.

13 The destiny of samskaras in European rendering happened to be far less adventurous and vague than that of *dharma*, and this is hardly surprising, for from the very start of modern Buddhology they were—and rightly so—associated with the much vaguer concept of Western culture, that of *will* or *volition*. That is, the concept which, after having been almost totally neglected in Cartesian tradition, and hardly noticeable in the tradition of classical German philosophy, appeared on the scene of European philosophizing, and assumed there its new function. It became the necessary and indismissible counterpart of individual consciousness, now directly opposing the latter, now permanently accompanying it as a complementary concept. Moreover, one may say that will, in its opposition to consciousness and reasoning, became an inalienable attribute of all romanticism of the nineteenth century, exceeding thus the confines of philosophy and changing into a very important *cultural* category. And it is Schopenhauer, von Hartmann and particularly Nietzsche, whose *critique* of their own (i.e., Christian) culture contained 'will' as an extra-cultural or meta-cultural category. [I.e., as a concept which might have been used in the evaluation and criteriorization of all cultures or, a concept from the point of view of which all cultures could have been viewed as one, or The Culture. This is particularly significant in view of the assumption that Buddhism, seen in the light of its 'initial' posulations at any rate, could itself be considered as 'a-cultural'.]

When later in the twentieth century this category became more and more associated with and merged into, that of the un-non-or sub-conscious (from P. Carus through Freud to Adler), it became thereby totally excluded from 'all that was conscious in culture', and served very often to denote the sphere of natural urges, instincts and impulses associated with the idea of 'natural' as opposed to 'cultural'. [What is important to bear in mind is that 'culture' here is used as a synonym of '*cultural reflection*' and is, therefore, totally divorced from what we call 'civilization'; the latter cannot reflect on itself by definition.]

Looking at such renderings of samskaras as those attempted by D. T. Suzuki and B. Nanjio, we are tempted to call their position on this point also 'cultural'. For theirs was the task of 'translating' the terms of Buddhist *philosophy* into those of Western *culture*, whatever their genuine aspirations might have been. And if looked at from such an angle, the whole problem can be described in the following manner: samskaras can be ascribed to dharmas as their most general predicate, but they cannot have an ontology of theirs, while dharmas can (when, of course, they are not predicated by samskaras). At the same time, dharmas, irrespective of whether they figure as phenomena or merely *relational* categories, are supposed to possess their own reality (regardless of the degree of relativity of the last), whereas samskaras *do not exist as such*, but only as a modus of some *other* being. And this is so, even given that samskaras are very often used in Buddhist texts in an absolutely *naturalistic* way. See particularly, Rune E. A. Johansson (1979, pp. 41–8). The tendency to naturalizing is revealed in this book with all possible sincerity, which, I think, is inevitable when one forgets ontological *secondariness* of samskaras with respect to dharmas. This secondariness was particularly stressed by B. Keith (1923, p. 74): 'We should not regard the samskaras as things in relation to mind (*saṅkhata*); rather the term has the more general signification of product, as well as of producing, and it is therefore naturally and directly applied to the whole world of external reality as well as to mental products'.

14 Otto O. Rosenberg, *Problems of Buddhist Philosophy*, Petrograd, 1918 (in Russian). See also German translation, *Die Probleme der Buddhistischen Philosophie* (aus dem Russ. Übersetzt von Frau E. Rosenberg), Heidelberg, 1924.

15 Th. Stcherbatsky (1923, p. 5).

16 That is, probably, why Kern used both terms as almost synonymous, when he spoke of the Abhidharma. See H. Kern (1896, pp. 47, 51).

17 So, the most difficult thing in the rendering of samskaras into any term, or even describing them by a group of terms, was the fact that in Buddhism—irrespective of this or that school, branch, sect or tradition—*samskaras were never opposed to consciousness taken in its phenomenal or transformational* (*pariṇāma*) aspect. As for their relation to dharmas, the situation becomes even more complicated, for, if taken strictly as *categories* (that is, as denoting concepts, not things or phenomena), they may play the role of the unique, in point of fact, *predicate* to dharmas. [As in the well-trodden, yet not at all understandable formulation from the *Mahā-parinibbāna-suttanta*: 'All dharmas (are) samskaric' (*sabbe dhammā saṅkhārā*).] But in this place dharmas figure also in their *phenomenal* aspect i.e., as 'things' rather than 'states of consciousness'. Because, if we take the *ontological* aspect of dharmas, then all of them would be seen as a-samskaric, not only those which are *asaṃskṛta* [on the strength of their 'such-ness' (*tathatā*) or '*dharma-ness*' (*dharmatā*)]. But of course, the main thing is that samskaras simply could not be used, unlike dharmas, as meta-terms. For what they, in fact, denote is the *concrete phenomenal characteristics* of dharmas—their (dharmas') potentiality and actuality of being connected, in time and space, with one another in various and diverse configurations. So, speaking of samskaras as *phenomena*, we may say, that they are such modes of conscious (dharmic) being, due to which one can perceive of one's conscious being as individual and personal (*pudgala*). While in the context of our (or, perhaps, any other) cultural reflexion, the will or volition would be seen as an attribute of the personal being directly opposed to its other attribute, consciousness. Not to mention the fact that an extreme technicality of samskaras in Buddhism had put this term far aloof from its previous (or contemporary, in Brahmanic ritualism) *cultural* meaning than was the case with the Schopenhauerian Will or Freudian 'subconscious'.

[*Will is not an Indian category*. But, there is something practically in each Indian *darśana* which could be identified with *will* by the way of *analysis*, but not the other way round! We must not seek—and cannot find—such a concept in India. But it should be possible to find *something* which would be what *we* call or would call *will*, e.g., desire (*icchā*) is a facet of ignorance (*avidyā*), one *edge* of which would represent for us (under the circumstances and as long as the context permits) the will. If we look at the concept of 'my body' as featuring a quality (*dharma*), or just quality in general, we may make a *conscious* effort to sort out the various wordly discrepancies (*viśiṣṭa*) constituting the impact which *māyā* may have on us by means of some personal *intentionality* (perhaps contained in *manas*, in vedanā, or in the samskaras in Buddhism). While we might discover a Shankarean aspect—edge—of *will* in such a process as that of putting various data together (my *body* and *my* body), ultimately even those of *tat tvaṃ asi*, we would in Buddhism find that *empirical* data are recognized and evaluated, however, in order to put an (ultimate) *stop* to the process of Dependent Origination. Moreover, setting aside the negative and neutral aspects of will taken as a *secondary* concept in any ancient Indian tradition, we may, perhaps, be faced by the possibility to define (as Simon Weightman tries) *will* in a merely *positive* way, as that which brings together some autonomously and isolatedly existing things. So, turning to the Upanishads, we will see that it is 'desire' (*icchā*) that brings the things about (separately), and after that a certain unnamed intentionality could bring them together.]

Another difficulty about samskaras is that their understanding from the very beginning was confined to two oppositions: 'energy/substance' and 'conscious/unconscious'. Such renderings of the term as 'synergies', or already mentioned 'confections' ('concoctions', 'co-actions', or, even, 'coefficients), tried to take into account their active, dynamic character, ignoring, both psychologically and soteriologically, their far more fundamental and universal *inertness*. That is, if looked at in the sense of a *mental microstructure*, they seem to be dynamic, but if considered in the context of the whole life of an individual, they remain the main factor preventing or impeding all radical transformations in a sentient being. There is no dialectics here, but mere taking into consideration the fact that samskaras cannot be thought of without objects (including 'dharmas as objects'), subjects (individual sentient beings, sattvas) and actions (including 'thoughts' understood as actions, not the other way around). Speaking generally, one may assert, that their 'existence' can be detected presently or traced in retrospect, only provided that we are *precisely* informed of a level on which such a work is going to be initiated, for this work is absolutely samskaric in its character, in its intentionality. The late R. Johansson asks: 'Are they material?'—and wittily answers: 'This question is not relevant. We know them only as conscious processes. We can study them through *introspection*'. The methodological confusion brought about in this passage is evident, and not less evident is its cause. For Abhidhammically speaking, they are *conscious* indeed, but not in the sense of their opposition to what is *not conscious*, for unlike the 'objective methodology' of modern psychology, the Abhidhamma does not deal with what is non-conscious, because the Abhidhamma is a 'theory of consciousness', and the rest simply does not exist in the sense of the Abhidhamma. Let alone the elementary fact, of course, that in the context of a modern psychological investigation, 'introspection' can be treated only as an *object* thereof, by no means as its method.

18 To call a *dharma* incomposite (*asamskṛta*) or composite (*samskṛta*) *category*, is a clear instance of such an ambiguity, but this is very often the case. See, Satkari Mookerjee (1935, p. 249).

19 T. R. V. Murti (1980, p. 192).

20 R. E. A. Johansson (1979, pp. 30, 59).

21 See in E. Conze (1967, pp. 76–81). This tendency is very clearly shown in his recently (1979) published autobiography.

22 For it is this law that stands as the cornerstone in any attempts to comprehend dharmas psychologically. See, for instance, R. E. A. Johansson (1979, pp. 7–8).

23 Ibid., p. 51.

24 Would not this remind one of a sort of Kantian 'thing for itself' the other way around, i.e., as 'a thought for itself'?

25 In his theory of 'living systems', G. Miller used to repeat that the expression 'the brain thinks' is as meaningless as 'the tongue speaks'. And of course, it had to be meaningless, for he was not able to separate, at least theoretically, the conditions of his own thinking from those to be attributed or denied to brain.

26 That is why it is so essential to name a *dharma* without any *contential* (i.e., semantic) associations, as if it were a name without 'the named', which, in fact, would already be a sort of meditation. The same can be said of its translation into another language.

27 Such as, for instance, 'flexibility of thought' (*cittamudutā*, △44).

28 It is implied here that each kind or form of the Buddhist (as well as any other) yoga is a kind or form of *thinking*.

29 In connection with this statement I would even take risk to say, that *no psychology can be learnt from the yogic psychology*, for the latter quite definitely implies a certain meta-psychological transformation, wherefrom there will be no return to a 'psyche' as a *natural* (i.e., psychological) object.

30 And this is extremely significant methodologically, for there can be no psychology without *reification* of the subject of psychical or mental phenomena. When this subject is *nominal*, we cannot make an object of psychology out of his mentality.

31 Unfortunately in this formulation I cannot avoid a certain ambiguity, for theoretically (i.e., Abhidhammically) speaking, consciousness cannot be conscious of anything but consciousness, thought and mind. This implies that either it is conscious of these, or it is conscious of nothing. On the other hand, however, it may be conscious of *objects* which, technically, are also *mental* but other than consciousness, thought and mind themselves. Therefore, 'the mind' can either be an object of consciousness, or an object of mind which is an object

of consciousness; whereas 'a tree' would be always understood as an object in the second sense only.

32 Or, as a matter of exactitude, not 'dharma' proper, but our approximate understanding of it. In order to avoid any psychological ambiguity I deliberately made this 'indication' (instead of a 'definition') sound in an Abhidhammic way.

33 Or, speaking more exactly, we may say that this is the most general aspect of time *to be deduced* from the concept of 'rise of thought' (*cittuppāda*). Two other aspects are 'psychological' and 'cosmological'. [They could be called, metaphysically of course, the 'microcosmic', 'macrocosmic' and 'cosmic' aspects of time in Buddhism.]

34 Not to speak, of course, about 'consciousness' in the sense of (6), i.e., as an object of 'mind' which is an object of the 'consciousness' in the sense of (2), etc.

35 Or, shall we say, they may have borrowed a psychological content, in which case they would be named the *mental* states in distinction from the states of consciousness (about their difference see in 5.0, 5.1, 5.7).

36 See in André Bareau (1951, p. 23 *et passim*). Although later on he has preferred to translate 'dharma' as 'a thing', see *Dhs.fr.*, p. 41 *et passim*.

37 This seems to me to be a tendency which might have begun as early as the time of the first Abhidhammic lists, the tendency towards *getting rid of content in dharmas*. This tendency is particularly clear in the *Aṣṭasāhasrikā Prajñāpāramitā* where any negation means that what is negated does not exist *as such*, i.e., even without being negated, and that negation itself is no more than an outer sign of this non-existence of *content*.

38 'En effet, la cessation et son objet ne sont pas en dépendence mutuelle, et il n'y a pas entre eux relation de cause à effet.' See A. Bareau (1951, p. 80).

39 'La cessation comme l'espace, est objet de connaissance sans être cause de la connaissance.' See A. Bareau (1951, pp. 82–3).

40 However paradoxical it might sound, but that is to what the *Prajñāpāramitā* theory of dharmas seems to be tantamount.

41 I am aware here that, speaking dogmatically, it is not possible to say 'all dharmas', for some of them are unthinkable. But in this case even their ineffability may be taken as an object of thought.

42 In exactly the same way as the whole sphere of 'yogic trance' (*dhyāna*) could be treated as one other factor conditioning the thinking. That is, probably, why in some of the lists of dhammas the 'five trances' (*Dhs.*, p. 45) are added to the 56 dhammas.

43 E.g., *Dhs.*, p. 21. It figures in Cases Nos. 1–8 as MV2 (see 4.0, 4.6).

44 Thus the knowledge, at least if taken in its relation to thought and/or consciousness, remains something more or less *accidental* in the Abhidhamma. It then becomes more understandable why the Buddhist theory of knowledge, or epistemology, came into existence so late.

45 And on the strength of the inevitability of some inner 'logical' rules hidden in each philosophical system, *dharma* would then 'partake' of the 'thingness' lost by thought. This seems to be of enormous philosophical interest and significance, and applies not only to *saṃskṛta*, but also to *asaṃskṛta* dharmas, particularly when they are investigated in the aspect of their *element* (*dhātu*). The last can be regarded with respect to dharmas, as approximating the meaning of 'material base'. In this very sense it is used even when referred to Nirvana in a purely religious context where the term *dhātu* denotes at one and the same time both the *bodily relic* of the Buddha and the *material basis* of Nirvana. So we read in an extremely interesting inscription belonging to the Kushan period: 'Of Him fully quenched this relic (*dhātu*)... with this body-relic (*śarira*) possessing the material basis of Nirvana (*Ṇirvaṇa-dhātu*) according to Tathagata's instruction...' See H. W. Bailey (1980, pp. 21–3). The concept of *dharmadhātu* itself might have been pertaining to the cult of relics prior to the time (first and second centuries A.D.) when it became the central notion of a new metaphysical theory wherein this cult found its reinterpretation. As such, the concept of *dharmadhātu* served as the metaphysical link tying together the concepts of 'sentient being' (*sattva*), Nirvana, and *dharma*. And this is particularly clearly expressed in the Tathagara-garbha doctrine where *dhātu* figures as the (Nirvanic) essence in each *sattva*. See here in Essay 4 (4.2.4 and note 31) and D. S. Ruegg (1980, p. 236).

46 I would even be inclined to go so far in my meta-philosophical speculation as to suggest that there cannot be a theory of knowledge without *cosmogony*, while in Buddhism we have no more than some glimpses of *cosmology*.

47 See A. Bareau (1951, p. 122). We can go on, saying...' and though not a samskrita dharma, is an asamskrita dharma', which would not be quite senseless, for to call Nirvana 'a dharma' can be seen not only as a way of saying or a philosophical mannerism, but a thing absolutely necessary for metaphysical consistency and completeness. The same would apply to *ākāsa*.

48 Of course, this does not mean that we need treat *karma* as a phenomenon because, strictly Buddhistically speaking, only where there are *two* (or more) individual streams of consciousness, the *karma-vāsanā* relation could be 'observed'. This in turn means that *karma* implies not 'thought as such', but on the contrary, thought (or consciousness) in terms of its *individuation and plurality* only. As for 'thinkability' of *karma*, this question seems to be even more complex for, as a general principle, it is thinkable, but while taken in its concrete factuality, it is not.

49 That is why both *rūpa* and Nirvana are totally akarmic, i.e., absolutely *neutral* with respect to *karma*. I am not touching here on other aspects of their rapprochement or of differences between them.

50 Where, by the way, 'a person' is neither a 'dharma' (by definition that there is no such 'dharma' as 'a person'), nor 'thought' (for they are juxtaposed to one another), nor even an object, for it is there only where 'a person' is opposed to 'an object' in his personal subjectivity.

51 The term is here arbitrarily chosen, for it may be rather *prajñā* or even *dhyāna*.

52 Not to confuse this with 'direct perception', which is totally out of question.

53 Here I am aware of the 'Abhidharmic fact' that, strictly terminologically speaking, it will be not 'this', but 'another' thought then.

54 For it would always be related to something else.

55 I am aware that this may induce one to think that *unrelatedness* to thought could be seen as something specific or, at least, allowing for a specific interpretation, but I think that 'the proof from the contrary' is very seldom, if ever, used in Buddhist theorizing.

56 I stick here again to a purely *formal* and *naturalistic* attitude of modern Abhidhammists. See, for instance, in *Dhātu-Kathā* (pp. XXVII, 96).

57 'Thing' here is not an 'object' in the sense in which the latter has been used so far. Nor is it used Abhidhammically, for 'a thing' here is not a *thing* in the Abhidhammic sense, but an *object* of *my* thinking about Abhidhamma. In my trying to establish some methodological links between the Abhidhammic approach and my own, I am stressing the distinction of my *idea* of object of thinking (*viśaya*) from that of Abhidhamma itself (*vatthu*).

58 A *dharma* figures in this interpretation as *a state of consciousness* conceived in the sense of Buddhist philosophy in general, and irrespective of all inter-scholastic differences, while a *dhamma* is here a technical term used in the context of the Pali Abhidhammic texts only. In saying this, I am entirely aware that there are many texts in the Pali Canon where 'dhamma' figures in the sense of 'dharma'. It is so, for instance, in the opening stanzas of Dhammapada (I, 1.2).

59 'A subject of thought' here, i.e., in terms of a meta-philosophical approach, means that I (or any other external observer) choose to think of a thought as attributed to someone who might be myself or somebody else. This attribution, however, is a matter quite secondary to the observation of thought itself.

60 It seems to me that the very term 'risen' (*uppanna*) might be seen or, at least, renderable as 'fact' in the context of such considerations.

61 Lilian Silburn (1955, p. 171) is gravely mistaken when she writes that 'taken as discontinuous and pure, the dhammas are entirely out of reach of activity of thought'. For the dhammas are *related* to both observing thinking and observed thinking and thereby, cannot be thought of as either cognizable or non-cognizable, not being included in the *system* of cognition. Her criticism of St. Shayer is futile on the two points: for one thing, the texts of Abhidhamma (as well as her own texts) are, formally, at least, 'the activity of thought' aimed at grasping the meaning of *dhamma;* for another thing, Abhidhamma itself does not yet know the *methodological* difference between a system of objects of knowledge and a system of knowledge: though it draws the frontier between facts and their interpretations quite clearly.

62 See above 6.2.1(1) and ref. 13.

63 Here, I am afraid, we would have to make distinction between 'individual' understood in the sense of 'subjective', and 'individual' thought of (or, thinkable) as a manifestation of the highest *objectivity*. I think that *ālāyavijñāna*, even taken in its *individual* aspect, would need to be understood in the latter sense.

64 Moreover, sometimes, as in *Vajracchedikā Prajñāpāramitā*, the idea of past, present and future time figures in connection with *one and the same* text (i.e., this very *sūtrānta*) spoken, understood, heard or explained at different times.

65 And exactly the same we see in the 'biography' of any Buddha (in saying this I mean 'all His existences'), where time is needed only to establish the *phases* in His Buddhahood. This idea is entirely contrary to that of Husserlian phenomenology where time figures as 'the sphere' for unique biographical situations, and assumes, thereby, a uniqueness of its own being. See in Alfred Schurtz (1973, pp. 308–9).

66 'Thinking, if you ask a philosopher, is something very difficult, so never ask a philosopher about it because he is the only man who doesn't know what thinking is...,' (C. G. Jung, 1976, p. 11). Well, we can conjecture, Jung might have known *how* one or another person was thinking, which did not make him know how one or another thinking *happened*, or even, whether it happened at all. The Masters of the late Mahayanist schools did know, at least, that two (or more) thoughts do not make the thinking, but *remain* as consciousness: 'What is called "consciousness" (*vijñāna*) is the "continuing thought"' (*Awakening of Faith*, p. 49).

67 See in Th. Stcherbatsky (1930, pp. 389, 400).

68 On this one thing more is to be said. Even such a 'linguistically minded' philosopher as Wittgenstein could not avoid a kind of very strong implicit psychologism. When Ernest Gellner sharply (and jokingly) criticizes him for 'an important but misplaced insight' concerning *emotional concomitants of thought* (not a quite unbuddhistic idea, by the way!), he sees this as a part or aspect of Wittgensteinian 'naturalization' of *all* ideas. Far more important, however, is that such naturalization cannot help assuming the form of a psychologism or even, cannot help but become a philosophy of mind. Being 'a simple and tired' philosopher (!) one cannot but admit (simply and wearily) that thought is less natural a thing than feeling, and that a 'mentalism' is a necessary and unavoidable concomitant of 'linguisticism'. To which a Vaibhashika-Yogachara philosopher of the 7th or 8th century A.D. would have untiringly objected, and said that the only thing that mattered was whether we dealt with thought or with its object (be it a feeling, a table, or a thought), and that no object could be less or more natural than another. See E. Gellner (1979, p. 220).

69 '(Consider) the samskaras as other, not as self' (...*saṅkhāre parato na ca attato*), *Thera and Therī* I, No. 177, p. 140; *Therī*, *tr.* p. 20. 'See the samskaras as other...' (*saṅkhāre parato* ...) *Thera and Therī* I, N. 101, p. 133; *Thera tr.*, No. 1224B (comm.) pp. 112, 292; *Therī tr.*, pp. 13, 83.

70 I have already been referring elsewhere (A. Piatigorsky, 1983, pp. 176–7) to an 'epistemological obsession' in the modern philosophy wherefrom any 'immediate experience' is excluded as not subject to a logical or a semantical analysis. That is probably why, if it does figure, it does so somewhere 'between' knowledge and belief: 'There may very well be cases in which one knows that something is so without its being possible to say how one knows it. I am not so much thinking now of claims to know facts of immediate experience...' (A. J. Ayer, 1956, p. 32). In a certain, and extremely naive way, Ayer asserts that it is a belief, not an immediate experience, that is one of the modes of knowledge. Or, if we rephrase it, if taken as one of the *conditions* of knowledge, a belief may have implied any modus of knowledge whatsoever. Ayer's epistomelogy, as well as that of his Oxonian colleagues of the post-Wittgensteinian period, is utterly *non-modal*. Dharmakirti knew, at least, that 'belief' is one state of consciousness, and 'immediate experience' is another, and that they were so, apart from and irrespective of, their being two different modes of knowledge.

71 This last statement stresses the fact that in the framework of a positivist methodology (which has, eventually, become a world-outlook of the modern culture and a method of its self-reflexion) thought itself is not an experience, and thinking, therefore, cannot be included in experiencing, while knowledge can. This is so, because thinking cannot be incorporated (as a part or an element) into any thinkable collective or cultural totality in respect to which

it would always be explored as 'absolutely other'. O. Neurath wrote in his dedication to Moritz Schlick: '...the Vienna Circle maintain the view that the statements... about the reality or non-reality of the external world and *other* minds are of a metaphysical character... they are meaningless... For us something is "real" through being incorporated into the total structure of experience' (1973, p. 308). Being quite 'external' to and 'other' than (in fact these two terms are philosophically one here) the Viennese approach, my approach tends to fix that which belongs to culture and to externalize it as 'mine' and 'non-thinking'.

A GLOSSARY OF DHARMIC TERMS

abhabba, impossibility, 3.1.1.1; 3.1.1.3.
abhibhuyya. mastering, having mastered, Tab. V, No. 46.
abhidhamma, see also *abhidharma*, Foreword, 1.2.1; 1.2.4; 1.2.5; 1, n. 12; 1.3.1.; 1.3.2; 1.3.3; 1.3.4;, 1.3.4.1; 1, n. 13; 1.5.3; 1.6; 1, n. 18; 2.1.0.4.1; 3.0.2.1; 3, n. 2; 3.2.3; 3.4.1; 4, n. 2; 4, n. 3; 4.1.3; 4, n. 11; 4.2.0; 4.2.3; 4.3.0; 4.4.0; 4.6.0; 4,n.55; 4.7; 4.8; 4, n. 58; 5.0.1; 5, n. 10; 5.1.1; 5.1.3; 5.2; 5.3.0; 5.3.1; 5, n. 16; 5, n. 17; 5.3.6; 5.3.7.3; 6 (*passim*).
abhidharma, see also *abhidhamma;* Foreword; 4.2.1; 4.6; 5, n. 20; 6 (*passim*).
abhijjhā, covetousness, Tab. IV, No. 145, △70, etc.
abhijñā, see also *abhiññā;* further or higher knowledge, 2.2.3.
abhiniropanā, 'application (of mind'), Tab. VI, No. 1, △6, etc.
abhinivesa, inclination; Tab. VI, No. 145, △64.
abhiññā, see also *abhijñā;* 'further' (or 'special') knowledge, higher knowledge, 2.2.3; Tab.V (*passim*); 5.4.2.
abhippasāda, 'assurance', 'reliance', Tab. VI, No. 1, △11, etc.
abhisamecca, 'having realized', 2.1.1.2.
abyākata, indefinite, indeterminate, 3.3.2.4; 4, n. 55; 5.0.2; 5.0.3; Tab. IV; Tab. VI; 5.1.2.
abyāpāda, 'non-maliciousness', Tab. VI, No. 1, △32, etc.
acalā bhūmi, 4.2.4.1.
acintya, unthinkable, 2.2.5; Tab. V; 5.7.4.3; 6.0.6.11; 6.5.
adandhanatā, 'non-sluggishness', Tab. VI, No. 1, △41, etc.
adassana, 'not seeing', 'blindness', Tab. VI, No. 145, △71.
adharma, as a Jaina category of 'static'; 5, n. 26.
ādhipateyya, domination, dominated, Tab. V, No. 111; 5.1.3.
adiṭṭha, unseen, Tab. VI, No.119, △59.
adosa, non-hatred, Tab. VI, No. 1, △32, etc.
adukkhamasukha, 'neither suffering nor pleasure', Tab. V, No. 12; Tab. VI, No. 5, △2a, etc.
adussanā, 'non-hating', Tab. VI, No. 1, △32, etc.
adussitatta, '(state of) not feeling hatred', Tab. VI, No. 1, △32, etc.
advaita, non-dual, 1.3.4.2.
advaita-vedānta, 1.3.4.2.
advaya, non-dual, 1.3.4.2.
āhāra, nutrition, Tab. V, No. 138.
ahirīka, shameless, Tab. VI, No. 145, △74.
ahirīkabala, 'power of shamelessness', Tab. VI, No. 145, △68, etc.
ajimhatā, 'undeflectedness', Tab. VI, No. 1, △49, etc.
ajīva, also as a Jaina category: 'non-soul'; 5, n. 26.
ājīva, mode of life, way of living, livelihood, Tab. VI, No. 119, △62, etc.
ājīvaka, 3.0.4.
ajjhatta, individuality, subjectivity, 2, n. 27; 2.4.5; Tab. V (*passim*); 5, n. 17.
akakkhaḷatā, 'non-rigidity', Tab. VI, No. 1, △43, etc.
akaraṇa, 'unmade', 'unaffected', Tab. VI, No. 119, △60, etc.
ākāsa, space, Tab. V, No. 107; 6, n. 47.
akathinatā, 'non-stiffness', Tab. VI, No. 1, △43, etc.
akiñcañña, (in comp.) nothing, Tab. V, No. 109.
akiriyā, '(leaving) undone', Tab. VI, No. 119, △60, etc.

apariyogāhanā, 'inability to compare'(?), 'non-penetration', Tab. VI, No. 145, △71; 'lack of grasp' (?), No. 155, △80.
apatta, unattained, unobtained, Tab. VI, No. 119, △59.
apilāpanatā, 'deep penetration' (by memory), Tab. VI, No. 1, △13, etc.
appamāda, undistractedness, 3.1.1.3.
appamāṇa, immeasurable, Tab. V (*passim*); 5.3.4.
appanā, 'fixation' or 'direction' (of mind), Tab. VI, No. 1, △6, etc.
appaṇihita, aimless, Tab. V, No. 131.
appapañña, one with little wisdom, 2, n. 16..
appaṭigha, 'unobstructive', 5, n. 24.
appaṭivedha, 'non-penetration', Tab. VI, No. 145, △71.
aprameya, immeasurable, 2.4.2.
ārammaṇa, see also *ālambana;* object, 2, n. 25; 4.1.1; 5.0.2; Tab. V (*passim*); 6.1.0; 6.2.3; 6.15.
ārati, abstaining, abstinence, Tab. VI, No. 119, △60.
arhat (*arahant*), 2.1.1.4; 2.2.4; 2, n. 20; 3.3.1.2; 3.3.3.5; 3.3.4; 4.4.4.
ariya, noble, Tab. V, No. 11.
arūpa, formless, 2.1.2.3; 2, n. 15; 5, n. 26.
arūpa-dhātu, formless element, formless existence, 4.4.1.
arūpāvacara, sphere of formlessness, Tab. IV; Tab. V, No. 168.
arūpin, formless, Tab. VI, No. 1, △18, etc.; 5.7.4.2; 5, n. 26.
aryapudgala, noble person, 4.4.0.
asacchikata, 'unrealized' ('not seen with one's own eyes'), Tab. VI, N. 119, △59.
asagāhanā, 'non-grasping', Tab. VI, No. 145, 71.
asamapekkhanā, '(being) unobservant', Tab. VI, No. 145, △71.
asambodha, 'unawakened', Tab. VI, No. 145, △71.
asaṃkheyya, see also *asaṃkhyeya*; incalculable, 2.4.2.
asaṃkhyeya, see also *asaṃkheyya;* incalculable, 4.2.4.2.
asammussanatā, 'unforgetfulness', Tab. VI, No. 1, △13, etc.
asampajañña, 'unawareness', Tab. VI, No. 145, △71.
asaṃskṛta, see also *asaṅkhata,;* 1.3.4.1; unconditioned, 1.5.4; 5.7.4.1; 6, n. 17; 6.2.3; 6, n. 45; 6, n. 47; 6.11.3. uncreated, incomposite, 1, n. 19.
asaṃskṛta dharma, see also *asaṅkhata dhamma;* unconditioned dharma, 1.1; 6.2.2; 6.9
asaṅkhata, see also *asaṃskṛta;* unconditioned, incomposite, 1, n. 19.
asaṅkhata dhamma, see also *asaṃskṛta dharma;* unconditioned dharma, 5.7.4.2.
asaṅkhata-dhātu, 'element of the incomposite', 5, nn. 23, 24; 5.7.4.3.
asaññā, non-notion, non-perception, Tab. V, No. 107.
āsappanā, 'evasion', 'fear', Tab. VI, No. 155, △80.
asāra, essenceless, 2, n. 14; 2, n. 29; 'non-entity', 4, n. 53.
asārāga, 'not infatuated', Tab. VI, No. 1, △31, etc.
asārajjanā, '(state of) not being infatuated', Tab. VI, No. 1, △31, etc.
asārajjitatta, '(state of) not feeling infatuation', Tab. VI, No. 1, △31, etc.
asāta, unease, disagreeable, uneasy, Tab, VI, No. 153, △2^b, etc.
āsava, influx, 3.3.1.2.
asithila, 'unfaltering', Tab. VI, No. 1, △12, etc.
asuropa, 'abruptness', Tab. VI, No. 153, △78, etc.
asvabhāvika, 'unnatural', 'natureless', 4.3.2.
ātman, see also *atta;* self, 1.2.2; 3.0.8.
atta, see also *ātman*, self, 1.2.2; 1.8; 2.1.0.2; 3.0.1; 4, n. 53.
attamanatā, 'uprisedness', 'exultation', Tab. VI, No. 1, △8, etc.

bodhi, awakening, 4, n. 42.
bodhicitta, thought of awakening, 4.2.0; 4.2.1; 4, n. 18; 4.2.2; 4.2.3.1; 4.2.3.2; 4.2.3.3; 4, n. 27; 4.2.3.4; 4, n. 29; 4.2.4.1; 4.2.4.2; 4.8.
bodhicittotpāda, rise of thought of awakening, 4.2.3; 4, n. 27; 4.2.3.3; 4.2.3.4.
bodhisattva, being of awakening, 4.2.1; 4.2.2; 4.2.3; 4.2.3.2; 4.2.3.4; 4.2.4.1; 4.2.4.2; 4, n. 31; 4. n. 37; 4.3.3.1; 4.3.3.3; 4.4.5; 4.5; 4.8.
bodhisattvabhūmi, stage of bodhisattvahood, 4.2.2.
bojjhaṅga, component of awakening, Tab. V.
brahman, Self, 2.1.0.2; 3.0.2.2; brahman, 2.3.3; 3, n. 8; 3, n. 9.
bsam-pa, see also *sems;* thought, 4, n. 21.
bskal-bzang, blessed period (of time), 4.3.3.1.
buddha, 1.7; 2.1.1.0; 2.2.1.0; 2.4.0; 2.4.2; 3.1.0; 3.1.1; 3.1.1.1; 3.1.1.3; 3.1.2; 3, n. 7; 3.3.2.1; 3.3.2.3; 3.3.2.4; 3.3.2.6; 3, n. 16; 3.3.2.2; 3.3.3.5; 3.3.4; 3.4.2; 4.2.3.4; 4.2.4.1; 4.2.4.2; 4, n. 37; 4.3.3.1; 4.4.4; 4.4.5; 4.4.6; 4.4.6.1; 4.5; 4.8; 5.3.7.3; 6.0.6.3.
buddhi, idea, awareness, 6.15.
byang-chub-tu sems, see *bodhicitta;* 4, n. 23.
byāpāda, maliciousness, Tab. VI, No. 153, △79.
byāpajjanā, 'causing harm', Tab. VI, No. 153, △78, etc.
byāpajjitatta, 'harmful(ness)', Tab. VI, No. 153, △78, etc.
byāpatti, 'maliciousness', Tab. VI, No. 153, △78, etc.

cakkhudhātu, 'element of sight', 4.8.
cakkhuviññāṇa, 'eye (or sight-)-consciousness', Tab. III; Tab. V, No. 157.
cakkhuviññāṇadhātu, 'element of eye-consciousness', Tab. VI, No. 157, △2[c], etc.; 5.1.2.
caṇḍikka, 'churlishness', Tab. VI, No. 153, △78, etc.
cāra, procedure, process, Tab. VI, No. 1, △7, etc.
catur, four, Tab VI, No. 119, △60.
catuttha, fourth, Tab. V. (*passim*).
cetanā, intentionality, intention (of thought), 3.3.1.2; 3.3.2.4; will, volition, Tab. V; Tab. VI, No. 1, △4, etc.
cetas, psyche, 1.2.6.1; 3.1.1.3; 4, n. 11: the psychical, Tab. VI, No. 1, △2, etc.; 5.1.3.
cetasika, psychic, 2, n. 8; 4, n. 2; Tab. VI, No. 1, △2, etc.
cetayitta, '(being) intended', Tab. VI, No. 1, △4, etc.
chanda, intention, desire, Tab. V, No. 111.
chandatā, desire, Tab. VI, No. 1, △12, etc.
cintā, thinking, Tab. VI, No. 1, △15, etc.
cintitvā, 'having thought', '(was) thinking', 3.3.2.4.
cintya, 'thinkable', 6.0.6.11.
citkarma, 'conscious karma', 'karma of thought', 5.2; 5.3.7.3.
citta, thought, Foreword; 1.2.2; 1.2.6.1; 1, n. 12; 2.0.1; 2. n. 11; 2, n. 18; 3.0.1; 3.0.3; 3, n. 5: 3.3.2.4; 4.1.0; 4. n. 2; 4. n. 11; 4, n. 15; 4.2.0; 4, n. 18; 4, n. 20 ('sentientness'); 4.2.3.2; 4.4.0; 4.8; 5.0.1; 5.0.3; Tab. III; Tab. IV; Tab. V (*passim*); 5, n. 6; Tab. VI, No. 1, △5, etc.; 5.1.0; 5.1.2; 5.1.3; Tab. IX; 5.3.3; 5.3.4; 5.6.1; 5.7.2; 5.7.3; 5, n. 27; 6.0.1–2; 6, n. 3; 6.1.1; 6.1.3; 6.3; 6.5; 6.10; 6.12.3; 6.15.
cittakammaññatā, 'workability of thought', ;Tab. VI, No. 1, △46, etc.
cittalahutā, lightness of thought, Tab. VI, No. 1, △42, etc.; 6.1.4
cittamātra, 'thought only', 1.3.4.1.
cittamudutā, 'flexibility of thought', Tab. VI, No. 1, △44, etc.; 6, n. 27.
cittapāguññatā, 'fitness (or good quality) of thought', Tab. VI, No. 1, △48, etc.
cittapassaddhi, 'composedness of thought', Tab. VI, No. 1, △40, etc.

cittasantāna, continuum (or stream) of thought, 2.4.3; 4.1.3; 5.3.0.2; 5.7.4.5.
cittassekagatā, 'one-directedness of thought', Tab. VI, No. 1, △10, etc.
cittavṛtti, 'fluctuation of thought', 6.15.
cittotpāda, see also *cittuppāda;* rise of thought, 3.1.1.1; 4.2.3.
cittujukatā, 'straightness of thought', Tab. VI, No. 1, △50, etc.
cittuppāda, see also *cittotpāda;* rise of thought, Foreword; 1.5.3; 3.1.1.1; 4.1.0; 4, n. 11; 5.0.1; 5.3.7.3; 6.1.0; 6.2.1.

dandha, slow, Tab. V. (*passim*).
darśana, sight, vision, system, 6, n. 17; 6.0.6.10.
dassana, sight (space of sight), vision, Tab. V.
deva, god, deity, 2, n. 13.
dhamma, see also *dharma;* the Buddhist teaching, 1.6; 3.1.0; 3.1.1; 3.1.1.3; state of consciousness, 2, n. 7; 3.1.1.1; 3, n. 8; Tab. II; 4, n. 2; 4.1.3; 4, n. 55; 4, n. 58; Tab. V (*passim*); Tab. VI, No. 1, △18, etc.; 5.1.1; 5.1.2; 6 (*passim*).
dhammārammaṇa, 'dharma-object', 5.1.2; 6.0.5.
dhammavicaya, 'investigation (or 'search') of Dharma', Tab. VI, No. 1, △15, etc.
dhāraṇatā, 'mindfulness', Tab. VI, No. 1, △13, etc.
dharatā, 'endurance', Tab. VI, No. 1, △12, etc.
dharma, phenomenological unit, factor, Foreword; state of consciousness, Foreword; 1.1; 1.2.4; 1.2.5; 1.2.6.1; 1, n. 12; 1.3.4.1; 2, n. 7; 2.1.0.4.2; 2.1.1.0; 2, n. 26; 3.2.0; Tab. II; 3.2.3; 3.3.1.1; 4.2.1; 4.4.0; 4, n. 52; 4.4.6.3; 4.6.1; 4, n. 55; 4.8; 5.0.1; 5.0.2; 5.0.3; 5, n. 6; 5, n. 8; 5.1.0; 5.1.1; 5.1.2; 5.1.3; 5.2; 5, n. 12; 5.3.0; 5.3.0.1; 5.3.2; Tab. IX; 5.3.3; 5.3.4; 5.3.7; Tab. X; 5.3.7.1; 5.3.7.2; 5.3.7.3; 5.4.1; 5.5; 5.6.1; 5.6.2; 5.7 (*passim*); 6 (*passim*); the Teaching, Buddha-Consciousness (Dharma), 1.7; 3.0.5; 3.3.5; 6.0.6.3: as a Jaina category, 2, n. 18; 3.0.5; 5, n. 26.
dharmadhātu, 4.8; 6, n. 45.
dharmadhātu-kāya, body made of the dharma elements, 4, n. 31.
dharmamātra, 'dharmas only', 6.11.1.
dharma-megha, 4.2.4.1.
dharmaparyāya, discourse on *Dharma*, exposition of *Dharma*, 6.14.2.
dharmatā, 'dharma-ness', 4.8; 5.7.4.0; 6, n. 17; 6.11.2.
dharmavāda, theory of dharmas, 5.7.4.0; 6.0.6.6; 6.0.6.8; 6.0.6.10–11.
dhātu, plane, sphere or element of existence, 2.1.0.4.3; 4, n. 18; 4,8; 4, n. 58; Tab. V; 5, n. 6; Tab. VI, No. 1, △2, *et passim;* 5.2; 5.7.0; 5.7.4.1; 6, n. 45.
dhīra, stable, 3.1.1.1.
dhiti, firmness, Tab. VI, No. 1, △12, etc.
dhurasampaggāha, 'strong grip of the burden', Tab VI, No. 1, △12, etc.
dhyāna, see also *jhāna;* trance, absorption, 5.1.3; 6, n. 42; 6, n. 51; 6.15.
diṭṭhadhamma, 'seen dharma', 'present dharma', 4, n. 55; Tab. V, No. 229; 5.3.7.
diṭṭhi, view, Tab. V; Tab. VI, No. 145, △64, etc.
diṭṭhigahana, 'thicket (or 'tangle') of views', Tab. VI, No. 145, △64.
diṭṭhigata, '(all) views and opinions', Tab. V; Tab. VI, No. 145, △64, etc.
diṭṭhikantāra, 'wilderness of views', Tab. VI, No. 145, △64.
diṭṭhisaññojana, 'fetters of views', Tab. VI, No. 145, △64.
diṭṭhivipphandita, 'scuffle of views', Tab. VI, No. 145, △64.
diṭṭhivisūkāyika, 'distortion of views', Tab. VI, No. 145, △64.
domanassa, mental sorrow, Tab. V, Nos. 12, 153; 5.6.3.
domanassindriya, 'faculty of mental sorrow', Tab. VI, No. 153, △77; 5.6.3.
dosa, hatred, Tab. VI, No. 153, △78, etc.; 5.7.4.2.

dran-pa, memory, remembering, memorization, recollection, 4, n. 46; 4.3.3.4; 4, n. 52.
dubbaṇṇa ugly, Tab. V, No. 65.
duccarita, misbehaviour, deviation, Tab. VI, No. 119, △60, etc.
duḥkha, see also *dukkha;* suffering, 6.11.2.
dukkha, suffering, 1.2.5; Tab. V; Tab. VI, No. 5, △2[i], etc.
dukkhasamudayanirodha, stopping the production of suffering, 1, n. 5.
dukkhindriya, faculty of suffering, Tab. VI, No. 222, △83.
dummajjha, 'stupidity', Tab. VI, No. 145, △71.
dussanā, 'hating', Tab. VI, No. 153, △78, etc.
dussin, 'one who is seeing', 2.4.2
dussitatta, 'feeling hatred', Tab. VI, No. 153, △78, etc.
dutiya, second, Tab. V (*passim*).
dvedhāpatha, 'standing at the crossroads', Tab. VI, No. 155, △80.
dveḷhaka, 'being ambiguous', Tab. VI, No. 155, 80.

ekabījin, 'single-seeder', 2, n. 26..
ekodibhāva, fixation of mentality, Tab. V, No. 10.

gabbha, womb, 2, n. 16.
gabbhaseyyā, womb, 2.2.1.0.
gāha, grasping, Tab. VI, No. 145, △64.
gati, course, direction, mode, 2.1.0.4.3; 5.2.
ghānaviññāṇa, 'smell-consciousness', Tab. III; Tab. V, No. 159.
ghānaviññāṇadhātu, 'element of smell-consciousness', Tab. VI, No. 159, △2[e] etc.; 5.1.2.
grong-'jug, transference, 4.3.3.2.
guṇa, tendency, property, 2.5.

hadaya, heart, Tab. VI, No. 1, △5, etc.
hāsa, 'mirth', Tab. VI, No. 1, △8, etc.
hatavikkhittaka, mutilated (corpse), Tab. V, No. 106.
hīna, inferior, little, Tab. V, No. 111.
hirī, shame, Tab. VI, No. 1, △37, etc.
hiribala, power of shame, Tab. VI, No. 1, △29, etc.
hirīyati, 'he is ashamed', Tab. VI, No. 1, △29, etc.
hoti, 'he is', 6.15.

icchā, wish, desire, 6, n. 17.
iddhi, supernatural power, 4, n. 37; Tab. V, No. 138.
indriya, faculty, Tab. V, No. 138; Tab. IV, No. 1, △5, *et passim*; 6.0.6.9.
iriyanā, 'moving on', 'progression', Tab. VI, No. 1, △18, etc.

-ja, born of, Tab. V (*passim*); Tab. VI, No. 1, △2, etc.
jānāmi, 'I know', Tab. V, No. 46; 5.3.7.
jhāna, see also *dhyāna;* trance, Tab. III; Tab. IV; Tab. V (*passim*); 5.1.3; 5.2; 5.3.3; 5.3.4; 5.3.5; 5.3.6; 5.3.7.1; 5.4.1; 5.5; 5, n. 22; 5.6.1; 6.0.6.4.
jīva, also as a Jaina category; soul, 2, n. 12; 2.4.0; 2, n. 29; 3.0.4; 4.3.0; 5, n. 26.
jīvita, 'living', Tab. VI, No. 1, △18, etc.
jīvitindriya, faculty of living, Tab. VI, No. 1, △18, etc.
jivhāviññāṇa, 'taste-consciousness', Tab. III; Tab. V, No. 160.
jivhāviññāṇadhātu, 'element of taste-consciousness', Tab. VI, No. 160, △2[f], etc.
ñāna, knowledge, 2.5.

lakṣaṇa, see also *lakkhaṇa;* mark, sign, 1.2.3; 1.3.4.1; feature, symptom, 1.2.5; 2.0.1.
lama, 4, n. 51.
las-can, see also *karmapa;* 'possessor of karma', 4.3.3.1.
lobha, greed, Tab. VI, No. 145, △70.
lohita, red. Tab. V, No. 89.
lohitaka, red (corpse), Tab. V, No. 106.
loka, world, 2.1.1.3.
lokuttara, 'supramundane sphere', Tab. IV; Tab. V; 5.1.1.
lubbhanā, 'greediness', Tab. VI, No. 145, △70.
lubbhitatta, 'feeling greed', Tab. VI, No. 145, △70.

maddavatā, mildness, softness, Tab. VI, No. 1, △43, etc.
mādhyamika, 1.3.4.2.
ma-dran/pa, 'non-memory', 4, n. 52.
magga, see also *mārga;* way, Tab. V (*passim*); Tab. VI, No. 119, △6^{a}, etc.
maggaṅga, 'component of the way', Tab. VI, No. 119, △6^{a}, etc.
mahāpurisa see also *mahāpuruṣa;* Great Person, 3.1.2; 4.4.0.
mahāpuruṣa, see also *mahāpurisa;* Great Person, 3.0.8; 4.2.3.2.
mahāyāna, 1.3.4; 1.3.5; 4.2.3; 4.2.4.1; 4. n. 37.
majjhima, middle, medium, Tab. V, No. 144.
mama putta, 'my son', 3.3.2.3.
māna, conceit, pride, Tab. V.
manas, mind, mentality, Foreword; 1.2.5; 1.2.6.1; 2, n. 18; 3.0.1; 3.0.9; 3, n. 5; Tab. II; 3.3.2.5; 4, n. 11; 4.3.0; 4.3.3.0; 4.4.1; 4.8; Tab. VI, No. 1, △5 etc.; 5.1.3; 5.3.3; 5.7.2; 5.7.3; 6.0.3–4; 6, n. 17; 6.1.3; 6.15.
mānasa, 'the mental', Tab. VI, No. 1, △5, etc.
manāyatana, basis of mind, Tab. VI, No. 1, △5, etc.
manindriya, faculty of mind, 1.2.6.1; 2.1.0.4.1; Tab. VI, No. 1, △ 5, etc.; 5.1.2.
mano, see *manas*.
manodhātu, 'element of mind', 4.8; 5.0.2; 5.0.3; Tab. III; Tab. V; Tab. VI, No. 162, △2^{h}, etc.; 5.3.3.
manomaya, mind-made, 1.2.5.
manomaya-kāya, mind-made body, 4, n. 31.
manovilekha, 'mental perturbation', Tab. VI, No. 155, △80.
manoviññāṇadhātu, 3.0.2.1; 'element of mind-consciousness', 4.8; Tab. III, Tab. V; Tab. VI, No. 1, △5, etc.; 5.3.3.
manusiyapajā, humankind, genus humanum, 2.1.2.2; 3.1.1
māraṇa, death, (also 'causing death'), 3.3.1.2.
ma-rig-pa, ignorance, 4, n. 52.
mātikā, tabulated or numerical expression, 5.3.0; 6.15.
matta, only, as far as, 6.1.1.
māyā, 'illusion', 6, n. 17.
medhā, sagacity, Tab. VI, No. 1, △15, etc.
mettā, compassion, 2.1.1.3.
micchā, wrong, Tab. VI, No. 119, △62, etc.; 5.3.0.1.
micchāājīva, wrong mode of life (or 'livelihood') Tab. VI, No. 119, △62, etc.
micchādiṭṭhi, wrong views, Tab. VI, No. 145, △64, etc.; 5.7.4.3.
micchāpatha, wrong path, Tab. VI, No. 145, △64.
micchāsamādhi, wrong concentration, Tab. VI, △No. 145, 10^{b}.
micchāsankappa, wrong construing, Tab. VI, No. 145, △6^{b}.

pahāna, giving up, abandoning, Tab. V, No. 119.
pahāsa, 'merriment', Tab. VI, No. 1, △ 8, etc.
pajā, progeny, 2.3.4.
pajānanā, understanding, Tab. VI, No. 1, △ 15, etc.
pakati, see *prakṛti;* 4, n. 56.
pālanā, 'keeping', 'conservation', Tab. VI, No. 1, △ 18, etc.
pamāda, distraction, 3.1.1.3.
pamodanā, 'delightfulness', Tab. VI, No. 1, △ 8, etc.
pamoha, 'utter delusion', Tab. VI, No. 145, △ 71.
pamojja, 'delightful', Tab. VI, No. 1, △ 8, etc.
pāṇa, life, animate being, animal, 2, n. 12.
pāṇabhūta, animate being, 2.1.2.2.
pāṇaka, small(est) animate being, 3.3.2.4.
pañcama, fifth, Tab. V (*passim*).
paṇḍara, 'clear'(?), Tab. VI, No. 1, △ 5, etc.
paṇḍicca, 'erudition', Tab. VI, No. 1, △ 15, etc.
paṇīta, perfect, excellent, Tab. V; 5.1.3.
paññā, see also *prajñā;* knowledge, 're-knowledge', wisdom, 2.2.3; 3.1.1.3; Tab. VI, No. 1, △ 15, etc.; 5.1.1.
paññā ābhāsa, 'lustre of wisdom', Tab. VI, No. 1, △ 15, etc.
paññā āloka, 'lamp of wisdom', Tab. VI, No. 1, △ 15, etc.
paññābala, power of wisdom, Tab. VI, No. 1, △ 15, etc.
paññāpajjata, 'splendour of wisdom', Tab. VI, No. 1, △ 15, etc.
paññāpāsāda, 'palace of wisdom', Tab. VI, No. 1, △ 15, etc.
paññāratana, 'jewel of wisdom', Tab. VI, No. 1, △ 15, etc.
paññāsatha, 'sword of wisdom', Tab. VI, No. 1, △ 15, etc.
paññindriya, faculty of wisdom, Tab. VI, No. 1, △ 15, etc.
pāpaka, sinful, Tab. VI, No. 1, △ 29, etc.
papañca, confusion, humdrum world, 2.2.6.
parakāyapraveśa, 'entering into another body', 4.3.3.2.
parakkama, exertion, Tab. VI, No. 1, △ 12, etc.
parakkamatā, exertion, Tab. VI, No. 1, △ 12, etc.
parāmāsa, 'being affected', Tab. VI, No. 145, △ 64.
paramatthato, 'in the ultimate sense', 4, n. 2.
parato, 'as other', 'as strange', 6, n. 69.
pariṇāma, modification, transformation, 4.3.2; 5.3.1; 5, n. 19; 6, n. 17.
pariṇāyika, 'guide', Tab. VI, No. 1, △ 15, etc.
parisappanā, 'indecision', Tab. VI, No. 155, △ 80.
parisuddhi, extreme purity, Tab. V.
paritta, not large, limited, Tab. V (*passim*); 5.3.4.
pariyāpanna, 'included in...', 'belonging to...', Tab. VI, No. 119, △ 6[a], etc.
passaddhi, 'composedness', Tab. VI, No. 1, △ 39, etc.
passambhanā, calmness, calming down, Tab. VI, No. 1, △ 39, etc.
passami, 'I see', Tab. V, No. 46.
passati, 'he sees', Tab. V, No. 46.
paṭhama, first, Tab. V (*passim*); 5, n. 6.
paṭhavi, earth, Tab. V (*passim*).
paṭiccasamuppāda, 'interdependent co-origination', 1.3.3.
paṭiggāha, 'grasping strongly at...', Tab. VI, No. 145, △ 64.
paṭigha, reflex, reaction, Tab. V, No. 107.

paṭipadā, course, process, Tab. V (*passim*); 5.4.2.
paṭipanna, 'entered', 3.1.1.1.
paṭipassaddhi, 'complete composure', Tab. VI, No. 1, △39, etc.
paṭipassambhanā, 'complete tranquilization', Tab. VI, No. 1, △39, etc.
paṭipassambhatatta, 'completely transquillized', Tab. VI, No. 1, △39, etc.
paṭissati, 'recalling', Tab. VI, No. 1, △13, etc.
paṭivirati, 'totally refraining', Tab. VI, No. 119, △60.
paṭivirodha, utter enmity, hostility, Tab. VI, No. 153, △78, etc.
patoda, goad, Tab. VI, No. 1, △15, etc.
paṭṭhāna, setting forth, advance, Tab. V.
patti, attaining, obtaining, Tab. V, No. 142.
pavicaya, 'research', 'investigation', Tab. VI, No. 1, △15, etc.
pekkhamāna, observing, 2.1.1.4.
phala, fruit, result, 3.1.1.1; 3.1.1.3.
phassa, touch, 5.0.3; Tab. V; Tab. VI, No. 1, △1, etc.
'pho-ba, transfer, transference, 4.3.3.2; 4, n. 46 ('stream').
'pho-bo, 'priest performing the ceremonies connected with *bat-do*', 4, n. 46.
phrin-las, 'activity', 4, n. 43.
phusanā, touching, Tab. VI, No. 1, △1, etc.
pīta, yellow, Tab. V, No. 89.
pīti, joy, Tab. V (*passim*); Tab. VI, No. 1, △8, etc.
piya, pleasant, 2, n. 25.
prajñā, see also *paññā;* knowledge, 're-knowledge', wisdom, 2.2.3; 6, n. 51.
prajñāpāramitā, 2.1.0.2; 2.1.1.0; 2.4.3; 4.2.1.
prakṛti, see also *pakati;* 2.5; 'nature' 'pristine', 'promordial', 4, n. 56.
pramāṇa, means of cognition, 6.0.6.10.
pratītya-samutpāda, also see *paṭiccasamuppāda;* 'interdependent origination', 5, n. 20; 6.0.6.11.
pratyeka-buddha, also see *pacceka-buddha;* 4.2.4.1.
pudgala, see also *puggala;* individual, person, 1.8; 3.0.8; 4.3.0; 4.5; 5, n. 2; 6, n. 17; 6.6.
puggala, see also *pudgala;* individual, person, Foreword; 2, n. 12; 2, n. 21; 2, n. 26; 2.4.5; 3.1.1.1; 4.1.2; 4.4.0; 5.1.1; 5.3.0.2; Tab. IX; 5.3.4; 5.3.7.2; 5.3.7.3; 6.1.0; 6.2.1; 6.5; 6.8; 6.10; 6.15.
puḷuvaka, infested with worms (corpse), Tab. V, No. 106.
purisa, see also *puruṣa;* person, Tab. IX.
puruṣa, 'male entity', 2, n. 28; person, 2.5; 3.0.8; 4.2.3.2; 4.3.0.

rāga, passion, Tab. V, No. 142.
ratana paṇīta, excellent jewel, 3.1.1.3.
rig-pa, awareness, 4.4.0.
rnam-shes, see also *vijñāna;* consciousness, conscious principle, 4.3.3.0; 4.3.3.2; 4, n. 46.
rūpa, form, 2, n. 8; 2.1.2.3; 4, n. 2; 4.8; Tab. V (*passim*); 5.1.3; 5.7.4.2; 5, n. 26; 5.7.4.3; 5. n. 27; 6.5; 6, n. 49.
rūpāvacara, 'the sphere or form', Tab. IV; Tab. V, No. 166.
rūpa-skandha, also see *rūpa-khandha;* 2.3.1.
rūpin, possessing form, Tab. V, No. 90.

sa-, with, Tab. V (*passim*).
sabbasatta, 'all sentient beings', 2.1.2.3.
sabbaso, wholly, altogether, Tab. V.

sacca, truth, Universal Truth, 3.1.1.3; Tab. V, No. 138.
sacchikiriyā, experiencing, eye-witnessing, Tab. VI, No. 119, △ 59.
saddahanā, 'having faith', 'believing', Tab. VI, No. 1, △ 11, etc.
saddhā, faith, Tab. VI, No. 1, △ 11, etc.
saddhābala, power of faith, Tab. VI, No. 1, △ 11, etc.
saddhindriya, faculty of faith, Tab. VI, No. 1, △ 11, etc.
-sahagata, accompanied by..., Tab. V (*passim*).
sakkāya, individuality, 2, n. 27; 2.4.5.
sakkāyadiṭṭhi, view of one's self (as real), 3.1.1.1.
sallakkhaṇā, discernment, Tab. VI, No. 1, △ 15, etc.
samādhi, concentration (of thought), 3.1.2; Tab. V (*passim*); Tab. VI (*passim*); 5.3.0.1; 5.3.7.1; 5.3.7.2; 6.15.
samādhibala, power of concentration, Tab. VI, No. 1, △ 10, etc.
samādhija, 'born of samadhi', Tab. V (*passim*); 5.3.7.1.
samādhindriya, faculty of concentration, Tab. VI, No. 1, △ 10, etc.
samāpatti, 'acquisition', Tab. VI, No. 1, △ 29, etc.
samatha, quietude, Tab. V; Tab. VI, No. 1, △ 10, etc.
samatikkama, transcending, overcoming, Tab. V, No. 107.
samaya, occurrence, casse, Foreword; 4.1.2; 4, n. 10; 4.1.3; 4, n. 26; 4, n. 27; 4.2.3.4; 5, n. 2; 5.3.1; 5.3.7.2; 5.7.4.5; 6.2.1; 6.15.
sambhavesi, those seeking for becoming, 1.1.2.2.
sambhoga-kāya, Body of Enjoyment, 4.4.6.
sambojjhaṅga, 'component (or constituent) of complete awakening', Tab. VI, No. 119, △ 8[a], etc.
saṃjñā, see also *saññā*, apperception, cognition, 1.2.1; 1.2.6.3; 1, n. 17; 2.2.3; 3.0.2.1; 6.5.
sammā, 'genuine', 4, n. 37; right, correct, Tab. V; Tab. VI, No. 1, △ 6, *et passim;* 5.3.0.1.
sammā ājīva, correct livelihood, Tab. VI, No. 119, △ 62.
sammākammanta, correct action, Tab. VI, No. 119, △ 61.
sammādiṭṭhi, correct view, Tab. VI, No. 1, △ 15, etc.; 5.7.4.3; 5.7.4.4.
sammāsamādhi, correct concentration, Tab. VI, No. 1, △ 10, etc.
sammāsaṅkappa, correct construing, Tab. VI, No. 1, △ 6, etc.
sammāsati, correct recollection, Tab. VI, No. 1, △ 13, etc.
sammāvāca, correct speech, Tab. VI, No. 119, △ 60, etc.
sammāvāyāma, correct endeavour, Tab. VI, No. 1, △ 12, etc.
sammoha, 'complete delusion', Tab. VI, No. 145, △ 71.
sampajāna, 'conscious', 'self-conscious', Tab. V, No. 11.
sampajañña, (being) 'conscious' or 'attentive', Tab. VI, No. 1, △ 15, etc.
sampanna, acquired, originated, 2.2.6.
sampayutta, 'associated with...,' 'conjoint', Tab. V (*passim*); 6.3.
samphassa, contact, Tab. VI, No. 1, △ 1, etc.
-samphassaja, 'born of contact with...,' Tab. VI, No. 1, △ 1, etc.
samphusanā, contact, contacting, Tab. VI, No. 1, △ 1, etc.
samphusitatta, 'contacted', Tab. VI, No. 1, △ 1, etc.
saṃsāra, 1.3.4.1; 2, n. 16; 4, n. 47; 4.4.7.
saṃsaya, hesitation, doubt, Tab. VI, No. 155, △ 80.
saṃskāra, see also *saṅkhāra;* 'complex', 'compound', 'synergy', etc.; 2, n. 8; 6 (*passim*).
saṃskṛta, see also *saṅkhata;* 'conditioned', 'composite', 'complex', etc.; 1.3.4.1; 5.7.4.1; 6.2.3; 6, n. 45; 6, n. 47; 6.11.3.
saṃskṛta dharma, conditioned dharma, 2, n. 7; 6.2.2.

skandha, see also *khandha;* 4, n. 18; 4.4.0; 5.7.4.1; 6.16.
socanā, sorrow, 2.2.1.1.
somanassa, 'mental gladness', 'joy', Tab. V (*passim*).
somanassindriya, faculty of mental gladness, Tab. VI, No. 1, △17, etc.; 5.6.2.
sotaviññāṇa, 'ear (or hearing-) consciousness', Tab. III; Tab. V, No. 158.
sotaviññāṇadhātu, 'element of ear-consciousness', Tab. VI, No. 158, △2-, etc.; 5.1.2.
sprul-pa, emanation, 4.3.3.1.
sprul-pai sku, body of transformation (see also *nirmāṇa-kāya*), 4.3.3.3.
śrāvaka, see also *sāvaka;* 4.2.4.1.
srotas, stream, 4, n. 46.
stūpa, 4.4.5.
subhaṃ, 'how beautiful', Tab. V, No. 92.
suci, purity, pure thing, 3.1.1.3.
sugata, well-gone, 3.1.1.1; 3.1.1.1.3.
sukha, pleasure, Tab. V; pleasant, Tab. VI, No. 1, △2, etc.
suññata, empty, void, Tab. V, No. 124.
śūnyatā, 2.1.02; emptiness, 4, n. 18; 4.2.3.1; 4.4.0.
śūnyavāda, 4.2.1.
susaṇṭhita, well-established, 2.3.2.
sūtra, see also *sutta;* 4.8.
sūtrānta, Buddhist text, 6, n. 64; 6.14.2.
sutta, 1.3.1; 1.3.2.; 1.3.3; 1.3.4; 1.3.4.1; 1.6; 1.7; 2.1.0.3; 2, n. 7; 2.1.0.4.1; 2.1.1.0; 2.1.1.1; 2.3.4; 2.4.5; 2.5; 3.0.2.1; 3, n. 2; 3.0.4; 3.0.8; 3.0.11; 3.0.12; 3.1.2; 3.3.3.6; 3, n. 17; 3.4.1: 3.4.2; 3.4.3; 4, n. 37; 4.8; 5, n. 14; 5.7.3; 6.1.3; 6.16.
suvaṇṇa, beautiful, Tab. V, No. 65.
suvatthi, well-being, 3.1.1.3
svabhāva, 1.3.4.1; nature, one's own nature, naturality, 2, n. 17; 6.0.6.11; 6.11; 6.11.2.
svabhāvataḥ, 'by (one's) own nature', 4.4.3.
svaprakāśa, 'self-illuminating', 4.3.2; 6.15.

tad, that, 2.1.0.1.
takka, 'ratiocination'(?), Tab. VI, No. 1, △6, etc.
tat tvaṃ asi, 'thou art that'; 1.2.3; 2.1.0.2; 6, n. 17.
tathāgata, 3.1.0; 3.3.1.2; 3, n. 16; 3.3.3.6; 4, n. 34; 4.5; 4.7; 4.8; 6, n. 45.
tathāgata-dhātu, 4.8.
tathāgatagarbha, Tathagata's embryo, 4.8; 4, n. 58.
tathatā, 'such-ness', 6, n. 17; 6.11.2.
tatiya, third, Tab. V (*passim*).
teja, flame, Tab. V, No. 45.
thāma, 'stamina', Tab. VI, No. 1, △12, etc.
thāmbhitatta, 'unsteadiness', 'vacillation' (?!), Tab. VI, No. 155, △80.
theravāda, 4, n. 37.
ṭhita, 'established', 3.1.1.1.
ṭhiti, state, 'stasis' ('a stabilized state'), Tab. VI, No. 1, △10, etc.
ti, three, Tab. VI, No. 119, △61.
titthāyatana, 'sectarian bias', Tab. VI, No. 145, △64.

uddhacca, excitement, Tab. V; Tab. VI, No. 156, △81.
uddhumātaka, 'swollen (corpse)', Tab. V, No. 105.
ujukatā, straightness, Tab. VI, No. 1, △49, etc.

vikkhāyitaka, 'fissured' or 'gnawed' (corpse), Tab. V, No. 106.
vikkhepa, perplexity, perturbedness, Tab. VI, No. 156, △81.
vikkhittaka, 'dismembered' or 'cut to pieces' (corpse), Tab. V, No. 106.
vimati, 'puzzlement (in judgement)', Tab. VI, No. 155, △80,
vinīlaka, 'discoloured (corpse)', Tab. V, No. 106.
viññāṇa, see also *vijñāna;* consciousness, 2, n. 7; 4, n. 11; 4.8; Tab. V; Tab. VI, No. 1, △5, etc.; 5.1.0; 5.3.2; Tab. IX; 5.3.3; 6.0.3–4; 6.15.
viññāṇakkhandha, aggregate of consciousness, Tab. VI, No. 1, △5, etc.; 6.1.4.
vipāka, ripening, 5.0.2; Tab. V, No. 157.
vipariyāsaggāha, 'grasping of inverted views', Tab. VI, No. 145, △64.
vipassanā, 'intuition', Tab. VI, No. 1, △15, etc.
vipayutta, dissociated from..., Tab. V (*passim*).
vipubbaka, 'festering (corpse)', Tab. V, No. 106.
virāga, dispassionate, Tab. V, No. 11.
virati, refraining, Tab. VI, No. 119, △60.
viratta, averted, 3.1.1.1
viriya, energy, 3.3.1.2; Tab. V; Tab. VI, No. 1, △12, etc.
viriyabala, power of energy, Tab. VI, No. 1, △12, etc.
viriyārambha, inception of energy, Tab. VI, No. 1, △12, etc.
viriyindriya, power of energy, Tab. VI, No. 1, △12, etc.
virodha, enmity, Tab. VI, No. 153, △78, etc.
viśaya, object of cognition, 6.0.6.9; 6, n. 57.
viśiṣṭa, discrimination, discrepancy, 6, n. 17.
vitakka, discursive thinking, 1, n. 17; reasoning, Tab. V (*passim*); Tab. VI, No. 1, △6, etc.; 6, n. 3; 6.0.6.10.
vitti, 'felicity', Tab. VI, No. 1, △8, etc.
viveka, separation, detachment, Tab. V; 5.3.7.1; 5.3.7.2.
vyāpāda, malevolence, maliciousness, Tab. V (also see *byāpāda*)
vyappanā, 'focusing (of mind)', Tab. VI, No. 1, △6, etc.

yajña, ritual, sacrifice, 3.0.8.
yakṣa, 2, n. 13.
yapanā, 'going on', Tab. VI, No. 1, △18, etc.
yāpanā, '(keeping) going on', Tab. VI, No. 1, △18, etc.
yathā bhutaṃ, 'as it is', 2.1.0.3
yathābhutatā, 'as it is'-ness, 6.11.1.
yid, see also *mahas;* mind, mentality, 4.3.3.0.
yogācāra, 1, n. 1; 1. n. 10; 1.2.6.2; 4.3.2; 4.6.0; 5, n. 15; 6.0.1.

LIST OF WORKS CITED

This is not a bibliography on the subject. Only those books and articles are here listed which have been directly referred to in the text [A.P.]

Anuruddha, *Abhidhammattha-Saṅgaha* (*Compendium of Philosophy*), trans. by Shwe Zan Aung, revised and edited by Mrs. C. Rhys Davids (London, 1910).

— *Abhidhammatha-Saṅgaha*, ed. and trans. by Narada Thera, Part I (Colombo, 1947).

— *Abhidharmartha Sangrahaya* (with a Singalese paraphrase), revised and edited by Pannomoli Tissa (Ambalangoda, Ceylon, 1926).

Aṭṭhasālinī, ed. by P. V. Bapat and R. D. Vadekar (Poona, 1942).

Awakening of Faith, attributed to Aśvaghosha, trans, with commentary by Y. S. Hakeda (Columbia University Press, New York, 1967).

Ayer, A. J., *The Problem of Knowledge* (Penguin, London, 1956).

Bachtin, M. M., *Aesthetics of Verbal Act* (in Russian, Moscow, 1979).

Back, D. M., *Eine Buddhistische Jenseitsreise* (Wiesbaden, 1979).

Bailey, H. W., *A Kharoṣṭrī Inscription of Senavarma, King of Odi* (Journal of Royal Asiatic Society, 1980, No. 1).

Bardo, The Tibetian Book of the Dead, ed., by W. Y. Evans—Wentz, according to Lama Kazi Dawa-Samdup's English Rendering (Oxford University Press, Oxford, 1960).

Bardo, The Tibetian Book of the Dead, a new translation and commentary by F. Fremantle and Chögyam Trungpa (Shambhala, Boulder and London, 1975).

Bareau, A., *l'Absolu en philosophie bouddhique* (Centre de documentation universitaire, Paris, 1951).

— *Étude du Bouddhisme* (l'Annuaire du Collège de France, 73e annee, Paris, 1974).

— *Recherches sur la biographie du Buddha dans les sūtrapiṭaka et vinayapiṭaka anciens* I (Paris, 1963).

Barua, B., *A History of Pre-Buddhistic Indian Philosophy* (Calcutta, 1921).

Bennett, J., *The Dramatic Universe*, Vol. III (Coombe Spring Press, Sherborne, 1976).

Beyer, S., *The Cult of Tārā* (University of California Press, Berkeley, London, Los Angeles, 1973).

Bhadra Kalpa Sūtra, A brief summary of *Mdo Bskal Bzang* (*aryabhadra kalpikā nāma mahāyāna-sūtra*), ed. by Sarat Chandra Das (Darjeeling, 1895).

Bhagavad-Gītā, ed., trans. and commentary by R. C. Zaehner (Oxford University Press, London, Oxford, New York, 1973).

Bhagavadgītā, a Bilingual Edition ed. and trans. by J. A. B. van Buitenen (The University of Chicago Press, Chicago and London, 1981).

Blue Annals, completed in A.D. 1478 by 'Gos-Lotsawa Gzhon-nu-Dpal (1392–1487), reproduced by Lokesh Chandra from the Collection of Raghu Vira (960 block-prints, New Delhi, 1974).

Blue Annals, trans by George N. Roerich, Part I (Calcutta, 1949), Part II (Calcutta, 1953).

Broad, C., in *The Philosophy of C. D. Broad*, ed. by B. A. Shillp (New York, 1959).

Buddhist Legends, trans. by E. W. Burlingame, Part I (Cambridge, Mass., 1921).

Burnouf, E., *Introduction a l'histoire du Buddhism Indien* (Paris, 1876).

Cassirer, E., *The Philosophy of Symbolic Forms*, trans. by R. Manheim, Vol. II (Yale University Press, New Haven and London, 1955).

— *The Philosophy of Symbolic Forms*, trans. by R. Manheim, Vol. III (Yale University Press, New Haven and London, 1957).

Colebrooke, T. E., *Miscellaneous Essays*, Vol. II (London, 1873).

Collins, S., *Selfless Persons* (Cambridge University Press, Cambridge, 1982).

Conze, E., *The Memoirs of a Modern Gnostic*, Part I: *Life and Letters;* Part II: *Politics, People and Places* (The Samizdat Publishing Company, Sherborne, 1979).

— *Thirty Years of Buddhist Studies* (Bruno Cassirer, London, 1967).

Cousins, L. S., *The Paṭṭhāna and the Development of the Theravādin Abhidhamma* (Centenary Volume of the Journal of the Pali Text Society, 1981, pp. 22-46).
Dasgupta, S. N., *An Introduction to Tantric Buddhism* (Calcutta, 1950).
Designation of Human Types (*Puggala-Paññatti*), trans. by B. C. Law (London, 1924).
Dhammapada, with Introductory Essays, Pali Text, English Translation and Notes by S. Radhakrishnan (Oxford University Press, Delhi, Bombay, Calcutta, 1980).
Dhammapada, Sinhalese edition (Sri Lanka, 1961).
Dhammapada, the Commentary, ed. by H. C. Norman, Vol. I (London, 1906).
Dhammasaṅgaṇi (Abhidhamma Piṭaka, Vol. I) Gen. Editor, Bhikkhu J. Kashyap (Pali Publication Board, Bihar, 1960).
Dhammasaṅgaṇi, traduction annotée par A. Bareau (Centre du Documentation Universitaire, Paris, 1951).
Dhargyey, G. N., *Tibetian Tradition of Mental Development* (Dharmasala, 1978).
Dhātu-Kathā (*Discourse on Elements*), trans. and explanations by U Nārada Māla Paṭṭhāna Sayadaw, assisted by Thein Nyun (London, 1962).
Eli [*alias* Manuel Capriles Arias, Caracas, Venezuela], *The Direct Path*, Vol. I: *An Outline of the Path* (Mudra Publishing, Kathmandu, Bodhgaya, Goa, Dharmasala, 1978?).
Feuerstein, G., *The Philosophy of Classical Yoga* (Manchester University Press, Manchester, 1980).
Gellner, E., *Words and Things* (Routledge and Kegan Paul, London, Boston and Henley, 1979).
Govinda, Anagarika, *The Psychological Attitude of Early Buddhist Philosophy* (London, 1973).
Grimm, George, *The Doctrine of the Buddha*, ed. by M. Keller-Grimm and M. Hoppe (Berlin, 1958).
Gudmunsen, C., *Wittgenstein and Buddhism* (London, 1977).
Guenther, H., *Saṃvṛti and Paramārtha in Yogācāra*, in *The Problem of two Truths in Buddhism and Vedanta*, ed. by M. Sprung (Dordrecht, Holland, 1973).
— *Tibetan Buddhism without Mystification* (Leiden, 1966).
Guenther, H., and Kawamura, L., *Mind in Buddhist Psychology*, being *The Necklace of Clear Understanding* by Ye-shes rgyal-mtshan (1713–1793), trans. by H. Guenther and L. Kawamura (Dharma Publishing, Emeryville, California, 1975).
Hartmann, E. von., *Philosophie des Unbewusstes* (2 Auf., Berlin, 1870).
Heimann, B., *Facets of Indian Thought* (London, 1964).
Hodgson, B., *Essays on the Languages, Literature and Religion of Nepal and Tibet* (London, 1874).
Hudson, L., *The Cult of the Fact* (London, 1972).
Husserl, E., *Die Krisis Europäischen Wissenschaften und die transzendentale Phenomenologie* (Husserliana, Band VI, The Hague, 1950).
Jaini, P. S., *On the Sarvajñatva of Mahavira and the Buddha* in *Buddhist Studies in Honor of I. B. Horner*, ed. by L. Cousins et al. (Dordrecht, Holland, 1974).
James, W., *The Principles of Psychology*, Vol. I (New York, 1910).
Jayasurya, W. F., *The Psychology and Philosophy of Buddhism* (Colombo, 1963).
Johansson, Rune E. A., *Citta, Mano, Vinnana* (University of Ceylon Review, Vol. XXIII, No. 1–2, 1965, pp. 165–215).
— *The Dynamic Psychology of Early Buddhism* (Curzon Press, London and Malmö, 1979).
Jung, C. G., *Analytical Psychology*, the Tavistock Lectures (London and Henley, 1976).
— *Memories, Dreams, Reflections*, ed. by A. Jaffe, trans. by R. and C. Winston (London, 1980).
Kariyawasam, A. G. S., *Bhūta* (*Encyclopaedia of Buddhism*, Vol. III, fasc. 1, Ceylon, 1971).
Karmapa: The Black Hat lama of Tibet, Nik Douglas and Meryl White (comp.) (London, 1976).
Karunaratna, Upali, *Bhavaṅga* (*Encyclopaedia of Buddhism*, Vol. III, fac. 1, Ceylon, 1971).
Keith, B., *Buddhist Philosophy* (Clarendon Press, Oxford, 1923).
Kern, H., *Manual of Indian Buddhism* (Strasbourg, 1896).
Khotanese Sūraṅgama-samādhi-sūtra, ed. and trans. by R. E. Emmerick (London Oriental Series, Vol. 23, London, 1970).
Kirfel, W., *Symbolik des Buddhismus* (Stuttgart, 1959).
Kolakowski, L., *Religion*, ed. by F. Kermode (Fontana Paperback, London, 1982).

Lamotte, E., *Passions and Impregnations of Passions in Buddhism*, in *Buddhist Studies in Honor of I. B. Horner*, ed. by L. Cousins, *et al.* (Dordrecht, Holland, 1974).
Law, B. C., *Concepts of Buddhism* (Amsterdam, 1957).
Lauf, D. I., *Secret Doctrines of the Tibetan Books of the Dead*, trans. by G. Parkes (Shambhala, Boulder and London, 1977).
Lévi-Strauss, C., *Tristes Tropiques*, trans, by J. and D. Weightman (Penguin Books, Harmondsworth, 1976).
Lévi-Strauss, C., and Charbonnier, G., *Entretiens avec Claude Lévi-Strauss* (Paris, 1961).
Mahā-Parinibbāna Sutta, Dīgha-Nikāya 2, *Mahā Vagga* (Nalanda Devānagarī Pali Series, 1959).
Mäll, L., *Une aproache possible du sunyavada* (*Tel quel*, 1968, No. 32).
Marasinghe, M. M. J., *Gods in Early Buddhism* (Sri Lanka, 1974).
Maslow, A., *Toward a Psychology of Being* (Princeton, 1968).
Masson, J., *La religion populaire dans le canon Pali* (Louvain, 1942).
Mookerje, S., *The Buddhist Philosophy of Universal Flux* (Calcutta, 1935).
Murti, T. R. V., *Saṃṛvti and Paramārtha in Madhyāmika*, in: *The Problem of two Truths in Buddhism and Vedanta*, ed. by M. Sprung (Dordrecht, Holland, 1973).
— *The Central Philosophy of Buddhism* (London, 1980).
Nanayakkara, S. K., '*Bodhicitta*' (*Encyclopaedia of Buddhism*, Vol. III, fasc. 2, Ceylon. 1971),
Neurath, O., *Empiricism and Sociology*, ed. by M. Neurath and R. S. Cohen (D. Reidel Publishing Company, Dordrecht and Boston, 1973).
Nyanaponika, Thera, *Abhidhamma Studies* (Kandy, Ceylon, 1965).
Nyanatiloka, Mahathera, *Guide through the Abhidhamma-Piṭaka* (Buddhist Publication Society, Kandy, Ceylon, 1971).
Obeyesekere, G., *The Rebirth Eschatology and Its Transformations*, in: *Karma and Rebirth in Classical Indian Traditions*, ed. by W. D. O'Flaherty (University of California Press, Berkeley, Los Angeles, London, 1980).
O'Flaherty, W. D., *Introduction* to Obeyesekere.
Pallis, M., *The Veil of the Temple* (Tomorrow, Vol. 12, No. 2, 1964).
Patterson, R. L., in: *The Philosophy of C. D. Broad*, ed. by B. A. Shillp (New York, 1959).
Penelhum, T., *Survival and Disembodied Existence* (London, 1980).
Piatigorsky, A., *A Word about the Philosophy of Vladimir Nabokov* (Wiener Slawistischen Almanach, Band IV, 1979).
— *An Introduction to Abhidhammic Psychology* in: *Works on Semiotics VI* (*Acta et Commentationes Universitatis Tartuensis*, No. 308, Tartu, 1973).
— *La riontologizzazione del pensiero nel Buddismo*, parti I, II, III (in Conoscenza Religiosa, Nos. 4 (1978), 1–2 (1979), 1 (1980), La Nuova Italia, Firenze.
— *Some Remarks on Other Stream*, in: *Buddhist Studies*, ed. by. P. Denwood and A. Piatigorsky (London, 1983).
Potter, Karl H., *Encyclopaedia of Indian Philosophies*, Vol. II: *Nyāya-Vaiśeṣika*, ed. by Karl H. Potter (Motilal Banarsidas, Delhi, 1977).
Puggala-Paññatti I, text ed. by R. Morris (London, 1883).
Rhys Davids, C., *Buddhist Psychology* (London, 1914).
— *The Milinda Questions* (London, 1930).
Richardson, H. E., in JRAS (1858, No. 3–4, p. 139).
Rosenberg, O., *Problemy Buddiyskoi Filosofii* (Petrograd, 1918).
— *Die Probleme der Buddhistische Philosophie* aus dem Russ. Übersetzt von Frau E. Rosenberg (Heidelberg, 1924).
Ruegg, D. Seyfort, *Ahiṃsā and Vegetarianism in the History of Buddhism*, in Buddhist Studies in Honor of W. Rahula (London, 1980).
— *Pāli Gotta/Gotta and the term Gotrabhū* in *Buddhist Studies in Honor of I. B. Horner*, ed. by L. Cousins *et al.* (Dordrecht, Holland, 1974).
— *La theorie du Tathagatagarbha et du Gotra* (Paris, 1969).
— *The Uses of the Four Positions of the Catuskoṭi and the Problem of the Description of Reality in Mahayana Buddhism* (Journal of Indian Philosophy, 1977, No. 5).
Śāntideva, *Bodicaryāvatāra*, with commentary by *Prajñākāramati*, ed. by P. L. Vaidya (Darbhanga, Bihar, 1960).

Schayer, S., *Contribution to the Problem of Time in Indian Philosophy* (Krakow, 1938).
Schurtz, A., *Collected Papers* I: *The Problem of Social Reality* (The Hague, 1973).
Silburn, L., *Instant et cause* (Paris, 1955).
Stcherbatsky, Th., *Buddhist Logic*, Vol. II (Leningrad, 1930).
— *The Central Conception of Buddhism* (London, 1923).
Stein, R., *La civilisation Tibetaine* (Paris, 1962).
Stenzler, A. F., *Ueber die Sitte* (Abhandlungen für die Kunde des Morgenlandes herausgegeben von der Deutschen Morgenländischen Gesellschaft, Band IV, No. 1, 1865).
Sūtra of Golden Light being a Translation of the *Suvarṇabhāsottamasūtra* by R. E. Emmerick (Luzac and Co., London, 1970).
Sutta-Nipāta, New Edition of Dines Anderson and Helmer Smith (published for the Pali Text Society by Luzac and Co., London, 1913).
Sutta-Nipāta Commentary II being *Paramatthajotikā* II, 2, edited by Helmer Smith, Vol. II (405–1149), London, 1917.
Sutta-Nipāta, trans. from Pali by V. Fausböl [SBE, Vol. X, Part II, Delhi, 1973, (Oxford 1881)].
Suzuki, D. T., *Introduction to Zen Buddhism*, Vol. II (New York, 1974).
Thera-and-Therī Gāthā, ed. by H. Oldenberg and R. Pischel, 2nd edition with appendices by K. R. Norman and L. Alsdorf (London, 1966).
Thera-Gāthā, The Elders' Verses I, trans. with an introduction and notes by K. R. Norman (London, 1966).
Therī-Gāthā, The Elders' Verses II, trans. with an introduction and notes by K. R. Norman (London, 1971).
Thinley, Karma, *The History of the Sixteen Karmapas of Tibet*, ed. with an essay by D. Stott, foreword by Chögyam Trungpa, introduction by R. A. Ray (Prajña Press, Boulder, 1980).
Tucci, G., *The Religions of Tibet*, trans. from German and Italian by G. Samuel (Berkeley and Los Angeles, 1980).
Upatissa, Arahant, *Vimuttimagga, The Path of Freedom*, trans. from the Chinese by N. R. M. Ehara, Soma Thera and Kheminda Thera (published by D. R. D. Deerasuriya, Colombo, 1961).
Vallée Poussin, L. de la, *Buddhisme* (Paris, 1909).
— *Introduction à la pratique des futures Bouddhas* (*Bodhicāryavatāra*), trad. par L. de la Vallée Poussin (Paris, 1907).
Vimalakīrti Nirdeśa Sūtra, trans. by Charles Luk (Shambala, Berkeley and London, 1972).
Wittgenstein, L., *Philosophical Investigations* trans. by G. E. M. Anscombe (New York, 1978).
— *Remarks on the Philosophy of Psychology*, Vol. I, edited and translated by G. E. M. Anscombe and G. H. von Wright (Oxford, 1980).
Yamada, I., *Vijñāptimātratā of Vasubandhu* (JRAS, 1977, No. 2).

DATE DUE